Shephard's Watch

Shephard's Watch

Illusions of Power in
British Politics

Gillian Shephard

First published in Great Britain 2000
Published by Politico's Publishing
8 Artillery Row
Westminster
London
SW1P 1RZ

Tel 020 7931 0090
Fax 020 7828 8111
Email publishing@politicos.co.uk
Website http://www.politicos.co.uk/publishing

First published in hardback 2000

A catalogue record of this book is available from the British Library.

ISBN 1 902301 56 0

Printed and bound in Great Britain by St Edmundsbury Press.

Contents

Foreword

Being powerful is like being a lady. If you have to tell people you are, you ain't.

JESSE CARR

THIS BOOK EMERGED from a series of lectures I gave at Queen Mary and Westfield College in the autumn of 1999 and the spring of 2000. Without the inspirational encouragement of Professor Peter Hennessy, the book would not have been written. Peter has a knowledge of the Whitehall scene second to none, but in addition he possesses that priceless quality of the born teacher, enthusiasm. Whenever my own energy flagged, Peter was there to revive it for the task in hand. His students and colleagues are fortunate indeed. I am grateful for the quiet encouragement of Professor John Ramsden, and to the students who attended the lectures and contributed to the seminars. The fields of activity which will eventually benefit from the education they have received at Queen Mary and Westfield will be fortunate indeed.

If the book would not have been written without Peter Hennessy, it certainly would not have been published without Iain Dale and John Simmons of Politico's. Unfailingly calm and professional, Iain was also a great source of encouragement during the

1

writing of the book, frequently adding irreverent suggestions of his own. He and his team – Sean Magee, John Berry and Clare Barnes – incredibly made even the final deadline stages seem fun.

I owe special thanks to all my many friends in Whitehall, and in particular Sir Geoffrey Holland, Lord Butler, and Sir Richard Packer. I am indebted to all my friends and colleagues in both Houses of Parliament for peopling this book with their talents and foibles. Keith Simpson, MP for Mid Norfolk, has been a constant source of cheerful and practical advice. Robert Cranborne has been a fount of wisdom on the constitution, and on most other issues as well. I have benefited from the steady support of the South West Norfolk Conservative Association, and its agent, Shelagh Hutson. My constituency secretaries, Valerie Flindall, Lynn Fox, Mary Reeder and Pat Roome, have all played a part. Fiona Syms, and Adam Burt from Palace Computing, have given invaluable help, especially when the lap-top had one of its frequent mutinous turns.

My family have all helped in their own ways. My mother has been a keen man-in-the-street critic of the book's content. My step-son Neil and his wife Heather, both authors themselves, have provided a wealth of practical advice. My husband, Tom, has been production-engineer-in-chief, as well as purveyor of coffee and support at all times.

The inspiration for the book has come from my thirty years of fascination with the democratic process, and the tradition of public service which still illuminates so much of what happens in Britain. Unsung, not shored up by spin doctors, year in and year out, the elected, whether parliamentarians, councillors, those who run organisations large and small, from the local darts team to the Women's Institute, and the volunteers, from magistrates to play group leaders, give their time to make this country work. They use the democratic process without even thinking about it. It is second nature to all they do. From it comes their power to act to make life better for the rest of us.

GILLIAN SHEPHARD

July 2000

Climbing the Greasy Pole

Politicians are like monkeys. The higher they climb, the more revolting are the parts they expose.

GWILYM LLOYD GEORGE

FOR AS LONG as I can remember, I have been interested in power and who exercises it. One of my earliest memories is of the 1945 general election; I was five. When the result came through on the radio, people went out into the village street, calling to one another over their gates either 'We've won,' or 'They've won,' according to their political persuasion. I asked what had happened. 'They've got rid of Mr Churchill,' I was told. For a child of five, brought up during a war to believe that Mr Churchill was invincible – he had beaten Hitler, after all – to be told that there was a 'They' more powerful than Mr Churchill, who had somehow removed him, was a revelation indeed. That the ballot box had achieved this overwhelming change was something I came only later to appreciate.

Power in politics is the power to achieve change. This book seeks to explore the nature of power in politics, how it is exercised and how it is tempered by chronology, by the machinery of the state, by personality and attitude, events and context. It examines the ebbs and flows of power within Government, influences on individuals and Governments themselves, the effect of changing attitudes and circumstances on the exercise of power. It looks at the difficulties that militate against the power to achieve change, within political parties, Parliament, and the constitution. It concludes optimistically by expressing the hope that despite a mighty media, strong competition from a celebrity culture and attempts to marginalise and trivialise the democratic process, it is the electorate, through the ballot box, who will always win.

Them and Us

Power is best used quietly, without attracting attention.

MALCOLM X

My early fascination with power, in the immediate postwar period and in a remote rural area, began by observing the series of 'Them' who governed our lives. 'They' decided that electricity, but not water or sewerage, should be provided for the village. 'They' issued building permits, without which no house could be built. 'They' came to the Parish Room to allocate ration books, or to sell us subsidised meat pies and sausage rolls. 'They' decreed that you could not kill a pig. This, curiously, did not mean that no one killed a pig but, rather, that its products were described as something else and passed from hand to hand covered with a cloth.

Even someone as powerful as the headteacher of our primary school was governed by 'Them', to whom she referred as 'the Office', based in far-away Norwich. When dissatisfied, local parents spoke of 'Them' as the Norfolk Education Committee. If 'They' came to the school, even in the form of the 'Attendance Officer' or the school nurse, the headteacher got flustered. For 'Their' benefit, there was hung over the schoolroom fireplace an ancient, splendid timetable, bearing no relation to our school day and executed in perfect spidery handwriting. It was headed by an impressive coat-of-arms, and the words 'Norfolk Education Committee', although you could only read this in the summer when there was no fire burning. Why, I wondered, was our otherwise courageous headteacher apparently afraid of 'Them'? Who were 'They' and how did 'They' get to 'Their' position?

She was less nervous of the school managers, and so were we. After all, we saw 'Them' about the village regularly. They included the vicar, in his ancient pre-war Austin, the farmer's wife, and a prominent churchwarden – actually there because he was on the Parish Council – and famous for his eloquent renderings of *Gunga Din* at parish socials. But even in their case, there was the question 'Why *them*?' And why not, for example, the doctor, who was greatly respected? It was some time before I understood that they had been elected.

First Impressions

Power? I'm about to meet real power.

EDWARD BENNETT WILLIAMS on his deathbed

Things gradually became clearer. There were more general elections. By the time I was at grammar school in 1951, I was more aware of the electoral process. The general election of that year was clearly very important. Posters went up, news bulletins discussed the parties' chances, we took sides at school. It was obvious that something very important was happening. In the end, Mr Churchill reappeared as Prime Minister.

Civics lessons explained things further. The ministers whose responsibilities we learnt about were in the newspapers, on the radio. One or two even came to the county, and were pictured in the local paper opening fêtes or inaugurating housing developments. That their position and power were connected to the electoral process, to politics was obvious, although there was ambivalence in our community about politics. Of course, there were differences in political points of view, but there were other differences too. On the one hand there were those whose political views were open and known to all. They were the people who worked at election times, taking electoral numbers outside the school, driving the elderly and infirm to vote – 'Very kind of Mrs X, but she did-n't know which way I voted', was a comment heard not infre-quently afterwards. On the other hand, in our remote, close-knit and secretive community on the eastern edge of England, there was a whole tranche of opinion which regarded politics as something you did not talk about. Your views were your own business and no one else's. I was so conscious of this when I first helped in a gen-eral election that I could barely bring myself to ask people for their electoral numbers. I wondered at the courage of those who were so open about their beliefs, and so prepared to be publicly defeat-ed that they actually put themselves up for election, and had their names on posters and leaflets. To achieve change, was it really necessary to go through that process? And who else had power? Could it be exercised by people who had not been elected?

Local Power

> The people who know where the levers of power are have a duty to help those who don't and those who can't help themselves.
>
> GEOFFREY BRADMAN

In the fascinating yet clearly powerful world of county govern-ment at the time, politics did not seem to figure. Indeed the best-known people were not elected, but were officers of the County Council. Theirs were the names on public notices, school notice-boards and writing paper. They achieved change. They provided schools, offices, old people's homes and youth centres. They had the power to sack people and when things went wrong they sorted them out. My perception that officers held the power was correct in a pre–1974 shire county. Politics did not really figure in a council's deliberations, which left a power vacuum that able officers were quick to fill. Very different was the position in boroughs, no matter how small, where local politicians were prominent, and where political swings resulted in definite changes of policy, particularly in education. When I decided to leave teaching after a couple of years, it was to a shire county that I went to work, to the Office in fact. I believed that there I would find a source of power, a position from which to achieve things, that I could not find in the classroom. I thought that I would become one of 'Them'. And thus, in a very minor way, it proved. I moved from post to post, under the guidance of an inspirational Chief Education Officer, always in the field of education, but ranging from careers guidance, to administrator, to schools inspector.

Then came the local government reforms, introduced by the Heath Government in 1974, when everything changed. Norwich and Great Yarmouth were absorbed into the county of Norfolk and Kings Lynn, which had had a divisional executive for education, became fully part of Norfolk too. The politicians took charge. The gentlemanly atmosphere vanished, never to return. Debate became political. Officers were sidelined. Budgets were drawn up, not by council treasurers, but by council leaders. There was fierce debate with the Rate-payers' Associations. Local politicians were now taking decisions, making changes, entering into controversy. Shire counties became politicised, and with that change came power and responsibility for local politicians. Accountability took a little longer to learn.

I recall vividly drawing up a rationalised plan for the county's schools. Given that there were then more than 550, some with fewer than ten pupils, it involved school closures and amalgamations. It was hailed with enthusiasm at County Hall, and adopted by the Education Committee. I attended the first closure meeting, of a school with eight pupils, to support the local county councillor. The members of the public present, twelve in all, were deeply hostile to the proposal. The councillor capitulated. He explained that it had all been my idea, and that he would take it back to County Hall and have it overturned. That, for me, was a seminal experience. But it was not a deterrent. Rather, I thought I might have done better than he had.

Getting Elected

Power is fun.

DONNA SHALALA

Later, after leaving full-time work to get married, I decided to get elected to a council. Deciding which political party to attach myself to was never a problem. I had been born a Conservative, and if I had had any doubts, Margaret Thatcher would have dispelled them. Much more nerve-racking was the fact that I had to declare, publicly, that I was putting myself up for election. It seemed a very exposed commitment. Once I had recovered from seeing posters bearing my name all over the electoral division, and had been elected, I became fascinated by the operation of political power at local level. There was a direct correlation between raising finance and carrying out the policies to achieve change, while a balance had to be struck between local political necessity, the broader interest of the electorate, and of the county as a whole, and party political requirements. I was impressed by the commitment of councillors, and indeed of many in public life, to public service, and to the interests of the places they represented. Intriguing also were the ambitions of some of those with whom I served: they wanted to get into the House of Commons, and their speeches in the council were intended for a broader audience.

On the whole, though, there was a close and perceptible link between elected and electorate. You put forward your programme, you were elected, you raised or reduced the finance, and carried out the plan. If it was unpopular, or ran into trouble, you took the blame – more or less: even at that time local government was not master of its own destiny. Indeed, it is arguable that, since no national Government in Britain has ever taken local government entirely seriously, while yet relying on it to carry out perhaps unpopular policies, it never has been. Shockwaves of horror swept through local government when in 1967 the Labour Government insisted that all authorities draw up plans for comprehensive education. Even greater shockwaves resulted from legislation to that effect in 1976. In 1977 local government was expected to play its part in meeting the requirements of the International Monetary Fund when a seven per cent reduction was imposed on all spending programmes.

Things were hardly better when the Conservatives came to power in 1979. For a variety of never entirely explained reasons, Margaret Thatcher was said to dislike local government. Perhaps the open defiance expressed to her policies by a number of left-wing councils when she came to power contributed to this. She certainly felt, and rightly, that she had been given a clear mandate by the electorate to reduce public spending, and if local democracy got in the way, that was inconvenient for it. Indeed, the Conservatives went on to put an end, virtually, to local autonomy,

13

or at least local accountability, when they introduced the 1984 Rates Act. This gave the Government of the day the power to set local authorities' spending levels, thus rendering local decision-making redundant.

In many ways the Conservatives had been driven to it: such were the complications of local government finance, and so arcane had become the ways for it to circumvent national intentions, that something had to be done – as people always say when they know that the knock-on effects of a course of action are unfortunate. A future reform of local government and a restoration of its account-ability and transparency are not the subject of this book. Suffice it to say that the erosion of power at local level led me to wonder if it would be more satisfying to transfer to the place where, I assumed, power had gone: Westminster.

Into Parliament

Powerlessness corrupts. Absolute powerlessness corrupts absolutely.

ROSABETH MOSS KANTER

Many people told me that as a backbencher I would find life less stimulating than being at the centre of things in local politics. It was of course the case that having been part of both the executive and the legislature locally, I sacrificed the executive role when I became a Member of Parliament in 1987. In fact, I was on the backbenches for just a year. In 1988, a year after my election as Member of Parliament for South West Norfolk, I became that lowliest of polit-ical creatures, a Parliamentary Private Secretary (commonly known as a PPS) to Peter Lilley, then Economic Secretary to the Treasury. During my year on the backbenches, I had had the opportunity to

14

observe the workings of the Parliamentary party, the slates run for backbench elections from the various wings of the party, the dining clubs and other groupings, the role of the 1922 Committee. I had also seen how Parliament could work to curb the Government's wishes. There had been an important rebellion on the reform of Housing Benefit in 1988, which had forced the Government to change course. I had also seen, as a member of the Health and Social Security Select Committee, that ministers could be held to account by their peers. I was conscious of the groupings and whisperings that even then could be seen as the first threats to Margaret Thatcher's premiership. Power, however, did not seem to reside on the backbenches. While it was clear that there were individuals and groups who had the potential to exercise power within the House of Commons, I was far too new and too much of an outsider to be included, so when I became a PPS I was delighted to have been given my first leg up the 'greasy pole'.

As the most junior Treasury Minister's PPS, I was hardly an influential figure. However, it was a good vantage point from which to observe the operation of power. Nigel Lawson, then Chancellor of the Exchequer, was a powerful politician: he was formidably intelligent, intellectually self-confident and a good manager. Instructions emerged from his meetings and were carried out. There was no doubt in the Treasury about who was in charge. However, it was the period when stories of disagreement between him and the Prime Minister began to surface in the press and diary columns. In the Treasury power certainly resided with him. Within the Government, it seemed to reside with the Prime Minister. Yet the trappings of power surrounding my immediate boss, Peter Lilley, seemed to me constricting rather than empowering. Housed in a magnificent room in Great George Street, with his driver and

15

private office at his command, he nevertheless appeared to be at everyone's beck and call, weighed down with appointments, media commitments, and red boxes. As his PPS, I served with him on the Finance Bill. I had not seen until then the operation of the legislative process from the inside and Finance Bills are by definition complex. There is an immense amount of detail to be mastered for work in committee, but at the same time, delegations of interested parties have to be seen, and parliamentary colleagues kept briefed. Last-minute changes have to be made. Senior ministers and other departments must be kept informed. For junior ministers, it looked to me more like hard work than the exercise of power although there was a certain glamour about the late night sittings, the warm evenings, the Chancellor looking in from time to time, and the supply of drinks laid in by the Whips in a nearby room, for those with strong heads.

Into Government

> Power is based upon perception – if you think you've got it then you've got it. If you think you don't have it, even if you've got it, then you don't have it.
>
> HERB COHEN

Later in the summer of 1989, I was made a junior minister, at the Department of Social Security. Mrs Thatcher appointed me during the course of a Downing Street reception. Afterwards I realised that she had done this, not as a particular honour, but to save herself time the next day. She pointed out that she had started in the same job, Parliamentary Under-Secretary at the Department of Social Security, and that it was important to work on the detail. The next morning, I arrived in my House of Commons office at about 8.30pm to find phone calls waiting from my husband, my agent, and my constituency office. 'A rather short ministerial career,' I recall thinking, imagining it had somehow all gone wrong. But it was Number 10: the Prime Minister wanted another word. 'Just,' as she put it, 'to be quite certain. If I were you, dear,' she added (she always called you 'dear' if she was not sure of your name. She still calls me 'dear'), 'I would get straight round to the department, and get on.' This I did, only to shock the department to its roots, and terrify my predecessor, Peter Lloyd, who was still packing his belongings into plastic bags before leaving for his new job at the Home Office.

To be the lowest form of ministerial life at the DSS was not to drink deep of the cup of power. It seemed to me that officials had far more power than I did – apart from the really difficult decisions, that is. 'We only bring you the hardest ones, Minister,' someone explained kindly. Meanwhile, the officials' power over ministers was exercised through the diary and the red box. On that first morning, the diary secretary appeared bearing a huge book. 'I want all your phone numbers and addresses,' she said, 'because we need to know where you are at all times of the day and night.' With those words the door to freedom clanged shut. I wondered if the compensations of office would be worth it.

Reshuffles

It is certainly more agreeable to have power to give than to receive.

WINSTON CHURCHILL

My next move occurred after John Major became leader of the Conservative Party in November 1990. I remember going to

Downing Street to be offered my new job. The street was crammed with journalists and TV cameras, who had been following the dramatic events of the preceding few days of the leadership campaign. I fought my way in and was thrilled to be offered a job in the Treasury.

This was the first time I had seen John Major alone, or almost alone – the Cabinet Secretary was in attendance – since he had announced the members of his first Cabinet. It seemed strange at first that he was here in Number 10 as Prime Minister, still recognisably himself, but touched, nevertheless, with the aura of power which inevitably surrounds the office. He explained that he wanted me to go to the Treasury, where I had been a very junior PPS. He pointed out that this would be the first time that there had been a woman minister at the Treasury. We discussed whether or not I would have the title of Paymaster General. I thought this was a fine idea, but in the end the title was given to Chris Patten, who was made Party Chairman. I was given the title of Minister of State. We talked about some Treasury issues. It was obvious that there would be problems ahead, and he was well aware of them, but the overall feeling was of excitement and optimism. He wanted me to emphasise that my appointment was of importance to the cause of women. 'Go out and impress on the journalists that you are the first woman minister there has ever been at the Treasury,' he said.

My first live television interview was with John Cole, the then BBC political editor. 'What do you think you can contribute at the Treasury, as a woman?' he asked.

Quick as a flash, I blew it. 'As a *person*,' I said pompously, 'I have a year's ministerial experience, and was a PPS in the Treasury.' It wrongfooted Cole, who apologised on air for being sexist, and told me later that his wife had been furious with his question. But it wrongfooted the Prime Minister too, who was later accused, by Teresa Gorman and others, of missing the opportunity to put women into his Cabinet. I did not feel I had made the best of starts.

The Treasury was a Rolls-Royce department. Even quite junior ministers could feel powerful there, given the Treasury's power of veto over everything that moved in Whitehall. For example, in the Cabinet Committee which dealt with plans for future legislation, the Treasury minister attending was always of junior rank, but in a position to say 'The Treasury says no', quite often for arcane Treasury reasons, which were much more to do with the exercise of power within the confines of Whitehall than with the practicalities of what was being proposed. When I was at the Treasury there was a great dispute about the need for legislation on hedgerows. This was eventually achieved when John Gummer was Environment Secretary, but when Michael Heseltine was in that post there were grave misgivings about the need for such regulation, and the form it might take. The Treasury said no for quite a period until Heseltine noticed what was going on, and very charmingly but decisively put his foot down. I recall clearly a late night telephone call from him, in my room in the House, when after an entirely delightful preamble he made it quite plain that junior ministers were just that: junior.

So this feeling of power was an illusion, affording only delaying time until Cabinet ministers noticed what was going on, and moved to crush one's impudence.

The senior mandarins were for most part knights of the realm, and very important. Andrew Tyrie, now MP for Chichester, then an adviser at the Treasury, told me that during his time there he had seen a flow-chart of the Treasury organisation. The officials had been carefully charted. In a side column there appeared a list of ministers, in very small print. On one occasion when my husband came to collect me from the Treasury, security denied all knowledge of my existence. Not deterred, he asked to see a list of ministers. It was headed by the name of Nigel Lawson, who had left two years earlier. All the ministers listed below his name had also left. There was no mention of Norman Lamont, by then the Chancellor, or of any of us.

Notwithstanding this, those working in the Treasury get used to the scent of power, particularly at the time of annual public spending reviews and the Budget. Junior ministers, however, are wise to realise that no matter what their illusions of power, they are not in the Cabinet, and not, therefore, privy to what happens at the highest reaches of Government. Power, I thought, must reside in the Cabinet.

I entered the Cabinet after the 1992 General Election. I was at home in Norfolk when the call came from Number 10. I drove to my flat in London and waited there to be telephoned, with the television switched on so that I could see what was happening in Downing Street. I waited and waited. Eventually, after about four hours, I rang the Private Office in Number 10. 'Shall I come down,' I enquired, confident I would get an affirmative answer. 'Well', said the cautious voice at the other end, 'I think it would be better if you waited for us to call.' 'Another short career,' I thought. 'Out of the Cabinet before I start.' In fact, the Prime Minister was having difficulty with some parts of his reshuffle: some senior colleagues either did not want what was offered, or did not see that the time had come for them to depart. By the time I reached Number 10, I think the Prime Minister was quite relieved to see someone who was overjoyed with what was on offer. I was promoted to become Secretary of State for Employment. We both knew that unemployment was likely to rise in the next year, and that the going would be tough. But the most intriguing offer he made was that I should take charge of Women's Issues. It was the first time a Government had included such a set of policies and I was enthusiastic. I had had some preparation, having served as co-chairman of the Women's National Commission. I knew that in this area, which within Government was effectively a green-field site, I would have the power to achieve change because I would be starting from scratch.

At that time the Department of Employment was a wonderful place to start a Cabinet career. It was a hands-on department, with excellent officials used to running their own show and devising real solutions for specific problems. There were a lot of issues to deal with, not least the gap between training and education, the development of Training and Enterprise Councils, and the handling of some tricky European matters, including the Working Time Directive. It was not a large department, nor one in which you might become dizzy with the exercise of power. It was an economic department, where close working with the Treasury was required, and where much of what we might want to do could run across education policy, or the sensitive arrangements within the territorial departments. Not for the first or last time, I became aware that power in our governmental system was often more apparent than real.

In a Government that had been in power already for thirteen years, there was always legislation to bring forward that had been left on the backburner for political reasons or because time had not been available. Taking someone else's ideas through the legislative process does not make you feel mistress of the universe, although it has to be done, and rightly so, in a cabinet style Government with collective responsibility. Thus it was that I found myself abolishing Wages Councils. While I supported the policy wholeheartedly, I would not, if asked a year earlier, have said it would be my first priority.

As I moved about the ministerial system, I became aware of the different ethos of the various departments. While different from the Department of Employment, the Ministry of Agriculture, Fisheries and Food resembled it in one important respect – it, too, was a hands-on department. It was regarded by smart political commentators as dull, and by other departments as incomprehensible. Therefore the Minister was left alone for the most part to get on, which is certainly in its way a form of power. It worked particularly well with the Treasury, whose clever officials knew nothing about agriculture, and who usually gave in during the course of public spending rounds, simply out of boredom. MAFF's budget is so small compared with most other departments' that it is hardly worth fighting over. However, in no other department is there so close a link with European policy, or so much outside control over what is done. On average the Minister spends one week in four in European meetings, usually in Brussels or Luxembourg, and is severely constrained by what he can wring out of the labyrinthine European decision-making process.

There was much less European work in the Department of Education, which was my next move in the summer of 1994. Traditionally, ministers arriving at Education had been amazed by their lack of power, given that local education authorities ran schools and universities ran themselves. Much of that had changed, thanks to Conservative education reforms that had begun in the mid-1980s. While the reforms themselves were instrumental in transforming attitudes within the education system, and certainly contributed to raising standards, they did not equip the department with either the skills or the power for the more centralised running of education they presupposed. This was undoubtedly one of the reasons for the resignation of John Patten, my predecessor, who felt, with justification, that he had been required to implement reforms without the necessary administrative tools. The paradox of ministers making pronouncements on the running of an education system that others, namely local education authorities, have to carry out, is still not resolved. The position is unsatisfactory, and can only be put right by a thorough-going reform of local government and its responsibilities. Suffice it to say that any education minister who believes that those responsible for implementing his policies will meekly do his bidding is in for an important lesson about the real nature of power.

The Illusion of Power

> Men of power have not time to read; yet men who do not read are unfit for power.
>
> MICHAEL FOOT

So where *is* power? I am not in the habit of quoting Michael Foot or Aneurin Bevan that often, but to me, this anecdote is at the heart of the question.

Drawing on a Commons speech of Bevan's in December 1943, Michael Foot, his biographer, captured the motivating force of the young Bevan in Tredegar.

> 'Very important man. That's Councillor Jackson,' his father had said to him. 'What's the Council?', he asked. 'Very important place indeed and

they are very powerful men,' his father had replied. 'When I got older, I said to myself, "The place to get to is the Council. That's where the power is." So I worked very hard, and in association with my fellows, when I was about twenty years of age, I got on the Council. I discovered when I got there that power had been there, but it had just gone. So I made some enquiries, being an earnest student of social affairs, and I learned that the power had slipped down to the County Council. That was where it was, and where it had gone to. So I worked very hard again, and I got there, and it had gone from there too.' [1]

Many whom the public perceive as powerful empathise with that anecdote about Bevan. This book will attempt to discover whether Bevan was right.

Power Vacuum:

From Margaret to Major

The world is given to those whom the world can trust.

WALTER BAGEHOT

THREE PRIME MINISTERS and one President have mused in my presence on the nature of power and its mirage-like quality – the nearer you think you are to it, the more illusory it becomes. Pierre Mendes France remarked that to govern is to choose. But how far is the power to choose constrained by the personality and attitudes of those exercising it; circumstance and chronology; policy inheritance; Party baggage and personalities; events; Government machinery; by the momentum for change?

Power in politics is the ability to achieve change; it is conferred on Governments through the ballot box and bestowed by Parliament. On becoming Prime Minister in 1990, John Major inherited the handsome parliamentary majority of his predecessor, Margaret Thatcher, 95 seats overall and 143 over the Labour Party. A different personality might have felt able to stamp his own authority on such a Parliament, but, while he did not lack ideas, Major felt that it was not *his* majority and, since he was pledged to change key policies like the Poll Tax, that it was not his mandate either. When he had his own mandate in 1992, it was with a parliamentary majority of 21, which, in the end, proved not enough. The Conservatives learnt the truth of Bagehot's remark that 'All satire apart, the principle of Parliament is obedience to leaders. The penalty of not being so is the penalty of impotence'.[2]

Some argue that only the Governments of 1906, 1945, 1979 – and possibly 1997, although this remains to be seen – have been true forces for seminal change. One of John Major's misfortunes was that his administration was sandwiched between two of them and its reputation, in the short term, has suffered.

But any leader taking over from a giant figure like Margaret Thatcher eighteen months before an election, after eleven years in power, with a looming agenda of economic recession, a party split on Europe and on other issues, and beset by extraordinary events would have had difficulties. It is to Major's credit that he has emerged, still recognisably himself, and having laid the foundations in the economy, health, education, welfare and Northern Ireland to enable the new Labour Government to make a flying start. But his story and that of the Conservative Party in this period illustrates the perhaps reassuring truth that a strong parliamentary position is what matters in the exercise of power. That it did not feel like that to us at the time is beside the point.

Do certain personalities find it more difficult than others to exercise power, no matter how enthusiastic they are to achieve change? Should John Major have felt so constrained by the fact that his inherited majority was not his own? Before 1992 he spoke frequently of his desire for his own mandate. Rightly or wrongly, he seemed to feel that he could not apply the smack of firm Government until he had taken the Conservative Party to the country. In any case, he seemed hesitant about power. In his autobiography he says,

> After the pomp and circumstance of the Thatcher years, I was keen to present an antidote to that, to show people that it was possible to be prime minister without changing. I wanted to show that it was possible to be prime minister and remain a human being, just like the fifty-five million other human beings in the country, but with an exceptional job. In one sense, having power reminded me that it needed to be exercised in a way that did not make you different from other people. I think I felt quite differently about power than any Prime Minister this century.[3]

Those who supported Major as leader of the Conservative Party perceived that he indeed had a different approach from his predecessors: it was more up-to-date and in tune with the end of the twentieth century. He was chosen precisely because he differed from his immediate predecessor who, at the time of her downfall, had come to be viewed by many of her colleagues and Conservative activists as a political liability.

Some in the Parliamentary Party, ever ungrateful, forgot why they had picked him when things became increasingly hard later on. As is common with political leaders, he, like Margaret Thatcher, became more and more criticised for the very leadership style for which he had been elected in the first place. Interestingly, the public, with whom he remains very popular, has been less fickle.

John Major's view of himself, then, was at odds with a more conventional image of a prime minister. Those who knew him well understood this. It was an integral part of the man. On occasion, though, it made things difficult.

Before the 1992 general election, much thought was given at Conservative Central Office on how best to present his 'plain man', straightforwardness. We were helped by the knowledge that his election as Tory Leader had wrongfooted the Labour Party: they had decided on how to present the downside of Margaret Thatcher and had even prepared for a Hurd or Heseltine-led campaign. But they did not know how best to attack Major. Anthony Seldon quotes Neil Kinnock who said,

> Major came up from nowhere and we had no pre-existing strategy that could be used against him. The tactical dilemma was whether to portray him as a Thatcherite or attack him for the new things he was doing. The choice was basically for the former because the Tories wanted to project a new image and there was no point doing their work for them.[4]

Little did he know! From the day of Major's election as Party Leader, everyone had been wrestling with the same dilemma. Of course he was distinctively different from Margaret Thatcher but to emphasise that difference might split the party or alienate the many strong Thatcher supporters among our activists. Party strategists were not helped by Major's strong resistance to any hint that he should be made-over for presentational purposes. 'No point in me trying to do something people tell me to do. If it isn't me, it doesn't work. If I am comfortable with it, it will work to the best of my ability.'[5] This was infuriating to the style specialists, foremost among whom at that time was Shaun Woodward, later MP for Witney and a defector to the Labour Party in December 1999. But Major won out. For the 1992 election he adopted the soap box technique of addressing large crowds in a hustings style, using a megaphone or microphone. It served him well. The contrast between the simplicity of his approach compared with what came to be called the Labour Party's Nüremberg Rally, which took place in Sheffield the weekend before polling day, remains an enduring image of the campaign. It continues to colour, correctly, the public's view of Major as a straightforward, honest man, resistant to spin. They liked him for it then and they continue to do so.

Perhaps John Major's personality, attitudes and intermittent lack of confidence have made judgements of his premiership less positive than he would like. As Bagehot observes:

> Because the House of Commons has the power of dismissal in addition to the power of election, its relations to the premier are incessant. They guide him and he leads them. He is to them what they are to the nation. He will only go where he believes they will go after him. But he has to take the lead; he must choose his direction and begin the journey. Nor must he flinch. A good horse likes to feel the rider's bit; and a great deliberative assembly likes to feel that it is under worthy guidance.[6]

The Major Psyche

> An honest man can feel no pleasure in the exercise of power over his fellow citizens.
>
> JOHN MCLISH

Clearly, some of Major's own attitudes and personality traits were constraints. His style was consensual. In his autobiography, he observes: 'Margaret had been at her happiest confronting dragons. I chose consensus in policy making if not always in policy.'[7] This was not only a matter of his style: he was aware that he had inherited a deeply divided party. His first task as Prime Minister, the creation of a Cabinet, reflected both his style and the context of his leadership: he deliberately set about forming a Cabinet that represented all shades of opinion in the party. It would have been unthinkable for a man of his temperament to have excluded those who were not 'one of us'. It would also have been misguided, given the hopes within the party that he would be able to heal the divisions he had inherited. He was indeed consensual by nature, but he had to be if progress was to be made.

Those who were in the Cabinet before and after 1990 were much given to describing the different styles of John Major and his predecessor in handling Cabinet meetings. As Anthony Seldon puts it, 'The wisdom that she [Mrs Thatcher] began by announcing the conclusions whereas he would sum up after lengthy meetings has passed into folklore'.[8]

I did not join the Cabinet until after the 1992 election, although I had attended political Cabinets in the run up to the election, in my capacity as Party Deputy Chairman. I therefore had no opportunity to make comparisons.

Major was always keen, if he could, to arrive at a position where he could say that the majority view was X or Y. He did this even if

31

he disagreed with the consensual conclusion, as when public spending limits were finally set in 1995. He needed to feel that colleagues were on his side, and if this led to exasperation on the part of some for his lack of direction, he saw it otherwise.

> I went to a great deal of trouble to listen and respond to whatever people had to say. If, in the development of policy, I could reach a conclusion that I believed to be right, with a minimum of noise rather than a maximum, I would do so. If I can [sic] soothe wounds, I would do so.[9]

He demonstrated immense self-control at Cabinet, even when he was enraged by the latest series of leaks or briefings against him. The strongest sign of irritation he showed was to throw down his pencil. I have often wondered what the effect would have been if he had really given vent to his feelings – ruinous leaks in the press, I suspect, of the 'Major's lost it' variety. That, no doubt, is why he never did.

He described his first eighteen months in power as the time of greatest promise for him. A more ruthless character would perhaps have set out to trample on his policy inheritance and to carry out more positive changes of direction and personnel. He was sometimes perversely over-modest. But the circumstances of his election as Conservative leader – in the aftermath of the departure of a charismatic, adored and hated, controversial but undeniably world-stage figure – forced on him an even more cautious approach than he might now admit was necessary. He was certainly ambitious but he had not pursued his political career with the idea in mind that he would one day become Party Leader (unlike others with less credible pretensions). He had not sought to develop his ideas in pamphlets or articles and, although he was assiduous in his courtesy and attention to parliamentary colleagues, he never created a coterie of followers in the House. For the same reason, he never encouraged the expression of 'Majorism'. He seemed less than comfortable in making broad philosophical statements, preferring the concrete and actual rooted in his own experience. Broad themes – in his long-term enthusiasms such as education, opportunity, public services, a more relaxed attitude to Europe, control of inflation – emerged before the 1992 election, and were further developed afterwards. His tone, always moderate, was a true reflection of the man and it was certainly more in keeping with British attitudes than that of his predecessor, yet with the perversity that attends political fortunes, he was criticised for indecision and dithering, where she had been castigated for hectoring and bullying. In each case, the criticism was at odds with the reasons for which each had been elected leader in the first place.

Those of John Major's critics who found it convenient to accuse him of dithering, or of saying one thing to one group of colleagues and something else to others seriously misunderstood his leadership style. On many occasions he said that one of his principal aims was to achieve as much unity as possible in the Conservative Party, but he genuinely respected other people's views and had a real interest in what mattered to them.

Lancing the European Boil

> Successful conduct of economic policy is possible only if there is full agreement between the Prime Minister and the Chancellor of the Exchequer.
>
> NIGEL LAWSON

John Major's handling of the issue of a referendum on the Single Currency illustrates his style of Government. In 1994, he asked

Douglas Hurd, in extreme secrecy, to sound out colleagues on the possibility of holding a referendum on whether or not the UK should enter the Single Currency. Hurd reported back that they were overwhelmingly against (although I was not, I did not at that stage know which colleagues were with me). At the time there was much talk in the press that the Labour Party might announce that they were in favour of a referendum before we could, and the idea began to gain ground. It resurfaced around the time of the Madrid Summit in December 1995. At a reception held at Downing Street for the Clintons at the end of November 1995, a huddle of ministers, including Malcolm Rifkind and Lord Cranborne, developed around the Prime Minister and it was clear that some pretty heavy discussion was taking place. It was equally clear that if the Prime Minister had been able then to get collective agreement to announce such a plan, it would have made the Parliamentary context for the Madrid Summit much easier. It was also a rather risky place to hold such a high level discussion, in full view of the journalists and other Whitehall watchers there to greet the Clintons. In the event, the President was so charismatic that all eyes were upon him, and not on any other displays of body language in evidence. Even so, his presence, distinguished as it was, was not the important event at that reception. Not for the first time, I was struck by the multi-layered nature of political activity.

It was at around this time that James Goldsmith's Referendum Party began to make waves. It also made for nervousness in the Parliamentary Party. Wild talk – in the end not so wild – started in the House of Commons Tea Room about the number of seats that might be at risk. Still the Prime Minister was unwilling to raise the referendum idea in Cabinet, knowing that Kenneth Clarke, for one, was strongly against the whole notion. Interestingly, Ken had always maintained that he was against the idea of a referendum on constitutional grounds, rather than because he supported the notion of a Single Currency. Eventually Douglas Hogg raised the issue at a Cabinet meeting on 7 March 1996. The main subject for discussion that day was a paper on Britain's position for the Inter Governmental Conference to reform the institutions of the European Union and revise the Maastricht Treaty. It had been pre-pared in Cabinet Committee, under first Douglas Hurd's and then Malcolm Rifkind's chairmanship, and given the different views represented, much good-humoured progress had been made. In what appeared to be a spontaneous move, Douglas Hogg suggested that it would be a good idea for the Single Currency to be dis-cussed in the White Paper and the idea of a referendum was raised.

By now, Major was in favour of announcing one and could have driven the idea through straightaway. But he was aware of Clarke's opposition to the whole idea. He went round the table, asking each colleague for his or her views. Clarke, and to a lesser extent, Michael Heseltine, objected, but the overwhelming opinion was in favour. However, instead of summing up to that effect, Major asked the Foreign Secretary to prepare a paper giving the arguments on both sides, thus sparing Clarke any embarrassment before his colleagues.

Of course, it is possible to construe Major's decision as weak-ness, but I saw it as tact: Clarke was an able and senior colleague who, Major knew, felt extremely strongly on the matter, and one of whom he was very fond. He was also conscious of the dam-age Europhiles, led by Clarke, could do to Party unity. In the event he announced the policy change that afternoon through a planted Question in the House from Sir Marcus Fox, although in such a low-key way that a number of colleagues and most of the commentators missed it. His reputation for dithering was once again burnished, unfairly.

Major had great respect for the collective views of the Cabinet. He felt especially strongly that a Prime Minister should not over-rule his Chancellor. This might have been based on his own experience as Chancellor, but it is more likely, I think, to have come from his observation of the deterioration of relations between Margaret Thatcher and Nigel Lawson. This belief did not always serve him well.

The Power of the Treasury

> Those who have economic power, have civil power also.
>
> GEORGE RUSSELL

In the public spending round leading up to the 1995–6 financial year – pre-election year – I had had great difficulty persuading the then Chief Secretary to the Treasury, Jonathan Aitken, of the polit-ical importance of backing the Prime Minister's enthusiasm for education with realistic spending. Eventually I felt he had grasped how important it was to remind the electorate and the education establishment of all that we had done in the field of education. Our reforms had raised standards, made the whole system more trans-parent and emphasised the link between national success and edu-cation and training. We had plenty to celebrate, but a less than ade-quate financial settlement at this point before the election would merely concentrate the public mind on cash rather than policy.

I knew Kenneth Clarke would oppose me. He had a rooted dis-like of local authorities and all their works. I sometimes wondered if he had been bitten by an alderman when he was a child, as he was quite incapable of discussing local government rationally. He had also, perhaps, been scarred by his time at the then Department of Education, when he had been involved in pushing through radical reform in the teeth of fierce opposition from local authorities, Conservative as well as Labour and Liberal Democrat, and the teachers' unions. His battles were many and loud.

For whatever reason, he would not accept Aitken's recommendation, and a vigorously expressed debate took place in the EDX Committee, which handled public spending matters.

I was strongly supported by a number of colleagues, including, notably, John Gummer. The encounters between Gummer and others, especially Clarke, at EDX were so entertaining that an official said everyone should have a ticket to watch. Gummer was easily the most articulate of all colleagues, and could continue, in full spate, for hours on end given the chance. His diatribes became more and more outrageous as he progressed, culminating, usually, in everyone collapsing with laughter. On this occasion, however, Gummer was deadly serious. He had caught the mood from Tory councillors up and down the country. He knew that while disquiet about the previous year's financial settlement had been contained – just – further belt tightening, particularly close to an Election, would not work.

In the end the education settlement had to go to full Cabinet. Major was at pains to be a neutral chairman. Cabinet, narrowly, took the Chancellor's side. When Major closed the meeting he remarked that he hoped we would not come to regret the decision we had just taken. Sadly, we did.

That year, as the reality of the settlement came home we were faced with protests, demonstrations and strong complaints from our own Tory Councillors about the impossibility of the task we had set them. In the end, even Ken Clarke admitted that he had insisted on too tight a settlement but by that time, it was too late to persuade the electorate of our seriousness about education.

This was the more ironic given John Major's enthusiasm for education. In his autobiography he writes,

> An early pacemaker in domestic reform was education. In the spring, I
> told the Young Conservatives: 'At the top of my personal agenda is education. It is the key to opening new paths for all sorts of people – not
> just the most gifted – and for doing so at every stage of their lives. Not
> having had much education myself, I was keen on it.[10]

In this public spending round, John Major's personality, his consensual style, and his respect for the principle of collective Government prevented him from achieving one of his personal goals, something he may have regretted when it came to the election.

Cabinet Government

> Government is the only known vessel that leaks from the top.
>
> JAMES RESTON

It is commonplace in Government that many of the most important decisions are taken in Cabinet Committees, where battles are fiercely and knowledgeably fought. If agreement cannot be reached, the Prime Minister is told, and is asked on occasion by the Committee in question to decide the matter. At other times, the decision is taken by the full Cabinet. This was almost always true in the case of the public spending round. Yet, while all colleagues make a contribution to the Budget process, the

38

Chancellor's decision is final. It is on the morning of Budget Day, and not before, that he announces to the full Cabinet the contents of his Budget statement.

Some describe Cabinet meetings as a formality, believing that they merely rubberstamp the real action outside the overt process. Although some were much shorter than others, I always found them consumingly interesting, sometimes because of what people were not saying, rather than what they were. Alongside Cabinet meetings, there were political Cabinets, held more frequently in the run-up to elections, but attended by advisers and others from Conservative Central Office and without civil servants present.

The meeting on 20 March 1996, which had been planned as a political Cabinet[11] to discuss election strategies, became a crisis meeting to plan the Government's response to new information about BSE: that there could be a causal connection between BSE and Creutzfeld Jacobs Disease (CJD). The Prime Minister rang me before the meeting to warn me of what was to be discussed. At that meeting ministers and experts came together, in urgency and off-the-cuff, to formulate the most effective possible safeguards for human and animal health in the light of new scientific knowledge. Major chaired the meeting superbly. As usual, he had mastered the technical detail, knowing that this was a potentially serious development and that the scientific information was complex. Those who had not already wrestled with this problem, and that was most of the Cabinet, listened carefully to the experts' explanations. There was some discussion about whether statements should be made in the House that afternoon by Stephen Dorrell, the Health Secretary, and Douglas Hogg, the Agriculture Minister. I felt strongly that there should be two statements: human health was the most important consideration, but the implications for the agriculture industry would also have to be spelt out. My colleagues agreed. Major was at his best in this kind of situation: genuinely concerned for the public, and aware of the Government's responsibilities, he was calm and in command. While of course there was an explosion of public concern when the announcements were made, and while the problems were unprecedented and enormous, Major gave real leadership throughout.

The Emergence of Major

> A friend in power is a friend lost.
>
> HENRY O. ADAMS

Personality is only one factor which might constrain the exercise of power to achieve change. Circumstance and the context of a leader's emergence may also act as a powerful brake. This certainly applied to John Major.

The circumstances of his emergence and election as leader of the Conservative Party have been exhaustively chronicled. Those of us involved in his support team remember clearly how we used the arguments that he was a conciliator, a consensus man, someone who could bring together all elements of the party. We pointed out that he was a younger, family man, who could empathise with the electorate's concerns on health, jobs, education, and communicate with them in comprehensible terms. On the other hand some of the more experienced members of the team – I had been in Parliament only three years – were also aware that the nature of Margaret Thatcher's departure would cause problems for her successor and that the adoring support combined with the furious opposition she inspired would ensure that the task would be hard.

40

And thus it proved. Long-stay Governments get trapped in their own tramlines and when those tramlines have been put in place by a prime minister of great authority and appeal, the task of a successor is difficult indeed.

Guardian journalist Michael White emphasised that, as Major's rise had been so dependent on him being crowned as Mrs Thatcher's chosen successor, it was 'imperative for him to stamp his own authority on the Government he has inherited to prove that he is not "son of Thatcher"'.[12] Either way he was damned. If he strove to define and pursue new directions, he would be 'betraying the Thatcher inheritance'; if he did not, he would be caricatured as travelling with a back-seat driver. As it was, while he was a first-class tactician and politically adept, he found himself accused of lacking the necessary sense of strategy and even the ability to articulate such a strategy. He could see all too clearly that he was trapped by the circumstances of his elevation.

There was another factor. Because there had already been eleven years of Conservative Government when he took over as leader, he inherited ingrained attitudes and policies, preserved in shorthand definitions like 'wets' and 'dries'. Also, he had had no time to prepare. Of his position when he became leader, he wistfully wrote,

> Only now, years later, is it possible to understand how much was lost because I came into Number 10 from Government, without my own programme settled, rather than from Opposition, where my priorities would have been prepared and ready for action. The speed at which the incoming Labour Government was able to act in 1997 illustrates this point; their plans were ready to roll, giving an impression of dynamism, even where many of their policies were, in my view, unwise. I, by contrast, came into Number 10 after eleven years of Conservative Government and inherited policies some of which I had the pain of

41

> changing against the opposition of much of my own party, and the jeers
> of my opponents. I did not enjoy the luxury of working up my own
> programme at leisure. It had to be done at speed and amidst the frenzy
> of Government. Nor, after the Party had been so long in Government,
> could I create the image of a new agenda with a series of philosophical
> speeches on the principles of Conservatism. Yet people demand new
> ideas and new policies – and swiftly.[13]

Clearly, he believes that, if he had had the time to think out policies, strategy and tone, to assemble a dream team to work with him, everything would have been different. He perceives the constraints on his power to achieve change, imposed by the circumstances of his elevation. A long-term Government will show unmistakable signs of being institutionalised.

As a new backbencher with everything to learn in 1987, I was willing to accept party orthodoxy, believing that there must be reasons for it of which, in my lowly position, I knew nothing. But I was amazed to find when I became a minister, that orthodoxy often put paid to common-sense change.

Nothing was more crushing to a less than confident junior minister than to be told by a civil servant, 'No, Minister, we cannot do that. It isn't Government policy.' Soon I began to point out that ministers were the Government, not civil servants. On the other hand, after eleven years of a Government's life, the weight of received truth lay heavy. And when Margaret Thatcher was the Prime Minister, the iron hand of institutionalisation could seem heavy indeed.

The Power of the War Widows

People have power when other people think they have power.

WILLIAM WYNCHE FOWLER

While I was in my first Parliamentary Under-Secretary post with Tony Newton at the DSS, a furore arose on the level of war widows' pensions. We were bombarded with thousands of letters from MPs and others, pointing out the need for a rise and the inequity of the present arrangements. In fact, this was a Ministry of Defence matter and any increase would have to be paid for out of their budget. In the end, Newton took us at dead of night from our Regency surroundings at the DSS to the Stalinesque Ministry of Defence buildings to consult Tom King, then Defence Secretary, who claimed to have received no letters of protest, which might have been true, since we surely had all there could be. Paralysis seemed likely to set in, since we all knew that the Prime Minister was unlikely to favour a rise. Yet the issue became a great public cause, and all the tabloids positioned themselves firmly with the war widows.

Tony Newton was in an impossible situation; although he was convinced of the cause, he was attracting all the flak and was unsupported by colleagues. Finally, as Armistice Day approached, Dame Vera Lynn intervened and a media frenzy ensued. Mrs Thatcher was consulted and eventually agreement was reached. Tony Newton said afterwards, 'We did at least escape criticism from the Queen Mother.' The episode taught me a lot – not least about the rigidity of long-stay Government but also about how change can be achieved even between a rock and hard place.

John Major's arrival as Prime Minister immediately achieved more openness and more flexibility and the atmosphere relaxed to the extent that problematical issues could at least be discussed without danger of damnation for ever as a wet. Two of his early initiatives – unfreezing child benefit and awarding compensation to HIV-infected haemophiliacs – exemplify that change. Inevitably right-wing critics used them to lambast him for abandoning the 'true flame', as Anthony Seldon puts it.[14]

Soothing the Trauma

Unused power slips imperceptibly into the hands of another.

KONRAD HEIDEN

Also as a new Prime Minister, Major had to contend with the knowledge that we would face a General Election in less than eighteen months. While it was always true that the imminence of an election focuses the minds of backbenchers and erodes open dissent, there seemed to be an enormous amount to do, not least within the Party itself, to soothe 'the trauma of Margaret's dismissal', as Major put it.[15] There was little time to prepare.

If a leader is elected part-way through the life of a Government, he has to cope with the policies he has inherited. If some are deeply unpopular, he has also to plot a way through the forests of difficulties with colleagues, the public and the media, to remove them. The amount of time and effort this takes puts paid to achieving change; a problem that also faces every Cabinet Minister, one way or another, on first appointment. A new leader heading a newly elected Government is not constrained by this.

In 1997, commentators immediately rushed to compare Tony Blair's 'smack of firm Government' leadership style with that of his predecessor, who suffered in comparison. There was all the difference in the world between their circumstances.

As the euphoria of Major's elevation to Prime Minister died away, we all became aware of the policy inheritance with which we would have to deal. I had been appointed to the Treasury as Minister of State and could see the problems looming in the economy: inflation was approaching double figures, interest rates were at fourteen per cent and unemployment was rising. The Poll Tax would have to be dealt with, and Major's more emollient approach to Europe would do little to heal the splits so evident in the circumstances of Margaret Thatcher's departure. To cap it all, war was likely to break out in the Gulf. There were positive political legacies too: trade union reforms had transformed labour relations; there had been a great increase in personal wealth, with increased home and share ownership and savings. More privatisation in the public sector was breaking down the monoliths that had been so hard to shift in the past. Margaret Thatcher's brilliance and determination had made Britain a force to be reckoned with in the world, while the Labour Party under Neil Kinnock was regarded by many as unelectable.

There was a lot that was positive in Major's inheritance. Handling it, particularly with a diminishing parliamentary majority, would inevitably lead to a hardening of the party splits that were to dog Major for the rest of his premiership. Those in the Party who could never forgive him for not being Margaret Thatcher would continue to interpret every change from her approach as treachery. Some of those who had wanted to see her go perhaps hoped for greater distancing between his policies and hers. As John Major put it,

> The broad tradition of the Party was tolerant. If a certain shrill and censorious tone had set in, it was that tone which broke faith with our past. My predecessor was not personally unsympathetic but some, less

tolerant than she, saw 'Thatcherism' as a vehicle for intolerance and, sometimes, prejudice.[16]

Indeed, I believe the reinterpretation of Thatcherism by over-zealous, not always astute disciples caused far more trouble for Major than it had for Margaret Thatcher herself.

The abolition of the Poll Tax exemplified the nature of Major's inheritance. Its introduction had been deeply controversial within Government and in the party, and as a newly arrived junior Treasury Minister, I was startled to receive on my first day an admonitory lecture from a senior Treasury mandarin. He maintained that the Treasury itself would never have introduced a tax with 26 million losers. Nigel Lawson's opposition to the whole tax had made its introduction as difficult as possible.

Yet the notion that everyone should pay something towards the services they all used was attractive, not only in the party but in the country. As ever, it was implementation that dogged it from the first, but its abolition was regarded by some of the more fervent Thatcher supporters as yet another act of treachery. Its continued existence would almost certainly have meant defeat at the coming election and it had to be sorted out. And sorting it out had to be fitted in round the Gulf War.

Fortunately, John Major had had the vision to bring Michael Heseltine back into the Cabinet with the task of dealing with the Poll Tax and between them, he and Norman Lamont transformed a U-turn into, if not a political triumph, then at least a vanishing act for the hated tax. But the right wing of the party did not forget it.

Europe Again

Power only tires those who don't exercise it.

PIERRE TRUDEAU

As for Europe, Margaret Thatcher had become famous throughout the European Community, as it was then, for her intransigence, and her 'No, No, No' approach. But she had signed the Single European Act in 1985. In frequent protestations afterwards, including to me, she said that 'they had not told her' of its full implications for Britain's sovereignty. Here John Major describes his attitude to Europe:

> I was a pragmatist about the European Community. I believed it was in our economic interest to be a member. I welcomed sensible co-operation. I had no hang-ups about Germany. I accepted that being one of a Community of 15 meant that sometimes we had to reach a consensus that was not entirely to our taste. I was keen to rebuild shattered fences, to prevent Britain from being seen for ever as the odd man to be excluded from the private consultations that so often foreshadowed new policy in Europe.[17]

On becoming Prime Minister, Major discovered in his dealings with other European leaders what we all found in our EC negotiations: that Margaret Thatcher was regarded as the real odd man out and, with her, Britain. But the fact was that, in many ways, we *were* the odd man out. Our legal and welfare systems had developed in different ways; our democracy was exercised differently; and we had been a unified nation for longer than the other major states. Small wonder that we did not share the others' attitudes. But we were members, and the only way forward was to devise means of working with others that did not compromise us. From the start

47

Major recognised the importance for his own political survival and for the forthcoming election of the Maastricht negotiations of December 1991.

So did his supporters. Every effort was made to promote the outcome as positive to the press, the public and to the parliamentary party. As the final session at Maastricht drew to a close, elaborate arrangements were made to get instant feedback and briefing for the Parliamentary Party. Francis Maude, under Tristan Garel-Jones's direction, was put in charge, and a long night followed, of preparing briefing, telephoning colleagues, foreseeing and blocking loopholes, and dealing with British and foreign press. Initially, the opt-outs from European Monetary Union (EMU) and the Social Chapter were received enthusiastically at home – rightly so, since they were the result of Major's patient and dogged persistence in the negotiations, and formed the basis of a good deal for Britain. As things turned out, that initial enthusiasm turned into a later realisation of the difficult inheritance that Europe was for Major.

It is clear that he held a positive view of Europe and the opportunities it held for Britain. He was not a Europhile, but his opponents, some of whom were truly fanatical in their opposition to all things European, took every opportunity to paint him into that corner. In the end, it proved an impossible legacy. But it is one of the greatest of political ironies that Tony Blair swept to power having persuaded the electorate that the Labour Party's view on Europe was one of sensible pragmatism, the view for which Major's enemies blamed him for the Conservatives' electoral defeat.

Trouble at Home

> The first principle of a civilised state is that the power is legitimate only when it is under contract.
>
> WALTER LIPPMANN

Domestic policy making was no less hidebound, and Major had to contend with the absurd shorthand description of policy attitudes coined by Margaret Thatcher's supporters, wets and dries. To make over-enthusiastic statements about, for example, the public services was to damn oneself as disloyal to the Thatcher orthodoxy. Yet under her premiership, important reforms in education, health, and housing had been introduced, transforming standards of service and access to excellence. Public spending on these services rose also, although a great deal of effort was devoted to denying this.

John Major describes the eighteen months leading up to the election in April 1992 as 'the time of greatest promise for me in Government',[18] but afterwards his ambitions for change were 'displaced by the constant battles within the Party and by economic circumstances', [19] His 'effort to nudge Conservatism towards its compassionate roots' was interpreted as an attempt to undo the progress achieved by his predecessor. I had always believed that Conservative rhetoric during most of the Thatcher years had achieved the worst of all possible worlds for the Party. We trumpeted our concern for public spending in a way that resulted in a universal belief that we had done nothing but cut it – 'it's the cuts' became a mantra on every radio and television programme and at every public meeting – even though public spending increased. I believed in sound public services and thought that education, health and welfare were properly the responsibility of the State. So

49

did John Major. His childhood and education experiences had formed his views and attitudes to a profound extent and his concern for those who struggle with public services, those not affluent or confident enough to exercise choice, those who have had a difficult start in life, illuminated many of his social policies. Yet he and the party were never given the credit for them because, at the time, they were so at odds with the public face of Conservatism. As he points out with typical understatement in his autobiography,

> The public face of the Conservative Party carelessly, sometimes tactlessly, still allowed itself to be seen as not caring about improving the public sector. Many in powerful positions failed to acknowledge the work done by excellent teachers, nurses or transport workers. They too easily forgot how vital these skills were to the lives of nearly everyone in the country. Such views were politically self-defeating. They were also fatuous and absurd. The impression too often conveyed was that our support was grudging and our policy of privatising some parts of the public sector led people to believe we were hostile to all of it.

I shared this view. The public pronouncements and private hostilities of some colleagues were at odds with the investments in reforms and resources we had poured into public services. It was not 'macho' or 'dry' to pour scorn on local government or teachers. Indeed, to attract obloquy simultaneously from the left for being hostile towards the public sector and from the right for increased spending on it was a failure in policy and presentation of awesome proportions.

To party orthodoxy could be added the personal baggage of some Cabinet colleagues. Quite apart from the varying views on Europe, Major had to contend with other dyed-in-the-wool attitudes: Kenneth Clarke's real hostility to local councils and councillors, for example, and John Gummer's enthusiasm for them.

Managing differences of opinion in a corporate structure is the task of any leader but not every leader has to contend with public airing of those differences. A presupposition of a shared agenda may be possible in some organisations but not necessarily in Government.

A Matter of Trust

Trust your hopes, not your fears.

DAVID MAHONEY

John Major would have been helped if, like Margaret Thatcher, he had had a figure alongside him like Willie Whitelaw, whom he trusted and who knew his mind. Until the 1992 election, when he lost his seat, Chris Patten occupied that position.

Major relied heavily on Graham Bright, his trusted PPS. Bright was a likeable and astute man, with a sound business sense and a good feel for what was happening in the party within and outside Parliament. He was also said to be brutally frank with Major, which at times must have been difficult. However, some colleagues felt that he was not enough of a political heavyweight to be in such a key position. Major was also good friends with Robert Atkins, the entertaining and popular Lancashire MP, who had been close to Major since they entered the House together in 1979. Atkins was very much liked by colleagues, but again, they criticised him for lack of gravitas. Personally, I thought him a clever politician with his fingers on many a pulse.

It is the case that he lacked gravitas, but many would find that a relief in a context where far too many cultivate gravitas over substance. Tristan Garel-Jones, who was Deputy Chief Whip and then Minister for Europe, was both influential and supportive. He was deeply disliked and suspected by the Eurosceptic wing of the party, given his enthusiasm for the European cause. He was a fluent linguist, and had a Spanish wife, which caused him to be nicknamed the member for Madrid Central. He was a great observer of behaviour and spent long periods sitting, apparently innocently, on a bench in the Official Corridor, behind the Speaker's Chair, so that he could watch the comings and goings to ministers' rooms in the House, and keep a watch on any significant migrations which might be fledgling plots. But while Major was known to be close to these colleagues, and to a few others, they did not constitute a Willie Whitelaw, and as difficulties thickened, I was left with the strong impression that Major had come to feel he could trust very few, and they were not Cabinet colleagues.

John Gummer, John MacGregor, and I were frequently described as part of the East Anglian mafia. It is true that our common territory meant that we understood each other's political context. There was a fellow feeling between us. But I felt that I was too new a colleague to push my friendship with Major, even though I felt great sympathy for him as a man and as a politician. I also felt it best to remain on professional terms rather than become too close. Others doubtless felt the same. The result was that Major had a sense of isolation, which inevitably made his task harder, and also made it difficult for his colleagues themselves to feel they enjoyed his trust, except intermittently and when he had time to focus on them. Those of us who did support him throughout could not always find the means to do so.

To be Prime Minister at a difficult time is intensely lonely. To do that job without the fun and friendship which makes political life enjoyable is lonely indeed. Robert Cranborne, during Major's own leadership contest in 1995, was certainly trusted and supportive.

Nevertheless, Major did not feel close to Cranborne. It is a real sadness of John Major's premiership that a warm and affectionate man should have felt, mistakenly, so friendless by the end.

Harold Macmillan's celebrated reply, 'Events, dear boy, events', on being asked as to the most difficult feature of political success, might have been coined for John Major's premiership. Living through, in particular, the last two years of his administration, I began to wonder just what could possibly happen next. We engaged in two wars, and experienced incredible reverses and triumphs on Europe. There was a mortar bomb at Number 10, we left the ERM, we had mine closures, BSE and sleaze – each day brought something even more unexpected than the last. But there can be no doubt that everything was infinitely more difficult to handle because of the tiny and diminishing parliamentary majority. Apart from the problems of getting legislation through, it meant that groups of colleagues, even individuals, with axes to grind, gained a disproportionate importance in the scheme of things. They also took up unimaginable amounts of the Prime Minister's time. The constant airing of their grievances also added to his reputation for weakness and dithering – although those who accused him of this never produced solutions for the parliamentary problems we faced. They also forgot that Margaret Thatcher had undergone rebellions, which were legion on the Poll Tax but spectacular on welfare (National Insurance contributions), dangerous dogs, even the abolition of dog licences and football cards. Whips recount that on average there was a rebellion of serious proportions during most months, sometimes every fortnight, during her premiership, all of which were smoothed over because of the overall parliamentary majority.

The Long Parliament

> Power gradually extirpates from the mind every humane and gentle virtue.
>
> EDMUND BURKE

Once he had won the 1992 election, with a majority of 21, in sorry contrast to the one he had inherited, Major could see the problems ahead. He described prospects of success in 1997 as stretching 'the elastic of democracy too far'.[20] It was obvious to experienced MPs that, gruesomely, the average casualty rate of deaths, illness and mishap among their fellows would cause difficulties before the Parliament was over – and thus it proved. What was more, despite Conservative jubilation, there was a feeling of staleness and anticlimax after the election. It was as if the population had voted for us because they could not face a Labour Government, rather than because they wanted a Conservative one. The press and commentators, having been so conclusively wrong – with some honourable exceptions – in their predictions, would be out to get us. That proved to be the case too.

During the course of the 1992 Parliament, eight Conservative MPs died. Some of these died in particularly harrowing circumstances: Stephen Milligan was found asphyxiated in his flat, with an orange in his mouth. Iain Mills was also found dead in his flat. Others died totally unexpectedly, like Judith Chaplin, an outstanding Member, after just ten months in the House. Others were known to be in ill health, so that their deaths were not quite such a shock, but they caused great nervousness in the Parliamentary Party.

Some had the Whip withdrawn. Rupert Allason lost it over Europe in July 1993, and did not have it restored until a year later. In November 1994, the Whip was withdrawn from a further eight MPs, again on the European issue, and the Party remained without their votes on certain matters until May 1995. Richard Body, the fiercely independent MP for Boston and Skegness, resigned the Whip in November 1994 and it was not restored until January 1996.

There were also defections to other parties. Alan Howarth, who had been a whip when I became an MP in 1987, defected to Labour over welfare policies in October 1995. Emma Nicholson joined the Liberal Democrats at New Year 1996, a particularly wounding choice of timing since it made headline news over the holiday period. She had arrived in Parliament in 1987, the same time as me. We were among five women elected that time, the others being Ann Widdecombe, Teresa Gorman and Maureen Hicks (Wolverhampton North East, who lost her seat in 1992). Emma was full of confidence, the daughter of an MP, a member of a well-known family and the high-profile Deputy Chairman of the Conservative Party before the 1987 election. Emma is profoundly deaf and deserves all credit for having surmounted such a handicap with spectacular success. She was also very grand, and never bothered with the niceties of parliamentary life. She called me Elizabeth for our first two years in the House, following the principle that the second footman is always called William.

There were yet more defections. Peter Thurnham became an Independent in February 1996, and then joined the Liberal Democrats eight months later. George Gardiner joined the Referendum Party in March 1997. With the episode of the 'whipless eight' and the various by-election losses, the majority dwindled steadily throughout the Parliament from 21 to minus 3 by the end.

While the effect of that is obvious, in that every vote is a calculation of what can pass and what cannot, the time that handling
such a situation takes, from the Prime Minister, through Cabinet
and other insiders, right down to the Whips, can be imagined.
Tony Newton, who as Leader of the House was the
Government's business manager, bore the brunt of the work
heroically, (although at the cost of large numbers of cigarettes)
and lost his seat for his pains.

One of the major themes of this book is the importance of
Parliament in the exercise of political power. While power may be,
in part, an illusion for politicians, given the importance now of the
media, pressure groups and the effect of outside events, politicians
cannot exercise it without it having been conferred on them by the
ballot box, through Parliament. Even when a Prime Minister enjoys
a commanding majority in the House of Commons, Parliament
continues to scrutinise what his or her executive is doing and, at
times, to hold it in check.

John Major's power as Prime Minister after the 1992 election
was diminished by the dwindling parliamentary majority. The
Government had put into place a large legislative programme,
some of which was highly controversial. The effort that it took
cost dear in terms of the Prime Minister's time and energy, which,
given different parliamentary circumstances, he might have used in
campaigning, or even more careful examination of issues. Every
backbencher with a gripe used the parliamentary situation as a
means of getting his or her heart's desire. All of us were locked up
for hours with this or that pressure group, this or that splinter
movement, devising amendments, means of presentation, to bring
them on side.

Whips and Majorities

Power is not sufficient evidence of truth.

SAMUEL JOHNSON

Of course, parliamentary scrutiny is entirely legitimate – to scrutinise legislation is, after all, the task of parliamentarians and the aim
is to improve legislation, not to render its delivery impossible. That
of course is the role of Parliament. But there were those who saw
their task within the Parliamentary party as one of scrutinising and
revising party policy itself. While as a result of their election as
Members of Parliament, they had become members of a club with
rules and observances laid down, they believed that they had been
elected to change the nature of the Party and what it stood for.
Thus Alan Duncan pointed out to the 1922 Committee that
although the right held most of the Parliamentary party, the
Government was run from the centre left. Such attitudes led Major
to launch his own extraordinary leadership bid in the summer of
1995. He believed that to challenge his detractors to put up or shut
up was the only way to silence them, and to allow Government to
proceed. To an extent it worked, but too late to help the party
recover its electoral fortunes.

The Cabinet was equally hog-tied by the parliamentary situation. *The* priority for Cabinet Ministers was to be in the House for
votes, which meant that travelling, visiting, doing all the outside
things expected of them had to take second place.

I recall being invited to speak at the Cutlers' Feast in Sheffield.
This was a great honour, as I knew from my own connections with
Sheffield. It was an even greater honour in that the only women invit-
ed in the whole history of the Feast had been Queen Elizabeth I,

Margaret Thatcher and the Princess Royal. That day, of course, there was a voting crisis. The Whips said I would probably not be able to go. They finally confirmed that at around 4pm. I then had the really unpleasant task of telling the Master Cutler. Quite understandably, he was furious, could not see how anything could be more important than his event and took the whole thing as a massive insult by the Government. And so it was. My absolute disgust at the whole process was compounded by the fact that, in the end, there wasn't a vote at all.

Next day, I was confronted by a Whip, Irvine Patnick, who was a Sheffield MP. He said, 'My word, you have upset the whole of Sheffield, you had better write a really grovelling letter.' I had, of course, already done that, and sent flowers to the Mistress Cutler. Fortunately, history does not record the subsequent conversation with him, which was along the lines of 'A pity you, in the Whips' Office and privy to the discussions, did not think of that before.' The vocabulary was rather more imaginative.

On another occasion, I had been invited to Manchester University to speak at a business event for which people had bought tickets. Again, on the day there was to-ing and fro-ing by the Whips' Office – this time we were responding to two Opposition Day debates with votes at 7pm and 10pm. The university agreed to provide a plane to get me back for the 10pm vote. There was then some question of whether this would be allowed, first because there was a doubt about the validity of the pilot's licence – so confidence boosting – and, second, because we might not be able to land at City Airport. Finally, I threw obedience to the wind and left for the station.

At Macclesfield, my mobile rang: 'Just to let you know you'll have to be back for the 7pm vote. You have not been given permission to leave,' said the voice of the duty Whip. A vigorous exchange ensued and I went on my way. But these are the kinds of tensions that develop when a Government is working on a knife-edge majority. The whips were doing their job. I was doing mine. But such manoeuvres were sapping to morale, energy and the Government's standing with the outside world.

Parliament bestows power. Diminishing approval of what a Government is trying to do takes it away. Much has been written about the dramatic events with which Major's 1992 Government had to deal. The haemorrhaging away of the majority in Parliament was far more important to the Government's exercise of power than the personalities and tragedies which caused it to happen, yet it was the latter upon which comment concentrated.

In his autobiography, Major makes his own wry point about events. He describes his initial policy responses on becoming leader:

> A new, more friendly approach to Europe; a fresh education agenda focusing on vocational qualifications and training credits, an embryonic series of changes to improve public services, the replacement of the Poll Tax. All of these had to be welded to the continuation of existing policies and the struggle against a worsening recession. All of this was a sufficient agenda but it is not an exclusive list of the immediate demands which faced me. Within weeks of my election as Prime Minister, we faced an unavoidable obligation that dwarfed all domestic concerns. We went to war in the Gulf.[21]

This was an unavoidable obligation. Major implies (although he does not explicitly argue) that the Gulf War, important, vital even, as it was, consumed so much of his time and energy that preparation of his own programme, not to mention preparation for the forthcoming election and certainly the consolidation of his own

59

position, all had to take second place as he wrestled with a situation that threatened British lives.

The Troubles Start

> We give the impression of being in office, but not in power.
>
> NORMAN LAMONT

Leaving the Exchange Rate Mechanism, as Major says in his autobiography, 'was a political and economic calamity. It unleashed havoc in the Conservative Party and it changed the political landscape of Britain. On that day, a fifth consecutive Conservative election victory, which always looked unlikely unless the Opposition were to self-destruct, became remote, if not impossible.' Certainly the forces that led to Black Wednesday were outside the control of the Prime Minister, the Cabinet, Parliament, and the Bank of England. Its consequences were not only their responsibility but, the public expected, within their control. Major has subsequently said that he cannot see how he could have acted otherwise than he did. Since I was in Moscow on Black Wednesday itself, it is difficult to argue otherwise.

Interestingly, the British Ambassador in Moscow, presumably for his own reasons of not wishing to disrupt my visit, did not tell me what was happening at home that day. But I saw the news on Sky and Elizabeth Cottrell, my special adviser, rang to say I should get back as, in her words, 'The Prime Minister needs his friends'. Against stiff Foreign Office resistance, I insisted on leaving on the first available plane and arrived back in London just in time for the Cabinet meeting the next morning.

This extraordinary Cabinet meeting was held underground, in the 'War Cabinet' room which we had to use for several months while the Cabinet Room in Number 10 was refurbished after the IRA mortar bomb. The room was very small and stuffy and we were squashed together tightly. The mood was grave as the Prime Minister outlined the events of the preceding few days and asked the Chancellor to explain the actions he had been forced to take. Others, notably those who might have been expected to have misgivings about our course of action, were also asked to speak, like Ken Clarke and Michael Heseltine. There was strong support all round for the Prime Minister, although no one was in any doubt about the seriousness of the position.

The subsequent debate in Parliament on 24 September indicated what would be Major's problems for the rest of his premiership: attacks from his own side, increasingly effective because of the diminishing parliamentary majority. Major's lack of brass neck meant that he could not shrug himself out of the crisis. Conversely he blamed himself for it, considering resignation. In the end, he rightly decided to soldier on, his reputation for decision-making and resolve having been damaged once again.

Of the truly amazing revelations of sleazy behaviour on the part of Tory MPs and Ministers, there remains almost no more to be said – save perhaps that they have since been surpassed by the equally amazing revelations about Labour MPs and Ministers. But Major's way of dealing with them left him open to criticism. On each occasion, he was ready to believe the perpetrator, on each occasion he left himself exposed to accusation by the popular press of spinelessness. On each occasion, his own consensual sense of fairness and respect for others were brought into play and routinely rubbished by the press as weakness.

One extraordinary event in Major's premiership, however, did not come from outside but was manufactured by him. This was his own response to continuing problems and disloyalty within the

Parliamentary Party. He resigned as leader of the Conservative Party, and called an election for the post, in which he would be a candidate. Looking back on that episode, which was without precedent, I think that it was characteristic of many traits in Major's personality. While he was known to be cautious, he was also potentially bloody-minded. On occasion, he could lose his temper spectacularly. He was also a loner. The 'unpleasantness in 1995', which is how Robert Cranborne still refers to the episode, illustrates all those characteristics of the Prime Minister. They also illustrate what a man can do when driven to distraction.

Analysis after the event points to a number of reasons for Major's growing difficulties within the parliamentary party during the early summer of 1995. His critics identify the acceptance of the recommendations of the Nolan Report as one of the final straws. (The Prime Minister had set up, in October 1994, a committee to investigate standards in public life. This in turn followed the findings of the Scott Inquiry into events surrounding the 'Arms to Iraq' affair.) The Nolan Committee spread its investigations much more widely than perhaps the Prime Minister had envisaged, but commentators missed the fact that Major's attitude towards standards in public life was strongly coloured by his own uprightness, and disapproval of pork-barrel politics of any kind. When he received Nolan's recommendations, in May 1995, just after local elections had revealed a strong swing to Labour and the Liberal Democrats, he immediately announced his acceptance of their 'broad thrust'. The parliamentary party erupted. Some MPs were openly defying Major's leadership. Others saw Nolan as an attack on parliamentary sovereignty and their own integrity. Yet others claimed, inaccurately, that he simply did not understand the nature of outside interests, since he had never had any himself. Ill-tempered debates took place in the House to the advantage of the Opposition.

Small wonder that *The Times,* leader on 18 May 1995 declared, 'Morale among Conservative MPs has never been lower,' adding that the local election results had led to many 'contemplating defeat at the next general election and wondering what they would do with their lives afterwards'. There was a genuine gulf between Major's strongly held view that politicians should be seen to be putting their house in order, an honourable stance, and the view of many backbenchers that their rights were being diminished. With hindsight, although I recall pointing it out at the time, things might have gone better if more effort had been put into explaining to and consulting MPs on the whole issue of the Nolan Report in advance of its announcement.

The heavens opened. A leak of the conclusion of the Scott Inquiry, the affair of the Bosnian hostages, some well-publicised praise from Mrs Thatcher for Tony Blair, all combined with the sour parliamentary mood, to bring again to the fore talk of a leadership challenge to John Major. After a bad-tempered meeting between him and the Eurosceptic group Fresh Start, it was open season. All kinds of names came into the leadership frame, mine included, despite the fact that I was always adamant that I would never, in any circumstances, stand against Major. For their own reasons, and they were various, others continued to put my name around. I can now see that this must have been particularly hurtful to John Major – I had always been his strong supporter – but there did not seem the opportunity either to clear the air, or to clarify my own position without making things immeasurably worse. It would have been an open admission of the problems I knew he had.

The 1995 Leadership Election

A good indignation brings out all one's powers.

RALPH WALDO EMERSON

On 15 June the Prime Minister had to attend a G7 meeting in Halifax, Nova Scotia. His state of mind can only be imagined. Yet that very state of mind would have been coloured by his bloody-mindedness, and resulted in his 'put up or shut up' challenge to his critics. On his return from Halifax, on Monday, 19 June, his mind was made up, and he began to consult selected colleagues.

That evening I had a discussion with Robert Cranborne about the situation. I reassured him that I had no intention of standing against John Major, at any time, but added that in my opinion the situation was as bad as I had known. Two days later, Major himself consulted Cranborne, who eventually became his campaign manager in this strange leadership bid.

It is impossible to overstate the impact of the Westminster and Whitehall rumour machine at dramatic times like this. People eat, sleep and talk the crisis in question. It is not surprising that so much comment surfaces in the press, almost by osmosis.

On the morning of Thursday, 22 July, the Prime Minister rang me early at the Department. 'I wanted you to know that I intend to resign as Party leader this afternoon, in order to put an end once and for all to all this talk of leadership. If anyone thinks they can do better, they are welcome to have a go.' Part of me was amazed, and another part thought it entirely in line with Major's character that he should decide to go for broke in this manner. We had a warm, friendly conversation, during which he made it clear that not all

Cabinet colleagues were to be told before the announcement was made that afternoon. The subsequent Cabinet meeting was therefore a curious occasion. I announced that the NUT had voted against a strike by four to one. In other circumstances this would have been received as good news but in this strange atmosphere it fell rather flat.

Early in the afternoon, I was phoned by John Redwood. He said that he had just been given the news of Major's leadership challenge by Michael Howard. He asked me if I knew, and if so, when I had been given the news and by whom. I explained that Major had phoned before Cabinet. Redwood was incredulous and somewhat hurt. He said that he had had a meeting with Major a day or two earlier and that they had discussed possible ways out of the parliamentary difficulties. Clearly his arguments had not swayed Major.

My adviser, Elizabeth Cottrell, and I turned on the television to watch, in a suspension of belief, the Prime Minister with Brian Mawhinney and Ian Lang, his aides for this campaign, walk into the garden at Number 10 to make the announcement to an amazed press. John Major had taken the initiative, and at the same time, the political world by surprise.

Should he have thrown all caution to the winds in this way? Was it a legitimate exercise of his power as Prime Minister, or a tacit admission that he had lost it? It certainly smoked out those of his critics who were prepared to go public with their views. John Redwood gave his reasons for standing against John Major:

> I waited two or three days after the extraordinary declaration by Major. What made me stand was his friends briefing the press, saying no one on the right had the guts to stand, and that the right wing case was merely a straw man. I couldn't take that. I resigned because I thought he

was wrong to take the private arguments from the Cabinet into the public arena. Once he did that, I had to take him on in public.[22]

I have no doubt that Redwood was sincere in this statement but it was so far from how Major saw it as to be almost ludicrous. He truly believed that the Right was out to get him, and that Redwood was but one of a number of potential assassins.

The Party machine swung into action again. Cranborne took charge, organising early morning meetings with Alastair Goodlad, Ian Lang and Brian Mawhinney. I rang Cranborne at 6am each morning to let him know my view of the atmosphere in the party, and what seemed to be going on. The divisive nature of a campaign such as this, when we were in the process of governing the country, can only be imagined. For the duration of the campaign John Redwood and his supporters became the enemy, although this was dispelled once the 'unpleasantness', as Cranborne called it, was over.

On one occasion I had to stand in for John Major, who had been going to address a grand dinner at Beauvoir Castle. Cranborne organised a helicopter from my home in Norfolk so that I could fulfil that and my other engagements for the day. I took some evening clothes in a Selfridges bag, thinking, rightly as it turned out, that such a trip might not be conducive to elegant dressing. In the event, the pilot could not see where to land, we came down in a field several acres from the castle, and had to be rescued by a member of the family, who led me through the assembled grandly-clad throng, clutching my Selfridges bag, and wishing I was at the bottom of a deep well somewhere. When I came to speak to the gathering, I wondered, not for the first time, why they stuck with a parliamentary party that put them through episodes like this.

The media, once they had recovered from the shock of being taken at their word, followed all of us in the hope that we would in some way be caught out, betraying a confidence or an injudicious view. I recall a group of them, accompanied by someone in a John Major mask, invading a fête in my own constituency, in the hope of snatching a photo of me next to him, so that someone could fill in a damaging caption. The constituency trusties, bemused but stalwart, prevented it.

In the event, and when this distraction from the business of Government was finally over, Major polled 218 votes, against 89 for Redwood and 20 abstentions. It was enough. We were all instructed to go out on to St Stephen's Green to talk in the most positive terms to the legions of cameras and journalists camped there. We did so, and in Jeffrey Archer's words, 'It was sealed up on radio and television in the twenty minutes following the result, declaring it one of the greatest Tory victories for any leader.'[23]

It had been one way to exercise power. Common interest took over as the inevitability of a general election became clear to all. For the most part Conservative Party activists were unforgiving of the parliamentary party. Many took the view that the combination of publicly disloyal statements from MPs, mostly on Europe, sleaze and scandal, had forced the Prime Minister, whom they liked and admired, into this embarrassing manoeuvre. After the General Election, they exacted vengeance. There was a shift of power from the parliamentary to the voluntary Party in the modernisation of the Party that was to take place under William Hague.In the meantime, the peace between then and the election, was uneasy, but the Prime Minister had had his way.

Dream Teams

God is always on the side of the big battalions.

VICOMTE DE TURENNE

Most leaders say that creating the right Cabinets, politically and geographically representative of their parties, is one of the most difficult tasks they experience. It is never pleasant to have to tell colleagues that they must go. Indeed, given the complete lack of personnel skills that attend the parliamentary and political processes, it is amazing that Cabinets work at all. In most managerial situations, after all, it is safe to assume that senior colleagues embrace the aims of the organisation. In politics, however, many agendas, personal and collective, militate against that assumption. Yet to appoint those who will form the Government for which you are responsible is one of the most important jobs you will face. It is also the exercise of power at its most obvious. Or is it?

Maybe not. For one thing, the leader never starts with a fresh page. John Major found this when he created his first Cabinet in 1990 after his election as party leader. First there were those to whom he felt he owed his election and foremost among them was Norman Lamont, who believed he had masterminded the whole process. This may have been so, but others thought that, no matter what his role had been, he should not have been made Chancellor of the Exchequer. They conveniently forgot that Norman was, at the time that John Major became leader, the Chief Secretary to the Treasury, the post from which Major had himself moved on to become Chancellor. As Chief Secretary, Lamont had been responsible for public spending and had worked closely with Major on the preparation of his own Budgets.

Richard Ryder, who became Chief Whip, had also done much to get Major elected and most believed that as Chief Whip was the only position he wanted in politics, his was an appropriate promotion. In any case, he was supremely well-fitted to be Chief Whip. Ryder had been a junior Treasury minister and a minister at Agriculture. He was quiet, charming and an inveterate plotter. He was a good listener, with great knowledge of the Party and the way it functioned. He was very well suited to be Chief Whip but a combination of illness and family tragedy (he and his wife lost their baby son very soon after his birth) meant that he became, or seemed to become, increasingly detached from the political process. He may well have been relieved when finally he gave up his post in 1995.

For other appointments, speed was of the essence. Major's first Cabinet meeting was scheduled for only two days after his election. While he claimed that his aim to was to create a 'Cabinet of all the talents', other considerations were forced on him by the circumstances. Dream teams are usually just that, the stuff of dreams. For Major, the objectives were to heal divisions, if that were possible, and to avoid alienating Margaret Thatcher and her acolytes. He also needed to consolidate his support among the 'big beasts' in the party. Thus Kenneth Baker, who had played an ultra loyal role as Chairman of the Party during Mrs Thatcher's travails, became Home Secretary and Douglas Hurd remained as Foreign Secretary. Michael Heseltine was given Environment, with the task of sorting out the Poll Tax. Overall, Major moved nine of the twenty-two Cabinet Ministers, leaving thirteen in place. He gave the impression of wanting continuity, and on the whole the reshuffle was favourably received. However, his early experience as Party leader must have given him cause to wonder where power actually lies, even in the personal area of key Cabinet appointments. There were criticisms, some of which were justified, but peculiarly unfair at the same time. For all his talk of a classless society, the new Cabinet was still full of public school and Oxbridge-educated colleagues. Worse, he had somehow managed to appoint a Cabinet with no woman for the first time since 1963. Yet no one could have accused Major of sexism. He was strongly supportive of women and there was no hint of condescension in his makeup. At that time there were only seventeen women MPs in the Conservative Party and he rightly felt that none was ready to be promoted outright to the Cabinet. He was constrained by circumstance, at the very moment when he might have expected to exercise power in the most decisive way.

While he had more freedom of manoeuvre after the 1992 election, Chris Patten's defeat at the polls again prevented him from creating his dream team and because of the shrill reaction to the lack of women in his first Cabinet, he was obliged to bring at least one woman into the Cabinet. Lynda Chalker, who was in the Lords having lost her Merseyside seat, Virginia Bottomley at Health, Angela Rumbold at Education and I at the Treasury, were all Ministers of State. Lynda was by far the most experienced, and a first-class minister. She had been a front-bench spokesman when the Conservatives were in opposition, using her background discipline of statistics to great effect as a Social Security spokesman. But for all the time I knew her from 1987, she was at the Foreign Office, then at the Overseas Development Agency. She was hardworking, committed and very popular with the party in the country.

No doubt Major felt that it was just too difficult to have to justify a House of Lords Cabinet minister, so Lynda lost the chance she had so deserved. Virginia Bottomley was said to be reluctant to take on a Cabinet post, and I had been elected to the House less than five years before. In the event, he promoted both of us, Virginia to take on the huge job of Health Secretary at a difficult time, and me to the Department of Employment. At the same time he established that Employment should have a sector dealing with issues of concern to women, silencing his critics on that score.

The most unwilling colleague was Kenneth Baker, who, it was said, turned down the post of Welsh Secretary on being moved from Home Secretary, and for a time was deeply unforgiving in the hearing of anyone who cared to listen. No wonder Major wrote of the whole Cabinet process, 'My heart sank just a little. Reshuffles are a painful business.'

It is an interesting reflection that, despite the disparate backgrounds and well publicised policy disagreements within John Major's Cabinets, there was little personal animosity between its members. Handling and managing the various 'big beasts', and achieving consensus when he could, was one of Major's skills. A Cabinet including Michael Heseltine, Kenneth Clarke, John Gummer and Michael Howard, not to mention Lord Cranborne and Douglas Hogg who came in later, was not a personnel manager's dream, especially when leaks abounded and the press were eager to pounce on and expose any hint of a split. But one of Major's real skills, all too often billed by outsiders as weakness, was achieving agreement between widely opposed and sincerely held differences of view.

The rehabilitation of Michael Heseltine was a case in point. When I entered Parliament he had been a backbencher. He had left Government in a blaze of publicity over the Westland affair, and since then had been demonised by Thatcher loyalists. In my own Conservative Association, it would have been unthinkable at that time to have invited him to speak, although many local parties did.

We rarely saw him, but whenever he did come into the House, it was an event.

The view on the right of the Party was that he had been directly responsible for the departure of Margaret Thatcher, that he was a wrecker, a plotter, and not to trusted at any price. His supporters of course, denounced those accusations, on the grounds that her downfall had been based on a groundswell of opinion in the Party, and the reasons for it were far more complex than the activities of one individual.

The Heseltine Phenomenon

> The secret of power is the knowledge that others are more cowardly than you are.
>
> LUDWIG BORNE

During John Major's leadership campaign, in November 1990, we were kept informed of what was going on in the other camps (Heseltine's and Hurd's) by well-placed moles. Some of our supporters were suspected of acting as moles for them. When Major emerged as the victor, the rumour machine went into overdrive with speculation on whether he would offer Heseltine a job, and if so, which one. The purists said that if Heseltine was given a job it would only be a matter of time before he challenged Major, but Major knew that a big hitter like Heseltine was better in the tent of Government than outside it, and probably appreciated his skill and charisma. But what job would he get? The usual armchair experts opined that Major could hardly offer him the Exchequer, the Foreign Office, or the Home Office, given Heseltine's own leadership ambitions. On the other hand, they reasoned, Heseltine would be unlikely to accept Social Security or Agriculture. But they reckoned without the shrewdness of Major, and the political sophistication of Heseltine, who expressed a wish to return to the Department of the Environment, at which he had made such an impact under Margaret Thatcher. No doubt Major thought that someone of Heseltine's stature was needed to deal with the abolition of the Poll Tax – someone who could rightly claim that he had never supported it in the first place, and who had the brass neck to carry off the change of policy. Major might also have thought that if the policy change failed, Heseltine's reputation would suffer. It did not. After a successful stint at Environment, Heseltine was moved to Trade and Industry after the 1992 election, it was said at his own request.

In his appearance and in his style, Michael Heseltine embodies self-confidence and charisma. He has clear vision and strong views on certain issues and is pragmatic on others. He is not a detail man. The big picture approach describes his style perfectly.

He put in distinguished service at Environment, then Trade and Industry, but came into his own when he became Deputy Prime Minister in 1995 after the leadership election. His appointment to this post was a surprise to colleagues and commentators alike. They had failed to spot the development of trust between Major and Heseltine, and that Heseltine frequently took a middle position in Cabinet on issues that might otherwise divide colleagues.

Michael Heseltine is one of those politicians who attract attention from the press and the public. Others, like Chris Patten, Michael Portillo and Tony Blair, have the same gift. While it may be enhanced by image burnishing, and assiduous courtship of the most influential journalists, nothing can help those without it attract the same easy coverage. The question of whether a successful politician needs this quality to exercise power remains open. A powerful media image is a help but it is not as much of a help as its absence is a handicap.

One of Heseltine's strengths was his complete detachment from media comment. He understood the way the press worked, used it on occasion, but was never outwardly moved by what it said. Thus, he was quite without embarrassment in naming himself President of the Board of Trade in 1992. All kinds of 'Hezza for Prezza' jokes abounded in the press and in the House of Commons but he maintained throughout that the whole point was the job, rather than him. The title was abandoned by his Labour successor.

When he became Deputy Prime Minister, speculation came thick and fast: his office would be bigger than the Cabinet Room, the furniture had been specially made, he was giving himself airs above his station, John Major had better look out and so on. We were all summoned from time to time to appear before his Presentation Committee, whose modest aim was to co-ordinate Government announcements and activities. How ironic to reflect, in the light of the subsequent development of wholesale spin, that it was regarded with such suspicion by colleagues. Because it was Heseltine's creation? Perhaps, but would it have worked so well if it had been someone else's brainchild? Certainly not. Heseltine, as he continually and rather endearingly said, enjoyed the job of Deputy Prime Minister more than any other job he had ever done. He was enthusiastic about what he found going on across Whitehall. He was strongly supportive to colleagues when they were launching new initiatives.

By his personality, and the power he embodied, not from his position, but in his person, he was able to drive things forward. In persuading colleagues, he never used the Prime Minister as a big stick. Instead, he used the arguments he knew would work with individual colleagues.

His committee performed a useful function. It is hard, looking back, to imagine that any Government could manage without such a mechanism. However, officials and even some colleagues hated appearing before it. For a start, the surroundings were forbidding. Heseltine's office was vast. In the heart of the Cabinet Office, it had formerly been a conference room and contained equally vast furniture, cavernous sofas and enormous chairs into which the unwary might easily vanish before the Deputy Prime Minister's amused gaze from the heights of his own lofty but relaxed office chair. Whether he had deliberately organised such an intimidating field of operations, or whether the civil servants could only supply gigantic accessories from their store in Clapham, none of us ever knew, and Heseltine was not telling.

The point of all of this is that John Major brought Heseltine, who had previously been regarded as a threat by Major's predecessor, to his side. In so doing, he enhanced his own strength and that of his Government. Making Heseltine Deputy Prime Minister was a very skilful move.

The Cambridge Mafia

The purpose of getting power is to be able to give it away.

ANEURIN BEVAN

Another 'big beast', Kenneth Clarke, was regarded with affection rather than suspicion by the party, yet he was not always easy to manage. Through the robustness of his views, personality and physique Clarke has been a powerful figure in British politics over

75

the past twenty-five years. John Major famously remarked that Clarke would cross the road to pick a fight and few would doubt his relish for an argument.

Kenneth Clarke has an attractive personality. He is well read, has not an ounce of side, and enjoys a good laugh, not infrequently at his own expense. He has a quick mind, and is a fearless and entertaining debater. He has brought all these qualities to the many jobs he has done in Government and in Opposition, and is genuinely held in affection by that fabled beast 'The man in the street', if only for his sheer lack of political correctness, fondness for Hush Puppy shoes and a fat cigar. Of our many Parliamentary colleagues, there are few with whom I would rather share a dinner table.

But his open-mindedness on so many issues, which is a real strength, is on occasion outweighed by his inflexibility on others. For some reason, he has a real prejudice against local Government and all its works. This made difficulties for him when he was Secretary of State for Education. His strength and persistence were precisely the qualities needed in that post, yet soon he fell foul of the whole Education establishment, just as he had done with the Health establishment as Secretary of State for Health.

His aversion to local democracy is the more curious because it is at odds with his antipathy to big Government. The point is that real democracy, exercised at local level and left to get on with it, is a limitation on the powers of central Government, just the kind of principle one would have thought Clarke would have approved. Undoubtedly he would be insulted to be accused of a lack of enthusiasm for local self-determination, yet that was the impression he gave. Any discussion about councils, council funding, education, social services, or even trams, always ended with an onslaught from Clarke about the iniquities of local government, councillors' habits of using funds allocated to them for pet schemes of their own, their wastefulness, and their sheer inability to see things as he saw them. His attitude invariably led to epic battles with colleagues who had responsibility for local government, especially during public spending rounds.

He was a splendid Chancellor of the Exchequer. Confident, and with good judgement, he possessed the strength to push through change. He was a true democrat – after the Cabinet decision on a Single Currency referendum, he accepted that he had lost, although according to the press, he continued to brief them with his views on the matter. Within Cabinet, and on certain issues, he was a rock of resistance that had to be circumnavigated.

On public spending, one of Clarke's most obdurate opponents was John Gummer as Secretary of State for the Environment. It was not that Gummer was soft on public spending, or that he thought local government was without fault. Indeed, he engaged in furious battles with councillors up and down the land. But he could see that central Government should not make itself the target of criticism about local services, rather than the authorities that delivered those services. The debates between Clarke and Gummer on these issues were glorious occasions, made the more entertaining because they had known each other for at least thirty years, and knew how best to insult each other with great good humour.

Gummer is an unusual and highly capable man. He has a captivating personality, and is full of self-mockery. Even in departments where he had a hard time, like Agriculture, in the end he gained respect from those with whom he worked for his persistence and his courage. He thoroughly enjoyed his international work, and gained respect around the world for his pursuit of environmental policies. He was a ferocious debater, and could best anyone, either in the House or in public debate. He was also extremely loyal. He had the difficult task of being Party Chairman under Margaret Thatcher at a time when her popularity, and that of her Government, were waning fast. He was equally loyal to John Major and bore with fortitude the regular press briefings that said he was about to be sacked. He was never afraid of holding an unpopular or unfashionable view. In the end, he had the satisfaction of seeing his own strong environmental policies not only taken up by the Labour Government but publicly praised on all sides.

His success was not always achieved with perfect harmony. On one occasion he fell foul of a Norwegian Environment Minister, who referred to Gummer as a 'Dritsek' – a scum-bag in Norwegian. It happened during the summer recess when the papers are short of news, and before there was time to respond, the whole nation knew not only the story but the Norwegian for scum-bag. Gummer dealt with it cheerfully – he was more than capable of seeing the ridiculous side of high office.

Michael Howard was a different proposition. Very able, with a silky manner and personally kind and charming, he had been at Cambridge at the same time as Norman Lamont, John Gummer and Kenneth Clarke, but had not entered Parliament until 1983, by which time the others had achieved office. When he was a junior Minister in the Department of Trade and Industry he had won great respect for piloting through the House of Commons the Financial Services Bill. He entered the Cabinet as Secretary of State for Employment in 1990. He has strong right wing views on many issues, especially Europe, and as Employment Secretary was at Maastricht with John Major, and a key figure in negotiating Britain's opt-out from the Social Chapter. It is a mystery that he was not a popular figure with the media and in the country.

Efficient, articulate, and effective, with a lot of personal charm, he achieved a great deal in all his posts and was consistently high-profile. In Cabinet, however, he could be obdurate. This led others to take pleasure in inflicting defeats upon him, which sometimes happened in public spending rounds.

It is obvious that managing such 'big beasts' within a Cabinet, with the maximum of consensus and the minimum of leaking, is not an easy task. Yet there was strong agreement on so many fronts: the economy, the freedom of the individual, law and order, defence and, with the exception of Europe, foreign policy. That we came out of office without raging personal hatreds or mutual rubbishing is a testament to Major's style and mild-mannered approach.

Hiring and Firing

> Greater love hath no man than this, that he lay down his friends for his life.
>
> JEREMY THORPE, AFTER A CABINET RESHUFFLE IN 1963

Creation of Cabinets is one thing. Hiring and firing is another. Government reshuffles are something else, involving change right through the Parliamentary Party. With so many promotions and sackings, they are always dramatic and much-heralded in the press: knowledgeable commentators spend weeks mulling over who will be in or out. For those involved, the newspapers make more than usually uncomfortable reading. Anxious knots of people form in the corridors of the House of Commons. Jeers and taunts of 'Goodbye' from the other side, and unchristian thoughts from one's own, attend debates in the Chamber. There is a perceptible rise in tension.

No wonder that, when they can, prime ministers spring a sudden reshuffle on an unsuspecting world. Such a move is a useful weapon to distract attention from other difficult events, to give the smack of firm Government, or to refresh the team and bring on new talent.

On 27 May 1994 I had a full morning of engagements at the Department of Employment when a Cabinet reshuffle was sprung on the party and the public. The first I had heard of it was a word or two from officials that morning when I arrived at the office. Since I had been in post for only thirteen months, and in my first Cabinet post at that, I thought blithely that it could not apply to me, and carried on. Later that morning I had to deliver a speech at the University of the South Bank. I was just concluding, answering a question on whether I thought I was about to be reshuffled, when my driver, always a rather lugubrious man, appeared at the door, and said, 'Number 10'. He was a man of few words. The gathering was electrified. So was I.

We left. While I was in the car, the phone rang. It was John Gummer. 'I'm going to Environment,' he said. 'You may be facing a change.' I was. When I got to Number 10, the Prime Minister asked me to take Gummer's place at Agriculture. He told me that David Curry, the valued Minister of State at MAFF, was moving with Gummer. I asked if Michael Jack, then at the Home Office, might move with me to MAFF. Major agreed that he would sound him out, and in the meantime that I should go upstairs to have coffee with Norma. This I did, and took the opportunity to have a look at the morning papers. By the time all the necessary agreements for Michael Jack's move were in place, an hour had passed, and I emerged into Downing Street. The delay was later interpreted by the press as an initial refusal on my part to make a move, and an extreme reluctance to go to MAFF in particular. 'Major had to force her to agree' was the least of the press observations and, had my enthusiasm for agriculture not been well known throughout the industry, might have made my start in the ministry difficult. You cannot always believe what you read in the press.

It is an interesting reflection that while many political leaders bewail what they see as a lack of real power, in the area of hiring and firing, where it might be assumed that their power is undisputed, they frequently complain that it is the hardest thing they have to do.

One of the reasons may be fear of the political consequences, and where a colleague has strong personal support in the Party, it may be well founded. It is at least part of the calculation. Thus when William Hague sacked John Redwood from the Shadow Cabinet he might have been taken aback by the initial backlash from the media and activists. John Major, however, was criticised frequently for retaining colleagues in post when their credibility was diminishing.

One such case was David Mellor. He and Major were personal friends, who shared a great interest in sport, especially football, and a dislike of what they saw as the high snobbery of parts of the Tory Party. Mellor never achieved membership of the Blue Chip Club, for example, although Major became a valued member of it. Mellor told me that when they were first elected in 1979, he and Major spent time comparing their skills with those less gifted, but in their view more likely to rise, because of their birth, connections or education. As things turned out, neither had reason to complain, although Mellor became impatient when others he considered either his inferiors or his juniors in the House overtook him.

When Peter Lilley was made Secretary of State for Trade and Industry by Margaret Thatcher in 1990, Mellor sent for me to talk through where he might have gone wrong. I had a lot of sympathy for him. He was clever, funny, a lateral thinker, and a ferocious debater in the House. He was also a great self-publicist, although those who criticise politicians for that reason misunderstand the nature of the calling, especially nowadays. He thought Peter Lilley had been promoted purely on ideological grounds, and despaired that he, from the left of the Party, would never make progress. He was a prominent and articulate member of John Major's leadership campaign team. When Major became Prime Minister, he made Mellor Chief Secretary to the Treasury, where I became his colleague as Minister of State.

Mellor's manner was very non-Treasury. He believed in strong-arm tactics even when they were not warranted. He prepared for every public spending bi-lateral meeting with fellow ministers as if, someone said at the time, he was about to do several rounds with Muhammad Ali. After these meetings, he would recount with glee how he had humiliated this or that minister, and even more gleefully, the officials. In the House, he was always on top form. The notoriously boring wind-up at the end of a debate often fell to him. The press would have gone to bed, along with their first editions, and MPs crowded into the Chamber, often over-refreshed and sometimes over-tired and invariably emotional. Mellor turned these wind-ups into an art form and eventually the press took to reporting him, late though it was. He developed the Heseltine theme magnificently and unmercifully mocked the infamous Labour Party prawn cocktail initiative in the City before the 1992 election, claiming that 'never had so many prawns been sacrificed in vain'.

Mellor was a good colleague at the Treasury. He worked hard and was never short of an opinion and could deliver. He also

took on our boss, Norman Lamont, when he thought it necessary. An important part of the work at the Treasury was, of
course, the preparation of the Budget. Long meetings, known as
Budget overviews, would take place, starting at 3pm and attended by ministers, senior officials and advisers. Mellor was often
late for overviews. He would arrive, yawning, at around 3.30pm.
We all thought he was a late luncher but as things turned out, it
is possible he was otherwise employed. Whatever the reason, he
sometimes actually fell asleep, but he was one of those infuriating people who could wake in an instant, with an informed and
relevant comment on his lips.

Before the 1992 election, there was much talk of the creation
of a Ministry for the Arts and Sport – or Fun, as it was tagged.
Commentators were convinced from the start that Mellor, with his
ability and extensive knowledge of sport and music, would be its
first Secretary of State and thus it proved. He was outstandingly
good in this post. It is not easy to create a new ministry, especially
one that carves holes in others, but he simply got on with the job,
and became very high-profile.

Sadly, the end of his Cabinet career was even more high-profile
when it emerged that he had become involved with an actress, who
in turn seemed to have been involved with a tabloid newspaper.
When the affair broke, the media were awash with lurid details.
Mellor was typically straightforward about the whole thing, saying
that he had been 'very silly'. The usual hypocritical press demands
were made for his resignation. I felt they were testing Major, to see
if they could claim the scalp of Mellor, his close friend. In the end
Mellor did resign, not over his affair, but because of a suggestion
that he had accepted, and not declared, a holiday from a friend
influential in Palestinian circles. Major was then accused of not

having the guts to sack Mellor, of cronyism, dithering and finally giving in to media pressure. The truth was simpler. Major believed that people's private lives were their own, but when Mellor's acceptance of a holiday might have been represented as exposing him to outside influences, he had to act. Mellor left and was much missed.

Getting the Cane

> I hold it that a little rebellion, now and then, is a good thing.
>
> THOMAS JEFFERSON

Prime ministers, like other bosses, on occasion have to administer rebukes. I had my own taste of this in the autumn of 1996. There had been pressure within the Parliamentary Party for a free vote on the restoration of corporal punishment in the forthcoming Education Bill. Michael Howard, then Home Secretary, was said to be in favour, and various unhelpful press briefings pointed to the limpness of the Education Department over the issue, and a potential split between him and me. I was interviewed on the *Today* programme about the Bill, and the issue of corporal punishment came up. I said, not for the first time, that while I was personally in favour, it was not an option for the Bill because it was not Government policy, and because it had been outlawed at the European level. My statement had naturally enough been reported to Michael Heseltine's Presentation Committee and the Government machine went into overdrive.

Later that morning I had to open a new wing at a school in Surrey. While I was actually in mid-speech, and on the point of pulling the cord to unveil the statutory plaque, an overawed school secretary appeared to say that she had Number 10 on the phone. I had to decide whether to break off and go to the phone, or to say 'let them wait'. I thought the former course of action advisable. The Prime Minister was on the line. He was not pleased. He said that he could do without episodes of this kind, that the use of corporal punishment was not Government policy, and that for good measure, there were problems with Michael Howard as well, although he did not elaborate. I pointed out that I had on many occasions, not least at teachers' conferences, made it clear that while I might support corporal punishment, Government policy and European law did not. I added that I had said nothing more than that on the *Today* programme, and that while I regretted having caused an upset, we would not help matters by highlighting it. Unknown to me, the Number 10 press office were doing just that as we spoke, or anyway their version of it. It dominated the news for the rest of the day and the cartoonists for days afterwards.

The next day, John Major and I were due to visit a London school together. This had been long arranged, but with the perversity that seems on occasion to attend political activity it was heaven-sent for the media. We were scrutinised by what seemed every camera in the Kingdom for what might be interpreted as the merest hint of animosity between us. Subsequent photos of the occasion reveal two people smiling fixedly, like reluctant in-laws at a wedding. The spat did not last long.

John Major's achievements were many. They include the legacy of a strong economy, a consolidation of Thatcherism, with further privatisation, important reforms in the public services, including the principles of the Citizen's Charter, successful operations in the Gulf and Bosnia, a reduction in welfare costs, and a real way forward in Northern Ireland. In analyses of his Premiership, the question of whether a more decisive leader, one with more charisma, more ruthlessness, would have done better at that time is frequently asked. His critics invariably answer yes. My own belief is that any leader would have found the task well nigh impossible, and many would have done a less honourable job. Given the constraints placed on his exercise of power, by his own personality, the circumstances and timing of his election as leader, the policies and party baggage he inherited, events, and, above all, by his diminishing parliamentary majority, he emerged well thought-of by the public, leaving a solid foundation of policy success. In the end, the Conservative Party became ungovernable because of that parliamentary majority.

John Major said in his autobiography, 'It was right for Britain that the Conservatives won the 1992 election. And had the Party chosen to behave like a Party of Government in the five years after our victory, it would have been good for the Conservative Party.' So, back to Bagehot: [24] 'All satire apart, the principle of Parliament is obedience to leaders. The penalty of not being so is the penalty of impotence.'

Ministers and Mandarins

Bureaucracy is a giant mechanism operated by pygmies.

HONORÉ DE BALZAC

AN ENORMOUS VOLUME of comment and analysis over the last century has been written on the tensions between Westminster and Whitehall: the balance of power between elected politicians and permanent civil servants – the uneasy and shifting ebbs and flows of power between minister and civil servant that were immortalised in the TV programme *Yes Minister*. Each generation of office holders contributes to the bibliography. It is further enriched by vintage contributions from Brussels.

The major questions remain. Who is accountable, where powerful Government departments have been developing their own ethos for decades, and where the tenure of ministers is temporary? Are politicians, when they become ministers, given responsibilities not commensurate with their abilities and experience, and do civil servants therefore possess power to a degree not balanced by their public accountability?

The answer is, it depends. The principal question of accountability is clear. It is on politicians that power is bestowed, and not on civil servants, and politicians are accountable. As Margaret Thatcher memorably put it, when answering a question in the House of Commons on the role of Sir Alan Walters, 'Advisers advise, ministers decide.'

So, if the position is clear, why has so much attention been paid to it by so many, and why is its fascination so enduring?

The shifts and balances in power, so lovingly dissected by Whitehall watchers, depend on combinations of personalities within departments, the different ethos of departments, the relevance of the electoral cycle and parliamentary majority, and outside influences like the EU. What is clear is that when politicians become ministers, and in particular, Cabinet ministers, if they do not take the trouble to master their brief and the workings of their department, they can give up all hope of exercising power.

Are politicians, when they become ministers, given responsibilities for which their experience to date has not fitted them? Quite often.

What is the job description of a minister? Being a minister involves leadership – political, of course, but also managerial – of a large organisation, the department. It therefore involves administration, team leadership, time management, priority identification, meetings, decision and policy making.

In almost all cases it involves being a Member of Parliament, or a parliamentarian in the House of Lords. Parliamentary activities, especially when a Government's majority is small, are of vital importance. They are also a constitutional requirement. Even today reputations are made and lost in the House of Commons, which is an important power base for the ambitious.

For a minister, Government activities, such as work across Whitehall committees, presentation of Government policies via the media, at conferences and with specialist groups, are clearly important.

They are matched in the time they consume by party activities, up and down the country, working with activists, and others. Constituency duties are ignored at one's peril.

Then there is travel. Some ministers become infamous for the amount of high-cost travel they undertake. But for many, travel, and especially for work connected with Britain's membership of the EU, is important and has to be undertaken. There is little time to stand and stare.

Getting Elected

> Those who have been intoxicated by power can never willingly abandon it.

EDMUND BURKE

The starting point is election as a Member of Parliament, so it is worth considering how people are selected to become MPs, since it is the first step up the 'greasy pole' of preferment.

Horror stories about the selection process for MPs abound.

Ann Widdecombe remembers having been asked if she did not think she was too short to be an MP. As things have turned out, she could have rebuffed the question with characteristic firmness. At the time, she no doubt replied courteously but she has wondered aloud since if the same question would have been put to a man. There are some quite short male MPs.

Emily Blatch, now in the House of Lords, but at the time, an outstanding council leader, was asked if she realised that being an MP would mean she would need to be in London during the week.

Doreen Miller, also in the House of Lords and a prominent Conservative activist, was asked at a selection meeting if her husband knew she was applying for the seat. Knowing that things by then had gone beyond redemption, she replied, 'Yes, and so do my Mummy and my Daddy'. She was not, of course, selected, but she felt a great deal better for having hit back.

Judith Chaplin, the MP for Newbury who died so tragically and unexpectedly after only ten months in the House after the 1992 election, had been political adviser to Nigel Lawson and John Major. She had also been a prominent local councillor, had run her own business, and filled an economic post at the Institute of Directors. She was interviewed for a seat in South London and was introduced by the local Association chairman: 'Now please welcome Judith Chaplin. She is divorced, and is here tonight with her second husband, who lives and works in Norfolk. They have nine children between them.' She was invited to stand behind a lectern so high that it obscured all but her eyes, and address the assembled throng. As she said afterwards, 'I was not at my best.'

Of course, such ploys are not only used on women applicants; nor are they applied only by activists. At one selection process in East Anglia, the spouse of one applicant told another hopeful that the unemployment rate locally was low. (It was in fact at seneteen per cent, and a source of enormous local anxiety.) The hopeful did not check the information, and blithely announced in his speech that local people must be delighted that unemployment was so low. It was a low trick, but he was not selected.

Another young candidate proffered his CV to a selection committee. He had included his year's service as an Army officer, and his subsequent banking career. One activist, who had clearly taken against him, got up and asked, 'And just what were you doing in the three years between leaving the Army and joining your bank?' The question was so hostile that the candidate knew he had already failed and was sorely tempted to reply, 'Gosh, I was hoping no one would notice that. I was in Wormwood Scrubs, actually.' In fact, he had spent the three years in question at Cambridge, getting his degree.

The Conservative Party has now become more professional in the way it sifts those with Parliamentary ambitions. It has appointed a Vice Chairman, whose task it is to interview hopefuls, follow up references, make recommendations and pass on names to those running Selection Weekends. At such Weekends, candidates are observed in a variety of situations: debates, mock media interviews, in groups, presenting arguments, and being interviewed by people drawn from the business, voluntary and political worlds. The successful ones apply for seats when they become vacant.

The local party activists then come into play. For seats regarded as winnable, there are large numbers of candidates. The activists, who may not have performed this task for twenty or thirty years, sift the names and make a long list. They interview and select a shorter list, then make a final shortlist. On each occasion, the candidate has to speak and answer questions. The selectors will themselves have had little professional guidance. Many will take into account the candidate's experience in work or in the political or community sectors, but they are actually obliged by the process to select the one who makes the best speech and answers the questions most convincingly. Not a bad process, perhaps, for someone whose stock-in-trade will be precisely those skills, but not necessarily the best way to select someone who may eventually head a huge department, be required to take difficult decisions, master vast amounts of technical detail and be able to speed read.

Sir John Hoskyns, who had a brilliant career in Whitehall and in the private sector once remarked,

> Conservative MPs, and probably MPs from other parties too, are not interested in method. This is because they are at heart romantics.

One might add that it is also because they have not been selected for their attachment to method. Perhaps it is the selectors who are the romantics. He continues,

> They see Britain as a canvas on which the young MP can paint his political self-portrait, making his way in the world, until he holds one

of the great offices of state, finally retiring full of honour and respectability. Political life is thus about the triumphs and disasters of personalities. . . . For most [Conservatives] questions of policy analysis and formulation are thus of secondary interest until it is too late.[25]

In other words, politics attracts and tends to select those whose skills and qualities may only accidentally include management, administration, diplomacy, a sense of priorities and stamina, all of which are required, ideally anyway, in a minister. This certainly has relevance in the balance of power between ministers and officials within departments.

Becoming a Minister

Power tends to connect; absolute power connects absolutely.

PETER NEWMAN

Having become Members of Parliament, how are people chosen to become ministers? Is it a question of Buggins' turn, at the lower echelons? Seared on my memory is the conversation I had with the Conservative Chief Whip Tim Renton, when I was arguing the case for Ann Widdecombe to be promoted from backbencher to PPS. I felt very strongly about this. She was clearly outstanding for her energy and commitment, and was a splendid debater. Yet in 1990, she was still on the backbenches. The Chief Whip looked at me in disbelief. 'I have to tell you that the planning of colleagues' career paths is not the task of the Whips' Office,' he said, crushingly. The clear implication was that it was no one's task to plan MPs' career paths – unfortunate, I thought, since we were, after all, talking about the Government of the country. This story does have a happy outcome. Ann Widdecombe did become a PPS, to Tristan Garel-Jones, very soon after that, and entered the Government after John Major became Prime Minister, in December 1990. History does not relate if that particular Chief Whip has revised his opinion of Ann Widdecombe.

The story illustrates a fundamental point. In Britain for many decades there has been a determinedly amateur flavour to politics. Sir Alec Douglas Home's matchsticks, used to help explain the Budget process to himself, were only one manifestation of it. While Harold Wilson was reputed to have brought a more professional approach to governing, ministers were – and continue to be – chosen for their performing skills, their ability to perform well in the media; and meanwhile a political and geographical balance in the parliamentary party has to be maintained. All of these reasons are considered more important than anything that might actually be useful. Dull, worthy qualities, such as management or business experience, a business background, knowledge of a particular subject, are only gradually becoming valued for the political career path. And all of this impacts on the power dance between ministers and civil servants within departments, especially with newly appointed ministers.

Not all MPs want to become ministers. There is an honourable and respected tradition in Parliament either of pursuit of a particular interest – like Andrew Rowe and his expertise in the voluntary sector – or the ladder of Select Committee membership, or Standing Committee chairmanship, like Nicholas Winterton. There is, however, no shortage of candidates for preferment. Those who long for office have a variety of ways of making it plain to the Whips, who decide junior appointments. They make sure they are present at every possible vote, they offer to speak on Friday mornings, they put down questions when required; in short, they are as helpful and noticeable as possible. Some are courageous in pursuing what they want: one long-standing and able PPS made it clear to his whip that he expected promotion. He was given it, but into the Whips' Office. He turned down the offer, and a year later, became a minister. Not everyone would have had such a cool nerve or such an idea of their worth, but it worked.

It is also useful to have an influential supporter or two, or to be part of an influential group within the Parliamentary Party. During my first two or three weeks in the House I had dinner with Lynda Chalker. She anxiously enquired who had been successful in the Backbench Committee elections. The '92 Committee, chaired at that time by George Gardiner, was a right wing grouping that campaigned hard for the election of its slate of candidates for office in each committee. On that occasion, most of its candidates had been elected. This would have had a bearing on Lynda's work as a Foreign Office minister, because the Foreign Affairs Backbench Committee was influential. The same could be said of the Backbench Finance Committee. The others were less important, but to be elected an officer of one was important to individuals for their preferment.

Shuffling into Office

> He did not care in which direction the car was travelling as long as he remained in the driver's seat.
>
> LORD BEAVERBROOK

Before reshuffles the atmosphere within the House is electric. Everyone knows someone who has heard something. The fires of ambition are fanned by the press, which goes into overdrive. For journalists, the combination of personality politics, and *Schadenfreude* at the downfall of the mighty is irresistible. It is a form of role-play normally used in management training courses, the only difference being that journalists are never likely to have to manage anything more meaningful than a lap-top. It is peculiarly unsettling for a relatively new MP to find oneself mentioned in reshuffle speculation. One is caught between amazement, disbelief and hope. All one's friends ring with premature congratulations, not having seen the speculation for what it is. It is indeed heady, as long as it lasts, provided it culminates in promotion, and not unexplained silence.

Civil servants also read the speculation. But their information is rather more authoritatively based. There will have been discreet soundings of Permanent Secretaries, and of Cabinet colleagues. Hansards will have been scrutinised for any sign of form, or potential embarrassment. There will have been calculation about how this or that colleague might fit in, how they might complement the skills already to be found in the ministerial team. Groans or cheers will have attended the mention of each name. Strengths, weaknesses, awkwardnesses will have been described. The likely reaction to the workload, and parliamentary skills will have been discussed. A lot of people will have been in the know. I was astonished to find when I was appointed to my first junior ministerial post, that my constituency secretary had known about it for some time. It turned out that her sister was a Government driver. Drivers, of course, always know everything. It says a lot, too, for natural Norfolk discretion, that my secretary said nothing to me. My appointment was a surprise to me, as it is for all but the least modest. It follows that newly appointed ministers will not have had time for preparation. Their first appearance in the department will be of key importance in establishing who will take the lead in the power dance.

On my first appointment, I felt I needed an induction course, since I had studiously avoided speaking on Social Security in my time in the House, preferring to work on health, education and agriculture issues. There was indeed an induction process but it was short. It involved a meeting with Sir Robin Butler, then Cabinet Secretary, for me and the other two colleagues newly appointed to ministerial status, John Redwood and David MacLean. Sir Robin pointed out, admiringly, that Edwina Currie had set herself objectives when first appointed a minister. 'Very impressive,' said Sir Robin. I wondered what kind of world I had entered, where it could be considered exceptional to set objectives when starting a new job. It was only later that I realised that Edwina really had been an exception, compared with many others: as one pointed out, 'I made it clear to my Private Office from the start that I intended to make only politically advantageous decisions – best to be straight from the beginning.' Those were his objectives. Another startled his Private Office, on his appointment, by suggesting that he might be in the office on Tuesdays and Thursdays, so they would need to arrange the work around his availability. Yet another said that there would be no point in giving him a nightly box as he did not intend to do one. Officials could bring him the work at regular intervals during the day.

Officials, of course, would have heard it all before, accustomed as they were to dealing with new ministers, and indeed new Governments. A Permanent Secretary quoted in Peter Hennessy's *Whitehall* put it this way:

> For the first twelve months of a new Government, ministers are very suspicious of us, convinced we are in the pockets of their outgoing

rivals. Gradually, they begin to realise both that this is not so and that they need us. If you're lucky you then get eighteen months to two years of good Government. But, as the shadow of the next election looms, they start behaving in a political fashion again.

For those becoming ministers for the first time, the notion of wielding power can be heady. Before becoming an MP, Edwina Currie had been a health authority chairman. While being interviewed about her appointment as a Health Parliamentary Under-Secretary she was asked the stock question of how she felt about her promotion. She said excitedly, 'In effect, I have become my own boss.'

Andrew Mitchell, MP for Gedling, said of his first junior ministerial post at the DSS, that he had taken two thousand decisions. He was clearly conscious of the power he wielded, even as a junior minister.

It was not how the job struck me, even at Cabinet level. Perhaps among those who achieve high office, some see its possibilities and others its limitations. I belonged to the latter group.

Many are extremely image-conscious. I have heard so many stories from makeup people in television studios about the sheer vanity of, usually, male colleagues, obsessed with their 'best side'. One routinely shaved before every TV appearance, thinking that his dark colouring made him look sinister if his beard was showing through. Another told me, in all seriousness, that he had been advised to appear on television in a cornflower blue shirt – his own description – as it matched his eyes. I was not proof against this form of vanity myself. I found myself buying a vivid yellow jacket for my first Budget as a Treasury Minister. It was the object of great envy from David Mellor, who said, 'Oh, you are lucky, I wish I could have a jacket like that for the Budget. I'm stuck with a suit as usual.' With hindsight, and given the generally much more relaxed atmosphere these days, there would have been nothing to prevent him from wearing a jacket or shirt of any hue for the Budget.

On the other hand, it was as well not to be too vain during one's first days as a junior minister. For one thing, one knew nothing. Even the most junior official in the Private Office knew the jargon, and in particular the acronyms, that characterise each department. I have often been asked how new ministers seem so quickly expert in the brief. From my own experience, expertise comes from only one route, which is working at it – fast. While it may seem hard to have to take through the House half-completed legislation within days of being appointed, there is no surer way of getting on top of things from the start.

The House, moreover, is accustomed to such things and normally indulgent to the new minister who says, 'I don't know, but I'll get back to you.' Some find themselves answering Oral Questions on the day of their appointment – very macho, but it has to be done. After such an experience, anyone would support the proposition that knowledge is power.

Vanity is misplaced in a new minister because a new minister is often put upon. It is the role of an Under-Secretary to take home five boxes full of standard letters to sign every weekend, and sometimes every night as well. You are also the one to make the unpopular announcements. Tony Newton, recounting his junior days under Norman Fowler, never tired of saying how Norman took the good news for himself, and allowed others to take the flak for the bad. It is certainly true that when he was Employment Secretary, he established the pattern of doing a press conference and media round to announce the unemployment figures each month when they were falling dramatically. This did not seem quite such a good idea to me when I was Employment Secretary and they began to rise, to almost three million people out of work. On the other hand, to announce that they would not be announced would have been an equally bad idea. Thus is one a prisoner of the past and of perception.

On the other hand, the Private Office, whether the minister is junior or not, is full of enthusiastic officials dying to do their best for that minister, and convinced that he or she is extremely important. It is sometimes difficult for them to present the menial round as mould-breaking, but they all try. I recall a junior minister in the present Government bewailing the fact that that he had been expected to present awards to allotment holders. He had formerly been PPS to a senior Cabinet Minister, and found the contrast so hard to take that he gave up. In my experience, however, junior ministers wield very little power, nor should they, since there is so much to learn.

At Cabinet level, things are rather different. By that time, you have learned the form, experienced a number of departments, and with luck feel some enthusiasm for the job in hand. A lack of knowledge is still a handicap, but learning is easy and expertise always to hand, in the form of predecessors, or officials. The haphazard nature of the selection of ministers, for qualities which will help them only in certain aspects of their jobs, and with no particular thought for either their career paths or the best interests of departments, is smoothed away, usually, by the time they reach Cabinet level. They will have done a lot of learning on the job. That is when the power struggle, if there is to be one, begins between the politicians and the permanent officials.

The accountable but temporary politician and the non-accountable but permanent civil servant can make a formidable team. In many ways Britain has one of the best Civil Services in the world. At its best, it provides a collection of some of the top brains in the country, it is not corrupt, and is impartial. It is questionable, however, whether the effort it expends is matched to the needs of the day, and whether its culture precludes creative thinking. And, regardless of its excellence, it is not accountable. It is on ministers that the ballot box has conferred accountability. Does the system blur that accountability? How does the balance shift between the competent and the accountable? Is the system efficient? How does it work under pressure, from outside events, or parliamentary circumstances? Does the relationship between ministers and civil servants, nurtured in mutual dependency, or at times shared adversity, become too cosy? What constitutes a successful partnership?

A Different Style of Minister

> Power corrupts, but lack of power corrupts absolutely.
>
> ADLAI STEVENSON

There is no one way to be a good minister. Different types of ability and personality can combine to make one. Knowing something about the subject does not always make the best start, although it can be helpful, since the convert to a cause is sometimes its most enthusiastic exponent.

Nigel Lawson had been a financial and economic journalist so he knew plenty about what awaited him as Chancellor of the Exchequer. He was also efficient, with good organising skills and greatly respected by the officials with whom he worked. If asked, he might well have said that he did not enjoy the House of Commons. He was often disconcerted by dispatch box encounters with Gordon Brown, then Shadow Chief Secretary, deputising for the ill John Smith. Lawson was also famously impatient with those he regarded as lazy or incompetent. That he ran the Treasury when he was in charge of it was beyond question.

Michael Heseltine's qualities did not include a grasp of detail, or even recognition that it might help his cause. At the time of the mine closures, hard on the heels of Britain's exit from the ERM in the autumn of 1992, he was clear that the mining industry had reached the end of the line. It was a great shift in Britain's industrial economy that had to be faced. He was less clear about the need to think carefully about how to put in place measures to help the communities affected, and about the furore that would attend his announcement of the closures. In the event, he chose to make it on the day when I was in Wales presiding over a press conference concluding Britain's informal EU council on employment. It was disconcerting to be asked for details of the closures by journalists to whom I had hoped to present details of the council's conclusions. Of course, the general principles of the mine closures had been debated through Cabinet committee and correspondence but the consequent policy arrangements had not. They were skilfully put into place by the ever-ready and hands-on Department of Employment, but not before the Government had lost credibility on the competence front.

At the Department of the Environment, Heseltine caused deep shock by suggesting that planning appeals took too long to complete. He outraged an audience of councillors in the early eighties by saying that he had looked at some of the appeals cases. 'They are indeed complex,' he said. 'Some of them took me an hour and a half to decide.' The effect on his audience, locked into the wood and trees of local Government procedures, was electric. Even now, those words are quoted – and not admiringly. Yet that approach, the broad view, the vision, the grasp of what is important and what is not, was what made so much of Heseltine's work of lasting distinction. As Deputy Prime Minister to John Major after 1995 his remit enabled him to take an overview of the workings of Government and Whitehall. He was uniquely fitted to do so. His intervention into the workings of departments through his Presentation Committee was deeply resented and resisted. But many who grumbled could not see that Heseltine made an important contribution to breaking down the absurd departmental barriers that impeded the development of seamless Government. He also exhibited magnificent man-management skills, combining firmness of intent with delicate handling of colleagues', and their civil servants', sensibilities.

Tony Newton might be regarded in some ways as the mirror image of Michael Heseltine. A diffident man, with a truly awesome capacity for detail, he was loved by his civil servants and respected by the powerful and outspoken social security lobby groups. He brought in extensive social security reforms so skilfully that no one really noticed how radical they were. Yet he lacked self-confidence and was tormented by nerves before media appearances and on parliamentary occasions, but without exception did well, and always retained the respect of the House.

Kenneth Clarke's ministerial style was in complete contrast to Newton's. Given to sweeping generalisations and strong prejudices on some issues, he was macho, consistently unruffled and, indeed, apparently unrufflable. His sunny personality, self-mockery and roaring dispatch-box style made him an effective minister who was popular with the public. He was a stranger to political correctness, and loved more than anything else a good controversial row. His self-confidence and humour spread through all the departments he managed and he left regretful officials behind when he moved on.

Margaret Thatcher is spoken of with awe by those civil servants who remember working with her. She was seen as someone with an almost incredible capacity for hard work and mastery of detail. She always showed great concern for those with whom she worked and she was entirely professional in her approach. When Parliament was first televised, she is said to have spent time at the dispatch box after the House had risen, perfecting her technique before the cameras. Her attention to appearance was part of her professionalism – she simply thought that looking right was part of the job, and saved time in not having to answer accusations about her hair or clothes in the way that Shirley Williams was obliged to.

There are as many ministerial styles as there are ministers. Successful ministers need a broad overview, a sense of vision and direction, and an acute political sense. They can exercise power successfully without having a total grasp of the detail of their brief. Knowledge is a form of power, though, and while civil servants can provide it, that is no help when it is the minister who is being grilled by Parliament, or the media.

Civil servants are experienced in compensating for their ministers' deficiencies but even the most skilled find it hard going when a minister hates his job. Stephen Dorrell famously loathed his post at the Department of National Heritage, and seemed not to care who knew it. Yet he was a competent and enthusiastic Secretary of State for Health. Contrasting styles in the same job can be equally successful. The warm-hearted and emotional Tony Newton was deeply respected at Social Security, but so was Peter Lilley, with his dry analytical grasp of the complexities of the subject. Provided that the civil servants perceive the strengths of ministers, and provided that there is a positive relationship between them, the minister's position of accountability and ultimate power can be underpinned and supported.

The ability to adapt and compensate on both sides is at the heart of the partnership between the political and administrative process, and is a prerequisite in exercising power to achieve change. Each side of the partnership is aware of its own role, and the role of the other. The best departments and the wisest Permanent Secretaries operate with skill and sensitivity.

What is undeniable is the sharpness of the learning curve with which a new Cabinet minister is faced. Apart from the detail of policy areas, they must know the structures within the department itself, the key officials, and the nature of the department's relations with other departments, notably the Treasury. Then there are the specialist journalists and, of course, the groups and organisations with which the department has regular dealings.

From the moment one is appointed, these groups are on the phone to the Private Office asking for a diary slot as soon as possible. As a new Secretary of State, one may well have doubts about one's power and importance in the scheme of things, but it is the office that counts, and first encounters with such groups leave one in no doubt of that. And while the Government's policies and programme are the point of any minister's existence, relations with the relevant groups are important in that they help form public opinion of the Government's policies and, in today's world, are more convincing advocates than any politician. They matter. But they come with a health warning: because pressure groups, trade unions and professional lobbies have their own career structures and internal politics, the views their leaders express are not always those of the people they claim to represent. Careful judgement has to be exercised in interpreting their messages. It is also important for ministers to remember at all times that their electorate is broader than the pressure group concerned, even though its support and good opinion may be useful.

Pressures of Office

> Power is where power goes.
>
> LYNDON JOHNSON

When I was appointed Minister of Agriculture, the Prime Minister asked me to work to bring the farmers back on side. I was more than happy to do this, and was immediately in touch with the National Farmers Union, the Tenant Farmers' Association, and other representative groups, such as the fishermen, the Country Landowners' Association, and the various food processing organisations. The Ministry of Agriculture was then responsible for food and its safety, and consumers' organisations had to be brought in. There were also environmental and conservation interests. It was a time of change for agriculture, and I thought it important for farming's image to make clear that the Ministry did not regard itself as principally concerned with farming interests but rather with farming amid its changing context. Accordingly, I organised a number of occasions when the future of farming could be examined, not only with the obvious lobbies but also with academics and journalists. The Ministry was startled to be told that such occasions would take place over lunch. One would not have thought, given the initial resistance, that they were the Ministry of Food. But they buckled down, and we began to insert a broader view into the agricultural corridors of power.

Of course, relations between lobby groups and professional organisations did not always run smoothly. Many ministers bear the scars of encounters with their enraged customers, and we all developed our own ways of dealing with demonstrations.

Michael Jack was my talented Minister of State at MAFF. He was responsible for fishing policy, among other things, and like his predecessors, he had his fair share of upsets with the fishing community, in despair at the effects of the Common Fisheries Policy on their livelihoods. He and his wife accepted an invitation to a function in Torquay called 'the Crabbers' Ball'. He decided to meet the fishermen beforehand, at Brixham. He arrived to find a huge and noisy demonstration. Flour and eggs were thrown and his coat was covered with what amounted to a pancake mixture. When he put his hands into the pockets, he discovered that it was not his coat at all, but belonged to his driver, whose wife, seeing the incident on television, was not amused. Neither was Michael's, when later they booked into a hotel for what they hoped would be a romantic evening, only to find a Special Branch officer parked outside the bedroom door. 'I'll be here all night, right here outside,' he said comfortingly.

Nicholas Soames, the Parliamentary Under-Secretary at MAFF, won support wherever he went, with his outsize personality and gift for listening. He was particularly popular with the food industry, with his common-sense comments and zest for his job. Nevertheless, he ran into difficulties with the badger conservation lobby, and whenever he went to the West Country, he was pursued by enthusiasts dressed as large badgers. The same thing happened to me once or twice. It is hard to keep a straight face when conducting an interview with a six foot badger, no matter how sympathetic you might be to their cause.

When I went to the Department of Education, it was at an especially difficult time, and in the wake of the abrupt departure of my predecessor, John Patten. He was the fall-guy for a failure by Whitehall to recognise that it had not equipped itself to deal with the change of culture and activity implicit in the Government's education reforms. On the other hand, he had come into the job determined not to be seen as going native, and from the start had refused contact with the teachers' unions. Since the industrial action in the 1970s, the teachers' unions had been their own worst enemies and I frequently told them so. On the other hand, education and teachers were of such vital importance to the nation that they could not be put to one side. The Prime Minister told me when he offered me the job that he wanted me to bring peace to the education sector.

Dealing with Demos

Democracy means government by discussion but it is only effective if you can stop people talking.

CLEMENT ATTLEE

I stunned officials and teachers alike by ringing all the teachers' leaders the moment I got into the department and asking them to come and see me as soon as possible. It was not a question of going native, but good managerial sense. We had the usual ups and downs during my period of office, but on the whole I was able to be frank and constructive with them and they with me.

My time was relatively protest-free – with one spectacular exception, at the NUT Conference in 1996. The Conference had been boycotted for years by Conservative ministers, starting with Kenneth Clarke. I decided to attend, on the grounds that the NUT had called off their opposition to testing in schools, and because I felt it was time to demonstrate some goodwill from the government side. The Conference was held in Cardiff. On arrival we were unable to enter the conference centre through the front door as it was blocked by demonstrators, and the police claimed that they had only two officers available. We therefore entered by the back door, later written up by the press as a craven act. I was received in total silence, only broken half-way through by a row of delegates standing up, turning their backs and showing on their T shirts some slogan like 'End Tory Cuts'. I was quite relieved – when they got up I had been convinced they were going to moon at me, which would have done the profession no good at all. By the time we left, Cardiff police had had to find a few more officers, as the demonstration had caused gridlock throughout the whole city centre. This happy day out was compounded by a hostile profile in the *Daily Telegraph* saying, 'Gillian Shephard is too close to teachers.'

In the end, all of us became adept at conducting ourselves in demonstrations and swapped stories of those we had known. When Margaret Thatcher first became Prime Minister, demonstrations attended her wherever she went, as a sizeable section of the population was unable to accept the general election result. On one occasion, she visited Norfolk, and I was able to observe her technique at first hand. A line of official cars swept in. The demonstrators hurled their eggs, flour bombs, and tomatoes at the first cars, and ran out of missiles by the fourth, containing the Prime Minister, who waved at the empty-handed crowds as she sailed by, unscathed. I recommended this ploy to the French Employment Minister, Martine Aubry, daughter of Jacques Delors, when I was visiting her in Paris. I never knew if she adopted it, although the French have other ways with demonstrators.

John Gummer positively relished demonstrations. He tells a story of confronting three demonstrations against him on one single occasion, when he was delivering a speech on the environment at the University of Newcastle. The first was outside the lecture hall, with the usual calls of 'Maggie, Maggie, Maggie, out, out, out' to which we all became accustomed and would have missed, had they ceased. The second was during his speech, when five black-clad women stood up and solemnly displayed posters bearing the legend 'Women can be priests too.' Gummer continued to deliver his speech to the three hundred or so people there, and was leaving the rostrum at the end of his speech when he was approached by a man who struck him in the face with a plaice, saying 'Your fishing policy is crap'. We spent a lot of time afterwards wondering if the man had smuggled the plaice in under his coat, if it had originally been frozen, and how much more painful the attack would have been had it remained so. The aspect we most admired was the man's forethought. He had presumably been nursing the plaice throughout the whole occasion, which had lasted for at least two hours. On the other hand, it was a waste of good food.

The Well Oiled Machine

One day the don't knows will get in, and then where will we be?

SPIKE MILLIGAN

The ethos in different departments across Whitehall varies widely. To a new minister, predecessors are of vital importance in filling in the details about issues and personalities.

Some departments, like the Treasury, are full of clever people, accustomed to wielding real clout, in the form of 'The Treasury says no', but with no demonstrable need to run anything. When I was Minister of State at the Treasury, I decided to organise a series of breakfasts for businesswomen. The roof fell in. There was strong Treasury resistance – 'But why, Minister?' – and a total inability to provide a tablecloth or anything to eat or drink, much less to get anyone else to do so – 'You mean breakfast, Minister?' Finally, there was an anonymous briefing which resulted in a spiteful little item in the *Financial Times*, splendidly answered by a woman manufacturer of workwear, from Wigan, who wrote to the newspaper to ask if there would have been such disquiet if it had been a men's breakfast. The breakfasts went ahead. The women I met, from all over the country, provided a marvellous framework for the work I did later on with women's issues in my first Cabinet post. But in the early 1990s networking was an alien concept to the Treasury. I suspect that things may now have changed.

Other departments are at the other extreme. The Ministry of Agriculture, Fisheries, and Food is adept at running its own schemes, administering grants and regulations for its industries, but has almost no clout in Whitehall, being both unfashionable and arcane. However, it gets its own back, because so much of what it does is a total mystery to the rest, it can go its own way, not bothered by smart columnists.

An interesting contrast is provided by the former Departments of Employment and Education, now merged into the Department for Education and Employment. The old Department of Employment, formerly the Ministry of Labour, was a hands-on department, used to running directly the Employment Service and the services created from the Manpower Services Commission. The Education Department, on the other hand, was traditionally hands-off, where the services for which it was nominally responsible were either run by local government or, in the case of colleges and universities, ran themselves. There was a serious culture clash when the two were abruptly merged in the summer of 1995.

At the time of the mines crisis, which most would agree was not perfectly handled by the DTI, a Cabinet meeting agreed, finally, the list of closures, and a budget for programmes of training to help ease the economic transition. As we passed the Cenotaph, on our way back to the Department of Employment, I rang the formidable Sir Geoffrey Holland, the Permanent Secretary, to ask him to start work on the programmes. By the time I got back to Tothill Street, he and his most trusted advisers were closeted in a room, hard at work. The schemes were ready by four o'clock that day.

However, when nursery vouchers were introduced in four pilot areas in 1996, Education Department officials were simply not equipped, with the mechanisms or knowledge to get the work under way. In particular, their ignorance of local authority procedures was woeful, given that working with councils was supposed to have been one of the department's main tasks for at least a century. 'What do they mean, the committee cycle?' was one of the more astonishing questions from an Oxbridge-educated official.

Because the whole idea of nursery vouchers was completely new, we needed to ensure that those wishing for easy information could get it without having to approach forbidding institutions like councils, or even the department itself. So we installed a help-line, whose number was included in all the advertisements. We had regular updates from officials on the numbers ringing the help-line, and on other enquiries. The numbers using the help-line seemed to me to be rather low. No wonder. I rang it myself to see what it said. It turned out to be a recorded voice promising that someone would ring back later. No one did. Improvements followed in double-quick time. Did officials know? Had they rung the line? Who could say?

One of the problems experienced by John Patten was that the Conservative reforms, conceived by Sir Keith Joseph and introduced by Kenneth Baker and Kenneth Clarke, presupposed an administrative function in the department that was not there, as subsequent events proved. If a system has been set up on the assumption that local education authorities run schools, and if certain functions are then run from the centre – like inspection of schools, testing of pupils, a National Curriculum etc. – difficulties are likely to follow. It took some time and a number of staff changes before the necessary skills were in place to get the new systems working, but John Patten was sacrificed as a result. The received intelligence from the loftiest Permanent Secretaries that 'officials are there to do all that sort of thing' was not always well founded. If a minister is not aware of how things are made to happen, he may push the levers of power but no action will follow.

Clearly policy change that has been endorsed by the electorate is expected by departments, and usually skilfully handled. In my first Cabinet post at Employment, we set up a series of policies of interest to women, having first established a small team to deal with them. Rumours abounded in 1992 when the Conservatives won the election that an incoming Labour government had been planning a Ministry for Women. It was said that plans for such a ministry, including smart buildings, were far advanced, and had had to be swiftly dismantled after polling day. My own plans were less ambitious, but nevertheless involved some specific advances; and the department set to with a will, and the plans were put smoothly into place.

The nature of a department and the tools it has at its disposal to achieve change are important factors in the exercise of power.

Understanding them is necessary to achieve change, and to respond to pressure, whether of politics, circumstance or crisis.

Preparing for a Budget

A budget is a numerical check of your worst suspicions.

ANONYMOUS

The Treasury and the Department of Social Security are regulars for policy change that involves legislation. While other departments are always self-importantly thrilled if they have Bills, the two old faithfuls take it all in their stride, not least because part of the legislation annually introduced normally seeks to close a loophole left by the last legislation. When I was at the Treasury, it was still the convention for ministers and officials to go into 'purdah' during Budget preparation time. There are arguments for and against this practice of outlawing all comment on fiscal or economic matters in the pre-Budget period: those for, include insider trading and the sensitivity of exchange rates; those against, include the need for openness and for consultation on complex legislation. But whatever the arguments, 'purdah' was a blessing for ministers, at least, because it meant one less burden, in that there would be no media comment for the duration.

Under Norman Lamont, the Budget was prepared in sections, by each part of the Treasury, and overseen by long meetings held fortnightly at first, then weekly as Budget Day approached. I recall with pleasure the all-out opposition expressed by a number of Treasury knights ranged across the table from ministers when Lamont announced his intention to introduce a National Lottery. Their arguments against were so fluently and rapidly deployed that

115

in the end it became a huge joke, and the Chancellor concluded the session by saying 'Thank you. We are going to do it.' I do not recall anyone actually saying, 'That is very courageous, Chancellor', the traditional civil service way of expressing disapproval, but the air was thick as people resisted the temptation to do so.

Part of the Budget preparation involved serious away-days at Chevening, then the official residence of the Chancellor of the Exchequer. Chevening is a beautiful house, set in extensive park-land, close to Sevenoaks, whose orange street lights can be plainly observed after dark, somewhat shattering the illusion of a rural retreat. Norman Lamont made every effort to be a pleasant host, but the idea of such occasions being anything other than somewhat strained was a nonsense. For one thing, what other guests would arrive for the weekend accompanied by mounds of red boxes, briefings and heads full of battles to be waged? The determinedly casual atmosphere was accompanied by strict instructions on when ties should be worn. The ritual games of pool and darts between ministers and officials took place late at night, when most people would have preferred to be asleep. Wives were encouraged to attend, which posed the usual conundrum for my husband. He went once. The combination of fried food at every meal, cold bed-rooms, a surfeit of shop talk, showing off on the part of advisers, and nothing to do, defeated him. The final straw was that we were invited to buy pheasants shot on the estate just before our depar-ture. The eagle eye of the Treasury was not able to discern just who benefited from this private enterprise. Could it have been the tax-payer? And if not, then who?

The preparation of a Budget is the exercise of power to achieve change. Taxation is an instrument of economic and sometimes social change, which can take effect rapidly. Work on the Budget was one of the most satisfying experiences I had as a minister. One saw through the whole process, and had the pleasure, even if it was sometimes a little mixed, of witnessing its announcement in the ceremony and activity of Budget Day itself. I was at the Treasury for the Budgets of 1991 and 1992, and in that time managed to reform and simplify car taxation, among other things.

Crisis Management

> President Carter says he doesn't panic in a crisis, but that's not the prob-
> lem. The problem is that he panics without a crisis.
>
> CLAYTON FRITCHLEY

Legislating in response to a crisis is a different matter. Ministers are, like the rest of the population, affected by the event that has precipitated the need to legislate, but they are also conscious of the difficulty of introducing change that can make a difference, since legislation takes place after the event. This was the position after the Dunblane tragedy on 13 March 1996, when a man burst into a local primary school and gunned down children and teachers. The Government, like the nation, was gripped by the horror and drama of the event. It was clear immediately that we had to respond. The resulting legislation, although conscientiously prepared, had all the hallmarks of legislating in a crisis and in the end, satisfied no one.

An attempt to introduce identity cards for football supporters in the wake of a football stadium disaster did not reach the statute book but unleashed such fury among large sections of the population, normally unaccustomed to writing to their MPs, that the political effect was as bad as if it had.

During the early part of 1991, there were a number of fatal attacks by dogs on young children. These were appalling accidents which caught the attention of the nation. The Government was expected to do something. But the fact is that it is their owners who allow dogs to get out of control. The Government did its best. It brought in Dangerous Dogs legislation in July 1991. This introduced controls, among other measures, on the ownership and management of pit-bull terriers. But nothing could bring back the children, and the responsible dog owners' lobby was furious, believing that they were being penalised for the irresponsibility of a few. Indeed, on a rule of thumb basis, it is not often that one sees the results of the new law in the form of large numbers of muzzled dogs walking the streets.

Ministerial Priorities

> Unlimited power is apt to corrupt the minds of those who possess it.
>
> WILLIAM PITT (THE ELDER)

As in most other senior jobs, it is of paramount importance for a Cabinet minister to grasp quickly what is, and what is not, important. Norman Fowler, incredible as it now seems, was Secretary of State for Health and Social Security for six years. He survived splendidly, bringing in a complex reorganisation of the social security system, and many changes at the department. Throughout, he retained his good humour, his ability to speak well in the House and outside, and his popularity with colleagues. He was superbly professional. Those who worked with him, however, say that he was ruthless in doing only what he considered essential. Clearly he could not have survived otherwise, but this led to stories, maybe apocryphal, of mounds of unsigned letters and boxes that were the despair of officials.

John Gummer had a similar approach at MAFF. He spent eight years at the Ministry, and could be forgiven for thinking that he knew about every issue – he did, but he extended that attitude into a complete insouciance for 'doing his box'. From time to time, officials would fill the boot of his car with undone boxes, then take him off to visit some remote agricultural cause, stopping every so often to bring out more boxes for him to do while he was in the car. This made no difference to his competence as a minister: he was always well informed and enthusiastic. No doubt it made the officials feel better.

Unless one was firm, there was very little time to stand and stare in a busy department. All those who have been ministers have remarked on the need to be autocratic about the diary, otherwise it is filled with important-sounding but perhaps not essential meetings. I always found, too, that junior and London-based officials had only a hazy idea of how long it would take to get from A to B; the same was true of Ministry drivers. Dedicated as many of them were, I never found one who could map-read accurately, and many were inept at night driving in areas with no streetlights. Some drivers were legendary, such as the one who could not drive on motorways. His minister had to take the wheel!

Knowledge, forethought, and preparation are vital to the exercise of power. Unless new Cabinet ministers are aware that they may be kept so busy by zealous officials that all power is lost, they run the risk of becoming little more than automatons.

I was clear in my objectives when I entered the Cabinet as Secretary of State for Employment. I knew that unemployment was likely to rise and that the handling of forthcoming European legislation, like the Working Time Directive, would be difficult with parliamentary colleagues and the domestic press. I also knew that there was no escaping it in the longer term, although it might be possible to alleviate the burdens it would impose on British business. I wanted to bring education and training closer together, and to reduce the plethora of qualifications that had grown up around NVQs. I wanted to get close to business, and to make the department an economic arm of government.

I was also aware of how much I did not know. After my appointment to the post I returned to Norfolk in a thoughtful frame of mind. It was a Saturday. The peace lasted only until I drove into the yard. My husband had received dozens of phone calls from the press, wanting an immediate photo call. The Private Secretary rang to set up meetings for the Monday. I wanted an earlier start. I spoke to the Permanent Secretary, Sir Geoffrey Holland, and arranged to go into the office on Sunday evening for a quiet briefing session. I would then be able to get off to a flying start on Monday, when I knew dozens of cameras would be parked outside the department.

Sir Geoffrey Holland was an outstanding civil servant. He had planned and set up the Manpower Services Commission, with David Young, later Lord Young. He was accustomed to problem solving, was very hands-on and not in the least lofty. Whenever there were difficult meetings at the department, he would send out for chocolate biscuits to fortify us all, and he did the same that first Sunday evening. By the time I arrived at the office, immaculate files with neatly prepared briefing on the Department and outstanding issues were ready in piles. I noted with admiration that all mentions of 'he' in reference to the Secretary of State had already been changed to 'she' – within twenty-four hours. Despite its relatively small size, this department was run with Rolls-Royce efficiency.

The atmosphere was totally different from that in the Treasury. While no one could fail to enjoy the Treasury – its clever officials, the feeling of being at the centre of government, the interest and importance of the issues dealt with there – it was not exactly a cosy place. The building was hideous inside, with maze-like corridors, and decaying wires and switches hanging off the walls. There were creaky lifts. On one occasion, I organised a meeting for representatives of the car industry, including several groups who normally did not communicate with each other. The lift got stuck with them all inside it for at least forty minutes. When they got out, they were chattering nervously to each other in shared adversity. I always believed that that experience, which they thought I had arranged, played a significant part in the reform of car taxation. Several of those who were stuck still talk about the experience as a formative one. The main problem, they said, was that the lift was stuck in a position where they could see people's legs, and worse, smell delicious aromas floating from the coffee trolley, while the Treasury went on its way unconcerned. It could not have happened in the Department of Employment, where in a trice Sir Geoffrey would have had a task force in place, to get them out.

I had been very busy as Minister of State at the Treasury, since I was also at that time a Deputy Chairman of the Conservative party, and we were coming up to a general election. But I found it challenging and intriguing, when I got into the Cabinet after the 1992 Election, to know that the buck stopped with me. I listed my priorities in a dog-eared notebook which I have still.

I found I could not count on total support and unanimity of view from the junior ministers I inherited. For one thing, most of them wanted their own promotion, and spent time building their own support systems, which included contact with friendly

121

journalists. When disagreements arose, on policy, for example, such journalists might be co-opted to do down the Secretary of State. Dealing with this was just another aspect of management. I was determined from the start not to be surprised by anything a junior minister might have done, so I kept an eye on Answers to Written Questions, and some of the trickier correspondence. I also introduced regular 'Prayer' meetings, half with ministers and PPSs, and the other half with the most senior officials, which helped set the agenda for the week. I took control of my diary, believing that the use of my time was an important priority. I allocated blocks to policy preparation, speech writing, and strategy. Busy activity in a department can be confused with effectiveness, and at first I was guilty of it.

In some ways, priorities suggested themselves. The setpieces, of attendance at European meetings, Cabinets and Cabinet Committees, Oral Questions, which had to be carefully prepared, and conferences occupied blocks of time. Discussions and preparations for the public spending round were also time-consuming. Officials from the various parts of the department would prepare their priority cases, there would be numerous meetings, and detailed briefing before meetings of the special EDX Cabinet Committee dealing with public spending. I prepared even more conscientiously for encounters with the Chief Secretary to the Treasury, by then Michael Portillo, in his first Cabinet post.

It was amusing to have to go to the Treasury as a supplicant, having been an insider there. Treasury officials had intimidation down to a fine art. Visiting ministers and their officials were made to wait – standing – in the hall of the Treasury for an official to show them into the appropriate waiting room. On our first visit, I was so outraged by this that I led my party upstairs, and it was some time before officials could locate us, which made them late in getting us to the Chief Secretary. My officials were entranced. It was the first time anyone could remember the Treasury being wrong-footed at the start of the process. There was an enormous amount of posturing, which, while it was irritating, and a waste of time, was nevertheless worth going along with if it meant getting a good deal. And it *was* posturing, because we were really all on the same side on public spending, as the Prime Minister never tired of telling us. It was not the amount of public cash that was at stake, it was the judgement we made, individually, and collectively, about what was politically acceptable and what was not. The longer one stayed in a department, the more native one went – or so one's colleagues thought. On the other hand, cutting employment programmes at a time of rising unemployment was not easy, however clear it was that the economy, and only the economy, could provide real jobs.

In this work, the expertise of Geoffrey Holland and senior officials was invaluable. They were able to rearrange programmes, build on their experience of what worked and what did not, all the time moving towards the overall objective of bringing education and training closer together.

Women's Issues

Power is like a woman you want to stay in bed with for ever.

PATRICK ANDERSON

It was a wonderful chance for me, as a new Cabinet minister at Employment, that the Prime Minister had linked the job with a new one of responsibility for women's issues. Despite having had the first woman Prime Minister, the Conservative Party then was not really comfortable with women and their problems. There were still too many public school and military types around in the Parliamentary part, although John Major had no difficulty in working with women colleagues or in promoting women's interests.

I already had a good number of contacts in the field, partly because I had worked with Elspeth Howe on the Hansard Commission on Women at the Top. We had prepared a report that led directly to the launch of Opportunity 2000. This initiative signed up employers to work actively to promote women to senior positions. It reduced the effect of the 'glass ceiling', which had meant that women could go only so far and no further in the promotion stakes. Some interesting facts emerged from our work.

At senior level women were under-represented in almost every field – in politics, in the academic world, in business, and in the professions. Even in the media women were sparsely represented at the top. The upper echelons of both television and radio were almost exclusively male. There was a tricky line to tread in avoiding 'the Government must do something' approach, and the equally unsatisfactory 'market forces must prevail'. Getting the tone right was essential in order not to alienate all kinds of lobbies, many with opposing aims. It seemed clear to me that in an increasingly competitive world, no economy could afford to waste the skills and commitment of half its workforce. This was the approach we took, and it informed all of our thinking.

Elspeth Howe was a great character. She chaired the meetings from the Foreign Secretary's residence in Carlton Gardens, as her husband, Geoffrey Howe, was Foreign Secretary at the time. Always immaculately dressed, with splendid dangling earrings, she was brisk, efficient and determined. She was a great networker and had access to whomever she wanted for advice. She had brought some influential people into her team to produce the report: Lisanne Radice, Jean Denton, now in the House of Lords, Bob Reid, formerly chairman of British Rail, John Banham, then Director of the CBI, and Katharine Whitehorn, the journalist. The Commission published its report in January 1990 and Opportunity 2000 was launched. Seventeen months later, the Conservatives had established a policy initiative for women and I was in charge of it.

The media showed a huge interest in the work we did. Women journalists have told me since that they were always looking for stories of genuine interest to women, and were delighted when the new initiative was set up. They also told me that writing about policies for women was one way of getting back at chauvinistic news editors.

There was certainly plenty of hostility from around Whitehall, not least from within the parliamentary party. All of us swapped men stories when we arrived in the House of Commons. One prominent backbencher, Ivor Stanbrook, prided himself on not distinguishing between us. He always called me Betty, pointing out that he did not agree with women being in the House at all, so we might as well all have the same name. I often wondered what his wife was like. I also wondered how Betty Boothroyd might have reacted had he called her Gillian and used the same explanation. But I suppose he called her Betty, by his own logic.

On our side of the House an over-courtly approach to women was prevalent, of the 'God bless the dear ladies, we owe them so much,' variety. Even quite normal people like Ian Lang fell into this trap. At least a year after I arrived in the House, he rather charmingly approached me to say, 'I don't think we have met, but I do know you're Teresa Gorman.'

I suppose we were still something of a novelty, and we were certainly few in number, but I am not sure that things are that much better now, certainly in terms of attitudes, even though one in five of all MPs is a woman.

It was an unusual experience to be able to set up policies from scratch. Before the 1992 election, Angela Rumbold had chaired an interdepartmental working group to coordinate policies of interest to women and we had also worked closely with the Women's National Commission. The interdepartmental group, despite Angela's best efforts, was never very successful: there were regular rows over the future of child benefit, women's tax, and pension rights. The result was that nothing much was done. Now things could be achieved.

We began by asking a lot of questions. What would be most useful for women if they wished, as so many did, to combine work with looking after their families? What was available already? How much overlap should there be between schools, playgroups, and day nurseries? How much could we count on the excellent work already being done by the voluntary sector?

The answers came out clearly. Women wanted good, affordable, reliable childcare, at the times of the day when they were most under pressure. This was undeniably after school and, to a lesser extent, before school too. The work of the voluntary sector was much valued, but it was agreed that alone it was not enough. We decided to set up pilot schemes for after-school childcare, involving the expertise of the voluntary sector but with government funding. They were a great success, providing 64,000 day-care places.

At the same time, we felt that women needed to be made more aware of the professional, educational and training opportunities available to them locally. We organised a series of New Horizons for Women roadshows, using local Training and Enterprise

Councils, and our own network of the Employment Service. I was truly amazed, and delighted, by the response. We ran the roadshows in Bristol, Newcastle, Manchester and Birmingham, before I was moved on. Perhaps the greatest response was in Bristol, where women came from all over the south-west and from as far away as Truro. Universities, colleges, the Careers Service and voluntary organisations demonstrated what they could offer and there were presentations from local women, people who had done well in business or who had overcome particular odds. We prepared a video, which, among other people, featured a school dinner lady who had become a school governor. The video ended with a huge shot of her, saying 'If I can become a school governor, anyone can'. After the roadshows, our local employment officials, working with teams of others, carried on the work, and I have since met many women who were inspired by them to get qualifications or start up a business.

I learned a lesson then and have not forgotten it. Metropolitan reactions are not necessarily those of the rest of the country. Nationally, press and media present the views of metropolitan and London-based people, sophisticated, certainly, but also cynical and blasé. We invited some nationally known journalists to the road-shows. 'Goodness, these women like all this,' was one surprised comment. Generally speaking, local press and media are less uniform in their reactions than their London counterparts, and often more thoughtful and measured. What is a significant event in the locality for the regional media is just one more slog for the national journalist. Local presentation, and keeping in touch with local media, is vital.

Margaret Thatcher has been frequently criticised for not having done more for women when she was Prime Minister. Many would argue that becoming Britain's first woman Prime Minister, and a role model for the rest of the world, was to have done quite a lot. It is the case that she did not believe that women needed any special help in order to achieve, and she came from a generation of women who felt the same way. During the Second World War women had run schools, hospitals, local authority services and businesses as part of the war effort. Margaret Thatcher had attended an all-girls school and an all-women Oxford college, where people took it for granted that women achieved. Most observers say that she used her femininity to get what she wanted in politics. Her appearance was certainly part of her armoury, but so were her brain, her guts and her capacity for hard work.

By the early 1990s, however, women formed nearly half the workforce, and it had become vital to enable them to fulfil their role, first in trying to ensure that they were as well educated and trained as possible, and that they had sufficient childcare opportunities to make the combination of work and family comfortable. Employers needed to understand that what women brought to the workplace was as valuable, if differently structured, as what was offered by their male counterparts. This was a simple message, which to me made good sense. It was not always easy within Westminster and Whitehall to make others see that.

The process of government is at its weakest and most easily caricatured when interdepartmental co-operation is required. The women's policies launched by the Department of Employment were successful. Getting the equal opportunities principles adopted by the Government as an employer was something else. We would hold interdepartmental meetings at which ministers would be asked how they planned to introduce equal opportunities policies, and on what time scale. Resistance came from a range of fronts.

Libertarians believed that women, just like men, should simply operate in the workplace, and that no special arrangements should be made to accommodate their different career structures. Others thought the initiatives smacked uncomfortably of feminism and the 1960s, and would have none of it; yet others truly believed, despite all the evidence to the contrary, that a woman's place really was in the home, and that they were not needed in the workplace. And there were some whose officials resisted, as a matter of course, any attempt at cross-departmental working in Whitehall. Thus people would arrive at meetings determined to be as obstructive as possible, with a hostile briefing that they would deploy with an air of triumph. It took Virginia Bottomley, who headed – at the Department of Health – a huge workforce of a million people, most of whom were women, to shame the rest into action.

It was not only the Conservative Party that was ambivalent about policies for women: the Labour Party was driven to introduce all-women shortlists for selection of MPs. While these were eventually ruled unlawful, and they were certainly condescending to women, it was easy to grasp the reasoning behind the move. Much of the political process seemed weighted against women, not least the selection process for MPs. I was selected against a background of disappointment for many other equally qualified women who never made it to Westminster.

When I arrived at the House of Commons, women were still a rare commodity, which could explain why some of them adopted extreme attitudes just to be visible. It seemed to me that the best way forward was to adopt a low profile, especially with the press, to refuse to answer ludicrous questions of the 'Do you wear stockings or tights?' variety, and to get on with the job.

Others, notably Edwina Currie, took the other view. Edwina came into the House after a successful career in local government and as a Health Authority chairman. She was able, striking to look at and articulate. She seemed to take the view from the start that all publicity, no matter how trivial, was good. In some ways she might have been right – she certainly became very well known up and down the land. Moreover, given that she was only a Parliamentary Under-Secretary at the Department of Health and never achieved higher office, she got the Government's message across. She found Kenneth Clarke very difficult to work with. This may have been a mutual feeling. It is a pity that her huge talents have been lost to politics. Built up by the media, she was in the end destroyed by them. It is ironic that she has now joined them as a talk show host on Radio Five Live.

Harriet Harman suffered a similar fate. She was the darling of the press for a long time, with her beauty and the romance of her marriage to a trade union boss. 'Upper-middle class politician weds union boss', was the shorthand. She once asked me how I had survived, pointing out that both she and Virginia Bottomley had been savaged by the media. I said that I had deliberately played the Mrs Ordinary role in order not to attract the kind of attention I did not want. While this had meant that I was taken at my word, it seemed preferable to the avalanche of criticism that at times engulfed both Harriet and Virginia. Virginia and I were inevitably lined up by commentators as being in deadly competition with one another. She was certainly more spectacular than I, but since neither of us would play their game, they eventually lost interest.

It is difficult to generalise about women in politics. What is clear is that those who make it into the Cabinet are more diverse in every way than their common experience would seem to imply. It is not uncommon for male politicians to say, with whatever degree of self-deprecation they think appropriate, that they have come into politics to be in charge, or because they like the arguments. Most women say that they have come into politics because they want to change things. Margaret Thatcher was quoted on a number of occasions as saying that if you want someone to make a speech about a problem, ask a man, if you want the problem solved, ask a woman. A cursory analysis of the speeches of men and women MPs reveals this to be so. When filibustering takes place in the House, it is not normally women who indulge in it. Women's maiden speeches often concern themselves with detailed descriptions of their constituencies, and of what they hope to achieve as new Members. Men's are much broader brush in nature.

Civil servants will say those distinctions still apply when it comes to ministers. Women ministers are hard-working and conscientious, alive to the practical detail of policy implementation. Many are less interested in politicking between departments and colleagues than their male colleagues. Some are less confident. They have not necessarily served their apprenticeship in students' unions in universities, or in the world of trade union conferences. Command of rhetoric and enjoyment in defeating an opponent are less developed. On the other hand, the practical experience in local government which many of them have had means that they regard political debate as a means of getting something done, not as an end in itself, and most emphatically not as a game.

The women ministers with whom I worked in government were very different from each other. Margaret Thatcher combined an eagle eye for detail with an extraordinary capacity for hard work that left others reeling. She was also capable of distinguishing the important principle, and of articulating it in such a way that everyone else could too. Edwina Currie, who passed through the Conservative firmament like a meteor, had the most amazing capacity for spotting what was newsworthy and going for it. Like Margaret Thatcher, she believed that appearance was part of the job, and never looked less than glamorous and perfectly turned out. In the end, her ministerial career foundered on her unerring nose for a headline – in that instance about salmonella and the national poultry flock. Colleagues were jealous of Edwina's success. They would constantly point out that she had achieved it at the cost of becoming notorious, that she talked without engaging her brain. I always thought Edwina far too smart to have thrown away a career. I believe she achieved what she wanted, which was to become well known and successful. And she has.

There were other sorts of criticism of Virginia Bottomley. Again, they were mainly prompted by jealousy. She was said to be not very bright, to be autocratic and to use her attractive appearance to get what she wanted. When she first became a minister, she was fêted by the press. By the end of her career, they were attacking her for everything she did or had ever done.

Virginia was incredibly hard-working, committed to whatever brief she was given, and wholeheartedly loyal at all times. Indeed, the only time she admitted to rebellion was when she would not accept the Transport portfolio in the 1995 reshuffle, believing rightly that her talents would be better used elsewhere. She asked to be given the job of Secretary of State for National Heritage, which John Major agreed to. This was unfortunate for Jeremy Hanley, who had already been earmarked for the job. It was decided that he would not be suitable for Transport and so he lost his chance of joining the Cabinet. Brian Mawhinney eventually took on Transport – in such ways are Cabinet careers planned.

What all of us had in common was that in addition to the normal and expected criticisms of us as politicians – after all, who escapes – were the criticisms of us as women, our hair, our clothes, our make up – the constant comparisons of us to the detriment if possible of all. It made us wonder if the press were honest about their vaunted desire to see more women in senior political positions. They have been turned on their heads by the arrival of senior women politicians who do not care a fig what people say about their appearance, like Mo Mowlam and Ann Widdecombe.

The arrival of so many new women MPs after the 1997 election has disappointingly, not led to promotion for many or to the pursuit of women-friendly policies. Instead, it has led to some of the most trivial and demeaning press coverage I have known. There has been more press interest in MPs breastfeeding babies in the House than in what women MPs have to say, or what they have achieved since the 1997 election. There are two approaches to the somewhat male-oriented and quainter practices of the House of Commons: one is to accept that in becoming a member of a club for which privilege you have fought tooth and nail you must accept its rules, which you knew in advance and which can be changed from within; the other is to join the club, then criticise it for what it is, loudly. The experience of centuries should inform proponents of the second approach that the first has proved more successful.

Working Across Departments

> Power is the recognition of necessity.
>
> ABRAHAM ROTSTEIN

Cross-departmental working was at its most difficult when policies affected territorial departments. Local and regional politics, ingrained attitudes, special pleading, came into play and were followed, if things got really bad, by press briefings that undermined the enterprise or the reputation of the colleague involved. At the least, much time was wasted on wringing agreement out of other departments – for example, on agricultural or fishing matters, or the allocation of regional aid. Civil servants led these endeavours. On one occasion, John Redwood, then Secretary of State for Wales, and I exchanged and used each other's briefing notes at a cross-departmental meeting, just to see if officials noticed. They did, and the meeting went swimmingly well, made a lot of decisions and finished in record time. It was also clear that ministers were not interested in internecine war between England and Wales, simply in getting things done.

Interdepartmental stand-offs were, of course, much to the forefront when whole-government initiatives were undertaken. Take, for example, the Citizens' Charter, and the Deregulation Initiative, both launched from Number 10. In each case, the initiative was kicked off with a huge meeting in the dining room at Number 10; outside experts gave presentations, with responses from ministers. It was fascinating to watch the body language of unwilling or hostilely briefed ministers, wriggling under the gaze of the Prime Minister, senior colleagues and the interested eyes of the experts as Whitehall sensitivities and nonsenses were laid bare. It always seemed to me to be counterproductive if politicians fell for the insular departmental approach. To pursue such an approach was not helpful to the success of the Government, which should have been a matter of interest to ministers, if not to civil servants.

Some cross-departmental work went well. Tony Newton's Drugs Initiative, which had to have a whole-government approach was supported by everyone – partly because Newton was universally liked and respected and partly because it made excellent sense. Michael Heseltine launched an inter-departmental Competitiveness initiative. It was a good idea, but did not take off as it deserved to, partly because we were nearing the end of the Parliament, and partly because the British are not good with what appear to be abstract ideas.

I was always puzzled by colleagues' territorialism. While it was, of course, irritating to have one's budget plundered for a common cause, what should always have mattered most was the overall perception of the Government which might be enhanced by a cross-departmental initiative. We sometimes forget, at our own peril, that the public are neither interested nor impressed by Whitehall internalism, only by the policies that benefit them. But peculiar strength sometimes had to be exerted to achieve co-operative working, not only to overcome departmental resistance but sometimes that of colleagues, too.

It follows from this that while all kinds of personal qualities and skills can combine to make a powerful minister, it is essential that, to achieve change, the minister is conscious at all times that he or she is the decision maker, that the buck stops at their desk, that there is much to learn and everything to be gained by treating the Civil Service for what it is, the best support system, perhaps in the world, for the political process of government.

Parliamentary Priorities

> I once did a season at Butlins and that was very good training for the House of Commons.
>
> LIZ LYNNE

Nowhere is this more evident than in the balance which has to be struck between ministerial and parliamentary duties. It is to

135

Parliament that ministers are accountable. Almost all ministers are elected Members of Parliament. If not, they are members of the House of Lords and, for the most part, members of the political class – for example former councillors, trade union officials, academics or business people. They are aware that their function is political, and that their power depends on their support of a political party. In this, they are entirely different from civil servants, who are specifically not active members of a political party, and who, until the present anyway, are known to be impartial servants of the government in power.

Margaret Thatcher took Parliament seriously. She voted in more than one third of the divisions that took place during her time as Prime Minister, which is an astonishing record for anyone in that position. She frequently swept into the House at night after some evening function, dressed immaculately, attended by her current PPS, trailing clouds of Mitsouko and glamour around the lobbies. Hardly surprisingly she drew the line at all-night sittings, but often made an appearance when the rest of us were leaning wearily over the Tea Room tables in the early morning, presiding over the Augean stables we had created of our surroundings. She prepared carefully for all her parliamentary occasions, including the twice-weekly Questions, and was never less than excellent, if somewhat hectoring on occasion. On her last appearance as Prime Minister, she exclaimed, sounding surprised, 'I'm enjoying this, I'm enjoying this.' Perhaps that was because, despite her worst fears, her last appearance was a triumph rather than an ordeal.

Like Margaret Thatcher, in the past most senior politicians have taken Parliament seriously, even when, like hers, their governments enjoyed huge majorities. They have rightly perceived that, but for the will of Parliament, they and their governments would not be there at all. It has taken the government of Tony Blair to threaten the dignity and importance of Parliament and all that it represents.

Activities in Parliament are not of concern to departments. Naturally they prefer their ministers to perform well at the dispatch box, that votes are won, and that things go smoothly, so that Parliament and politics do not intrude on the running of the department. 'He's over in the House,' one would be told, in tones of mild disapproval, when tracking down colleagues absent from their departments, as if being in the House of Commons was not part of their job. The tale is told of one minister, deeply disliked by his civil servants and thought to be lazy, who had not bothered to read through a speech drafted by the department to be delivered in the House. Standing at the dispatch box, he completed page four, and turned over to page five, only to see a blank page except for the words 'You're on your own now, you bastard.' This anecdote has gone into Whitehall folklore, and is attributed to a number of ministers. It might have fitted a number of my acquaintance, who relied on their quick reactions and debating skills, rather than on careful preparation, to get them through the scrutiny process.

This certainly could not have been said of my first boss, Tony Newton, who was Secretary of State for Social Security when I became a junior minister in that department in 1989. He was meticulous, mastering all the detail of any brief and able to bite back at the dispatch box. He was once described by the columnist Matthew Parris as a 'feral gerbil'.

However, he was also nerve-racked before questions and debates, refusing to eat, and smoking enormous numbers of cigarettes. He infected the rest of us with pre-appearance nerves, especially me, as a brand-new minister not over-endowed with parliamentary confidence. In preparation for questions, he would preside over agonising occasions attended by ministers, PPSs, advisers, and senior officials, when the questions to be answered would be allocated to each of us, and there would be a brief discussion of the main points. I do not know how it happened, but without exception, he would pick out the questions I had to do, and say, either 'That is the most difficult question on the Order Paper this time, I'm glad it isn't me answering it,' or 'That MP [whoever it was] is the most tricky/knowledgeable/terrifying or awkward Member of the House'. All this would fill me with absolute dread, to the extent that I never enjoyed doing Oral Questions, during the eight years I was in government. I was wholly over-prepared, and undoubtedly over-defensive. On the day of Oral Questions, we all kept an eye on current news stories, hoping that we would not get caught out by a reference to something about which we should have known but had not had time to take in.

Like so much else in politics, Oral Questions are a theatrical game. The aim is not to elicit information but, if possible, to catch out the minister, to make a point, or to provide material for a constituency press release. PPSs would meet interested colleagues before Questions, to discuss likely topics, good responses, and to second-guess the other side. There was no doubt that a good PPS, with good party links, eased the passage of Questions and of all parliamentary activities. Backbench Committees, or more informal groupings – I called them claques – were invaluable for briefing and informing colleagues, for getting feed-back on policy developments and for keeping in touch with the mood in the party and in the country.

Written Questions are a different matter: they are genuinely used as a source of information, often for constituency consumption or for party research purposes. When a series of questions on, say, tax statistics, appears on the Order Paper, especially from a political opponent, it is important to take careful notice. As a Secretary of State, I spent quite a lot of time examining the questions being answered by junior colleagues to make sure that there would be no hostages to fortune. Sometimes there were. The old ploy of 'I will let the Hon. Member have a reply as soon as possible,' had to come into play. It is heartening that new ministers are learning these tricks too, and that they, too, can be caught out in being miserly with the truth.

More often than not, debates are important occasions. They are never as important in the outside world as politicians think, but that can be said of the whole political and parliamentary process. Performance in debates is judged more critically by colleagues on one's own side than by political opponents. The parliamentary commonplace that opponents sit in front of you, enemies behind may be a cliché but it is certainly true. The House can be supportive, dismissive, angry, amused, forgiving, all in the space of one speech. But when it is silent, it is menacing indeed.

Maastricht Misery

When you've got them by the balls, their hearts and minds will follow.

CHARLES COLSON

One of the curious facts about parliamentary debates is how often, when they are billed as really important, they become an anticlimax. The press will scream that such and such a minister is fighting for his or her life, and when the time comes, the whole occasion goes flat. This happened on 23 July 1993, on the morning after the Maastricht vote, when the Conservative Government had been defeated on its own motion to 'note' the Maastricht opt-out. The night before had seen extraordinary and dramatic events in the Chamber. Tension had been rising all week because the Eurosceptics were planning to vote for Labour's amendment preventing ratification of the treaty without the Social Chapter. The vote resulted in a dead heat, although it emerged the next day that there had been a miscount and that the Government had won by one. The next vote, however, was a different matter. The Government lost their own amendment to 'note' the Social Chapter by eight votes, with twenty-six Tory rebels voting against their own side. Given the timing of the votes at just after ten o'clock, this all made sensational television viewing. It was also a spectacular reminder of the power of Parliament.

It was not, however, unexpected. The Cabinet had been aware from the start of that week that defeat was possible. It met three times on Thursday, 22 July. The first was the usual formal meeting at which the forthcoming votes were discussed amid the usual business. The mood was one of foreboding. We could not tell how the vote would go, or quite what would happen if the Government lost it. However, since it was obviously best to keep up some atmosphere of normality, we completed the other business of the meeting. This was one of the Cabinets in which we could not avoid knowing how deeply the issue of Europe divided us. We were privately wondering if the events of the day would lead to some of us resigning. Indeed, if we lost the vital vote that evening, we might all be resigning. During the meeting the press were camped out in Downing Street. To avoid them, and further speculation, it was decided that we would reconvene at seven that evening in John Major's room in the House of Commons, not at Number 10.

At this second meeting, we had at least the satisfaction that only we knew we were meeting. The Chief Whip, Richard Ryder, gave us the latest assessment on the likely outcome of the vote. He forecast that the Government would lose. This was grim but, at the same time, ridiculous. How had we got to this point? The Maastricht Bill had made its way through all its House of Commons stages. The party had been enormously damaged by the parade of the Whipless Eight and other rebels, who had made their misgivings plain on every television and radio channel. Yet our activists were loud in their condemnation of the harm they were doing. The rebels were not supported by the party in the country. The majority of backbenchers wanted the Maastricht question to be dealt with and forgotten before the summer recess. There was a strong feeling that a handful of colleagues were holding the whole party to ransom, some with individual grievances that had nothing to do with Europe. Now the whole government might fall. We had to decide what to do in the event of the government losing the vote that night.

After a fair amount of discussion, we came to the conclusion that if we lost there should be a further vote on the Bill itself, as a vote of confidence, the next morning. None of us wanted such a vote delayed, and in any case to leave things until after the weekend would allow time for the rebels to regroup, and for the press to have an orgy of criticism and speculation. But the stakes were high. Steadily and calmly, John Major drove through his preferred option. Given that he was prepared to risk all in this way, no one should have been surprised when he resigned the party leadership in the summer of 1995. Here was a gambler.

The final Cabinet meeting of the day came after the votes. Since we had been warned by the Chief Whip to expect defeat, there was no surprise, only resignation on the part of some and hope on the part of the majority that we should be victorious in the confidence vote. There was no collective analysis, but we were asked to fan out around the House, into the Tea Room and the bars, to try to help assess the level of support for the government. I came across Sir Edward Heath in the Smoking Room. 'I blame the government, myself,' he said, heaving with laughter. I thought it quite the best response of the night.

The next morning, when the House reassembled, the mood was quite different from the frenzy and drama of the night before. Far from 'fighting for his political life' the Prime Minister spoke quietly, and despite an aggressive, triumphalist speech from John Smith, the Labour leader, the government won the day by 38 votes. Parliament had demonstrated its view of the government's handling of Maastricht. When it came to a vote of confidence, it did the same. The government stayed in place. In such circumstances, the cleverest civil servants can be of no help at all to ministers.

Select Committee Scrutiny

> Knowledge is power.
>
> SIR JAMES MURRAY

Select Committees were set up during the first Thatcher administration. They were designed to give a career structure for MPs that was separate from the ministerial ladder, and to some extent they have worked. Each department's work is scrutinised by a Select Committee, which has the power to examine specific topics, often controversial and in the news, but also the ongoing work of the department. The powerful Public Accounts Committee has the important remit to examine the financial handling of policies in all departments. Its reports can be of immense significance, and on occasion highly embarrassing to the government in power.

For a minister, an appearance before a Select Committee can be an ordeal. On the other hand, since such an appearance gives the opportunity to develop arguments instead of relying on short sharp soundbites, it can be a welcome change from argument in the Chamber. While the remit is scrutiny, Select Committees are sharply political, usually dividing on political lines when there is real contention. They can also be the scene of high drama, such as Edwina Currie's appearance before the Agriculture Select Committee in the wake of her claim that almost all British egg production was infected with salmonella. A larger than usual room had to be reserved for the huge numbers of journalists, colleagues and interested members of the public wishing to observe the proceedings. The atmosphere was that of a public execution, with Edwina dressed fetchingly in black and playing skilfully to the gallery. In the event, the drama was such that the chairman of the committee found himself unable to put the knife in, and the verdict was somewhat fudged. No one could have doubted on that occasion the power of Parliament to hold the government to account. Broadcasting of the most important Select Committee proceedings has also been of help in giving prominence to this vital, if sometimes unglamorous, part of the parliamentary process.

The scrutiny of Select Committees is rendered effective in that not only can they require the production of departmental papers, they may also spend considerable periods of time considering them and quizzing ministers and officials. When a government has a large majority, Select Committees are often one of the best means of opposition, or at least of holding the government to account. Especially effective are the Select Committees in the House of Lords: they are filled with former Cabinet ministers, permanent secretaries, academics and experts of every kind. Some of the most challenging encounters I have experienced have been with Select Committees in their Lordships' House, away from the glare of publicity but on the rack nevertheless.

Select Committees also examine controversial issues of the moment. At the time of the mine closures, the press quickly discovered that there was disagreement, at least on the handling of the matter, between Michael Heseltine and me. The chairman of the Employment Select Committee, Greville Janner, an able lawyer with a talent for publicity, launched a series of investigations into the policy, hoping to provoke dissension, although what there was had already been voiced in the press. Greville adored these occasions: he came dressed to the nines with a fresh buttonhole and an eye to the TV cameras, and set about effectively shredding his witnesses. What he was able to do in uncovering a sequence of events, through the vehicle of a Select Committee, would have been impossible in the rougher, but faster moving arena of the Chamber of the House of Commons.

Cabinet Committees

> Let us never negotiate out of fear. But let us never fear to negotiate.
>
> JOHN FITZGERALD KENNEDY

Departments provide a soothing and ordered environment for ministers from which to exercise power. The arguments are deployed for and against this or that policy, briefing is provided, pages of Questions and Answers. But the scrutiny of Parliament briskly returns the minister to the real world of opinion and opposition to his plans. Not for nothing does the Hansard Society describe Parliament as the link between the electorate and the Government between elections. If a minister forgets for a moment that he owes his position to the ballot box, and that there are limitations to his power, Parliament provides a powerful reminder.

The arena in which power is exerted within Whitehall is far from the public gaze, at Cabinet itself, or in the many Cabinet Committees that deal with every aspect of government policy. Commentators like to calculate the power exerted by a minister by adding together the number of committees they attend, and by working out the influence of those committees. Those who chair the committees, always a senior Cabinet minister according to what is being discussed, are also placed in a power pecking order. The committees are the workhorses of political and policy-making activity. In the Major administration, the EDX public spending committee was the most obviously powerful, but others, like the committee dealing with future legislative programmes and Michael Heseltine's presentation committee, were also important and influential. Officials took the committees very seriously, and piles of briefing, with offers of meetings, were in readiness for their minister to do battle. They were particularly keen for their departments to be engaged in legislation. To secure a Bill, or Bills, in the Queen's Speech was a real virility symbol for officials and some colleagues. I could never understand why. I always hoped, but in vain, that the Government would catch on to what I believed was the view of the public, that there were too many laws, and too much government interference.

One of the most successful committees I attended during 1995 and 1996 had been set up under the chairmanship first of Douglas

Hurd, then of Malcolm Rifkind, to prepare a White Paper laying out the Government's position on the completion of the Maastricht Treaty. All of us had gone through, first John Major's negotiation of the treaty itself, with Britain's opt-outs, and then the dramatic parliamentary sequel. We knew therefore that if we could achieve a consensus that actually meant something, we would have won a great prize.

For a time during the deliberations of the committee David Davis was the extremely able Minister of State at the Foreign Office in charge of European matters. His appointment had been inspirational: he was known to be a Eurosceptic, but was also a tough negotiator who carried clout in the Parliamentary party. He therefore had the respect of the more Eurosceptic colleagues for his views, while the Europhiles respected him for his skill and knowledge of the brief. Exchanges were frank and to the point, and gave the lie to press comment that we were paralysed by splits on Europe. We knew each other's views. There was no need for posturing, but for exploration of common positions, which was achieved with good humour. But as in Cabinet, it was important to be able to fight one's corner, confident of one's facts, if one was to win an argument within a group that might include several who had already done one's own job.

In Cabinet

> Rank is a great beautifier.
>
> EDWARD GEORGE EARLE

Behaviour in Cabinet was interesting to watch. In John Major's Cabinets, no matter what disagreements there might have been on policy, there was little personal animosity. Part of the reason for this was that many Cabinet members had known one another since university days, and were able to argue quite insultingly without giving serious offence. There was a fair amount of showing off too. Someone might say, 'I don't know if anyone heard me on the *Today* Programme this morning. I said X.' This went on for years, until one day, John Major said, 'I never listen to the *Today* programme.' There was a sudden silence, and a perceptible reappraisal round the table. I often wondered if he had just got tired of hearing of others' exploits. It is also entirely possible that he could not bear to listen to the spoken word in the mornings, like Richard Ryder, who only ever listened to music. We were in any case very aware of one another's views.

It was always interesting to hear of what others were doing. One of the weekly treats at Cabinet was to hear Douglas Hurd, effortlessly donnish, give his habitual *tour d'horizon* of world affairs. Others would describe events of note within their own portfolio, and there was always a report-back on meetings in Europe that people had attended.

John Gummer, despite his enthusiasm for matters European, seemed more frequently than the rest of us to be describing a row he had had within some European forum. As Peter Lilley once said, he did not really seem to like foreigners. Even so there was no excuse for the treatment he meted out to the French Agriculture Minister, a Monsieur Puech. Gummer insisted on taking him to the airport, with no Private Secretary, so that they could have a truly intimate conversation in the car. Gummer took the French minister to the City Airport. Unfortunately, the minister was due to leave from Heathrow. The plane departed without him. Gummer did not do this intentionally, of course, but Monsieur Puech did not forget. He told me about it when I, in turn, became his opposite number.

He had found the episode puzzling. No doubt he put it down to another manifestation of the ways of *la perfide Albion*, and determined to defeat us in the next European price fixing round.

Cabinet meetings were an important part of the week. For one thing, they were an element of the legislative process. Colleagues had to have Cabinet approval of new initiatives. Public spending agreement had finally to be sought from the whole Cabinet. Budgets were presented only on the morning of Budget Day, but in theory they could have been rejected by Cabinet even at that stage. On the other hand, much of the bargaining and horse-trading took place in Cabinet Committees in order to prepare for the final presentation at Cabinet.

Officials were always nervous about Cabinet. Folders, with briefing on issues that might come up, were conscientiously prepared, and one was anxiously asked what had happened on return to the department. When Cabinets overran, not only did officials get worried, the press outside began to speculate about rows that might be going on inside the building. On more than one occasion, the Cabinet fell to gossiping at the end of formal business, only to be stopped by John Major with the words 'We had better break up, or the press will be saying that the Government has fallen.'

Cabinets were also a corporate activity, which would have been familiar to any member of a management board. Competitive behaviour, careful watching of the demeanour of others, even the choice of whether or when to speak, all these were noted. They were also an opportunity to catch up with friends and colleagues in a crowded week, which was something I always welcomed. It was not clear to me at first if one should make comments on others' areas of responsibility. Michael Heseltine never had such scruples, opining on every subject under the sun, and referring to his own experience where relevant. While this clearly annoyed some, I always thought it was what Cabinets were for. Indeed it was interesting and helpful if colleagues spoke on areas for which they had once had responsibility. Collective memory and knowledge are surely too valuable to be wasted. Cabinet attendance also led to closer friendship with colleagues with whom one might not otherwise have much chance to work.

While I was Agriculture Minister, I sat opposite Robert Cranborne. I have kept some of our exchanges, which include his search for a rhyme for Osmotherly in a piece of doggerel he was composing. The best I could offer was 'was brotherly', or 'twas southerly', both of which were gratefully received and subsequently used. In such ways do Cabinet ministers keep their feet on the ground.

Out of Westminster

> Too bad all the people who know how to run the country are too busy driving taxi-cabs or cutting hair.
>
> GEORGE BURNS

This round of Whitehall activity was obviously time-consuming. It was also fascinating and mastery of it was essential to a successful stint in one's own job.

Almost as important was the round of purely political activities in which ministers are expected to engage. Cabinet ministers are constantly in demand to speak at party functions up and down the country, money-raising occasions, seminars, discussion groups, and conferences. When official engagements permitted, we usually bolted on to a ministerial journey a party engagement, during the course of which officials made themselves scarce. On one official visit to Scotland, when I had been asked by the Aberdeen Chamber of Commerce to address them, I arranged on each side of the engagement a party meeting. One took place in an enchanting small town, and the Private Secretary with me used her time to stock up with many Scottish delicacies, like haggis, smoked salmon and meat pies, all of which had to be got back to London. We both thought it might have been more convenient and certainly less expensive if convention had allowed her to attend my meeting, instead of singlehandedly shoring up the Scottish economy.

Much is written about the rubber-chicken circuit, and the pursuit of power by ambitious leadership contenders in the Conservative Party. It is true that there are always more invitations than one can accept; women ministers are especially in demand. But it is essential to accept as many as possible, not least because that is how to find out what the grassroots are feeling. I enjoyed visits to different parts of the country, and gaining an insight into what made things tick in any locality.

The way the Conservative Party functions in different parts of the country is fascinating. While obviously there is broad common ground on policy, there is the world of difference between the political contexts of, say, St Ives in Cornwall and Inner Liverpool. I found particularly valuable my contacts with local councillors, who were actually fighting the Party's political battles on the ground. I remain impressed by their commitment, knowledge and practical public service. Their enthusiasm for the Party, and their own local application of its policies, was endlessly interesting and heartwarming.

The Party Conference Experience

If you give audiences a chance, they'll do half your acting for you.

KATHARINE HEPBURN

The Conservative Party Conference is, of course, the place where national, regional and local politics come together, in the glare of national publicity and press comment. It is quite difficult to capture the atmosphere of a Conference, with so much common cause, so much loyalty and so much excitement squeezed into a few days at the seaside. For a Cabinet minister, the Conference, while in many ways a pleasure, is quite an ordeal, given the amount of activity that has to be packed in, and the constant scrutiny of the press, who are itching for you to put a foot wrong.

Some colleagues hate Conferences. For them, it is not what politics is about. For me, they were the essence of politics, and worth all the careful preparation they took. For one thing, they gave us the chance to judge how our message was going down with our supporters. For another, they gave them a chance to talk to us, and to equip themselves with the arguments they needed to support the Party. For many it was the chance to have a good time and to indulge in pure politics.

For the Prime Minister and Cabinet colleagues, the Conference is an important date in the political calendar. There are usually goals to be achieved: to cheer up the Party, to prepare for an election, to deliver important messages and, since the modernisation of the Party structures, votes to be taken on various issues. Apart from that, the Prime Minister and his colleagues are well aware that the whole of the national press is present and the Conference provides a vital shop-window for them and their ambitions. Ministers are judged on whether they have had a good or bad Conference, the length of applause earned by each speech is carefully measured and reported. Until I had to do it myself, I thought that giving a Conference speech, in front of a home crowd, must be easy. I was wrong. An enormous amount of time and emotion is expended on getting it right. Lights burn late into the night as drafts are revised and re-revised. After all, you will be performing in front of colleagues, that least indulgent of audiences, and the one most motivated by *Schadenfreude*.

Many have said that it is almost impossible to make good policy announcements at a Conference. What receives rapturous applause in the hall will not necessarily translate into good legislation. On the other hand, it provides a good opportunity to take the party's temperature, and for the party to make a judgement on how its parliamentarians are doing. It is also the right and expected place to float new policy ideas. That, of course, is precisely what makes civil servants nervous.

For them Conferences are part of that scrupulously screened-off area known as politics. Work on speeches, press releases and policy announcements has to be done with political advisers and people from Conservative Central Office. Obviously, officials have to be kept informed, if only because enquiries about new policies might be directed their way, and because they have to be compatible with the overall policy programme. They are incredibly nervous about what ministers might do away from the protection of the department. They would never admit it, but the television in the Private Office is on throughout the Conference, even if it is a forbidden political activity.

Political folklore abounds with anecdotes about public spending discussions overrunning the committee timetable allotted, and

Minister of State at the Treasury, 1991.

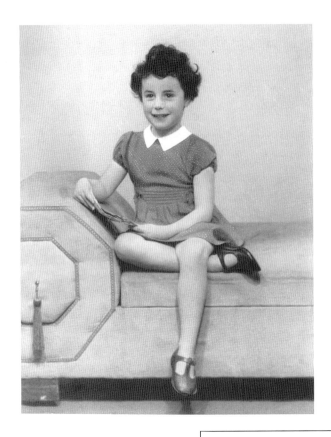

Aged five.

1977 election leaflet for
Norfolk County Council.

The Minister of Agriculture gets stuck in, 1994.

With Michael Heseltine at the Training and Enterprise Council
Conference, 1992.

At an Informal European Council of Employment Ministers, 1993. In
the centre is Irish Employment Minister Michael Woods.

At home with Tom after being appointed to the Cabinet, the Sunday after election day, April 1992.

My first day at the Department of Employment, the Monday after election day, 1992.

Dinner at Number 10 to celebrate John Major's victory in the leadership contest, December 1990

Major's Babes: John Major and his women ministers, Conservative Party Conference, 1991.

The Treasury team before the Budget, 1991.

At the Royal Agricultural show, 1994, launching a new policy on non-food crops.

Anyone for Beer and Sandwiches at the DfEE?

Peter Brookes' cartoon from *The Times*, April 1995.

© Peter Brookes, *The Times*

Richard Willson's view of the spending round, July, 1995.

Meeting young people, as Secretary of State for Education and Employment, 1996.

Photograph by Michael Rouse

spilling over into Conference week. It happened quite frequently but it helped achieve resolution of particularly intractable disputes between the Treasury and a department. On these occasions, officials had to visit us at the Conference, and their demeanour, a mixture of embarrassment and fascination, was a delight to watch. Less delightful was the nature of the meetings arranged in people's bedrooms, more often than not with the bed unmade and the remains of the previous night's carousing still visible in the form of stale sandwiches and dirty glasses.

In the Constituency

Two things control man's nature: instinct and experience.

BLAISE PASCAL

Although I was clear that there should be a division between Government and purely political activities for ministers, I have often wondered since if the amount of energy devoted to ensuring that the division was in place might have been used more fruitfully. I consistently found, no matter how excellent the particular Private Office, that it was impossible to make them really understand the importance of my constituency. For them I was a part of the office, their office, and their daily routine. The fact that I would not be there had it not been for voters in my constituency seemed to escape even the most brilliant of them. I found in Education that the invitations to events in my constituency were squirrelled away by the diary secretary, on the grounds that he did not know what to do with them. After a couple of months, I started to receive complaints that I had not replied to invitations. On enquiry, I found that they had been stuffed into a drawer, and filed as too difficult

153

to cope with. The official concerned did leave – but to promotion. I remain deeply shocked by that incident. Suffice it to say that even the most power-hungry politician will not get far if he fails to get re-elected, and neglect of the constituency can be one way of ensuring that failure.

Constituents have an ambivalent attitude towards Members of Parliament who become ministers. On the one hand, they are naturally proud that the person they selected to become their MP has had national recognition in this way. On the other hand, they are nervous that national activities may detract from con-stituency responsibilities and that they may see less of you than they think necessary for electoral success. I found routine work in the constituency a welcome relief after the pressure of whichever department I was in. Contact with all kinds of people with multiple interests and anxieties was life-giving after being closeted all week with officials who, of necessity, and through no fault of theirs, lived and breathed their particular special interest, whether it was pensions law, or the eradication of ragwort. To work in the constituency obliged one to keep up to date with all the issues being dealt with by ministerial colleagues and served as a useful discipline.

There were downsides, of course. In my constituency we held a quarterly Agriculture Committee, established by my predecessor, Paul Hawkins. In normal times, these were very useful occasions, enabling me to keep up to date with farmers' worries, and to lobby agriculture ministers on their behalf. This Committee had had the unwelcome experience of dealing with the first outbreaks of rhi-zomania, a sugar beet disease, and we had had considerable success in getting changes in the management of the disease from the then Agriculture Minister, John Gummer. We had a huge attendance at the first meeting of the Committee after I had become Agriculture Minister. It was only about half way through that I realised that this time the buck stopped with me, and I was the one being lobbied. The farmers were themselves, of course, a really invaluable source of information and advice. Officials would brace themselves at the Ministry for my return, full of impossible questions and demands.

Our Friends Across the Channel

The age of chivalry is gone and the glory of Europe is extinguished for ever.

EDMUND BURKE

In no area are ministers made more aware of the limitations on their power than in dealing with the European Union, and in no department is this more obvious than in the Ministry of Agriculture, Fisheries and Food. While I knew about this in theory when I became Agriculture Minister in late May 1993, I had no idea of just what it would mean in practice. It is a commonplace that United Kingdom agriculture has few domestic policies and many European ones. The task of the Minister, therefore, is to wrestle with the proceedings in Brussels, to deliver policies at home that are as relevant as possible to British farmers.

The first truth that dawns is that the whole process takes a great deal of time. Attendance at Agriculture Councils in Brussels or Luxembourg cannot be delegated to a junior minister, or an official. For one thing, the industry expects the Minister to be there. For another, only ministers can wheel and deal with other ministers when, inevitably, the Council turns into a Dutch auction at the end.

155

Thus, each month at MAFF, the following sequence of events would take place.

On a Thursday or Friday, there would be a major briefing session, involving all the commodity specialists in the Ministry – our beef man, our set-aside woman, and so on – and officials based in Brussels, who had to come to London to give the latest information about what each Member State hoped to get out of the ensuing Council of Ministers. There was generally much sabre-rattling at this meeting. 'The Germans are determined not to give an inch on rape payments,' officials would say, 'and the Italians will not move at all on milk quota.' Others would chime in for good measure, 'Number 10 particularly do not want you to upset the French, and the Foreign Office say that the Scandinavians are upset on a number of counts, so you will have to soft-pedal with them. And, by the way, the Scottish Minister has decided to come along, and you know how difficult that Scottish Office official can be on cereal payments. And it looks like being a long Council, so you won't have much time to prepare for Oral Questions, although if it does go on, you'll have to come back, even if it means rushing in to Questions at the last possible minute. And although we'll put all the briefing in your weekend box, it may be superseded by events, but we can talk about that on the way to Heathrow.'

Arrangements for travelling to Brussels or Luxembourg would then be discussed. Council meetings were generally held on Mondays, starting early in the morning, which meant leaving central London at around 5.30 or 6am to catch an early plane. Because MAFF was always strapped for cash (partly because it had to finance a permanent office in Brussels, regarded as MAFF's bad luck by the Treasury), at least five people would cram into the car, loaded with huge files, overnight bags and various other bits of paraphernalia, and last minute briefing would continue. Much as I loved the work at MAFF, its best friend could not claim that its policy issues were anything other than impenetrable, especially when they were being discussed in a crowded, steamed-up car on the way to Heathrow early in the morning.

Briefing would continue on the plane, crammed between the plastic food and drink, with officials swapping places to cover yet another issue before we arrived. Then on we swept into the centre of the town, only for yet more last minute briefing before the meeting actually began.

Often a bilateral meeting would have been fixed with another minister, or several, to elicit support, smooth the path, find out the state of play on their deals or where the European Commissioner stood on various issues. The whole event was invested with a sense of urgency that would have surprised those who thought MAFF a political backwater. It might have been, domestically, for the smart commentators, but in Brussels there was quite another perception.

Occasionally, there would be a demonstration. The one I recall most vividly had been mounted by the beekeepers of Europe. There were crowds of people dressed as bees, tents parked in the boulevard outside the building, decked with national flags, ministers queuing to be photographed with their own bee people, journalists swarming everywhere. It had very little to do with what was being discussed at the Council meeting, but enlivened proceedings a good deal, and provided photo opportunities for the politicians.

Once the preliminaries of the meeting got under way, the urgency died down. Ministers would settle down to revise their own briefing, while others set out their opening positions on the given issues, the whole being simultaneously translated, which gave an air of unreality to everything. Attempts to be humorous always fell as flat as pancakes. At regular intervals, coffee and tea would be served, sub-meetings would be set up, and ministers and their officials would keep an eagle eye on who was talking to whom, in case carefully arranged deals should be coming unstitched before their very eyes. If that happened to me, I would go straight up to the ministers concerned, and try to engage them in other conversations or eavesdrop on what might be going on. Negotiating in Europe certainly did not increase one's trust in mankind, or improve one's own behaviour.

On one occasion, when the meeting had been going on for four days and nights, my behaviour fell to a new low. At the time, Belgium was president of the EU so each Council was chaired by a Belgian minister. The chairman of the Agriculture Council was not the most impressive member of the Belgian government and towards the end of the marathon that the Council had become, it became evident that he had given his responsibility for brokering all the deals to the German and French ministers; not surprisingly, they were carving things up entirely for their own benefit. I asked to see him, and berated him for abdicating his responsibility, for acting in a way which was *anti-communautaire*, as he might have said, and in short for being thoroughly unacceptable. I did this in French so that there should be no misunderstanding. To my horror and amazement he burst into tears, wailing 'Oh, Madame, oh, Madame.' However, the sub-dealing ceased, and I noticed that he and the French and German ministers gave me a wide berth for the rest of the Council.

It seemed self-evident to me that while British farmers had done well out of the Common Agricultural Policy from the start of Britain's membership of the EU, and while it was vital that Britain should be represented competently in Europe, this way of doing business was not the most energy-efficient. For one thing, it is difficult to deliver change from a forum representing fifteen Member States varying, agriculturally, from Lapland to Crete. The inevitable result of days and nights of labour tended to be a fudge compromise that satisfied no one, and had nothing to do with an efficient agricultural industry or, come to that, protection of the European environment. All of us were aware that we had different political pressures in our own countries, but that seemed to me to be an argument against, rather than for the system by which the policy was delivered. Agriculture ministers working under these conditions had accountability; one had only to see the furious reactions from their farmers when they went home with what was regarded as a less than perfect deal on commodity prices. Yet they had almost no power, in any direct sense of the word. Such power as they had was so diluted by compromise as in the end to be practically meaningless.

However, on one dramatic occasion, it became obvious that the EU could deliver on an international scale. During my time at MAFF, the Uruguay round of the GATT process came to its conclusion, in December 1993. An enormous amount of work had led to this over a number of years, encompassing bargaining on all kinds of fronts, between nations and groups of nations, and involving all manner of commodities. I had had meetings with agriculture ministers from all around the world, all arguing their case and their own special hardships in support of it. At the same time, my colleagues were receiving similar delegations from ministers supporting other commodities, intellectual property, textiles, manufacturing and so on. The exercise was co-ordinated at European level by Leon Brittan, then EU Trade Commissioner, with the outstanding mix of flair and grasp of detail that has characterised his brilliant career.

159

Finally there was a so-called Jumbo Agriculture Council. It was attended, not only by agriculture ministers from around the world but also by foreign ministers. All the big players were there, including the Americans. The atmosphere was electric. It became obvious that this was Decision Day and that there would be neither time nor patience for the usual arguments about drought in Portugal or floods in Northern Italy. Douglas Hurd attended as the UK's senior minister and for the purpose of the meeting I became his PPS, passing notes about the underlying motives and pressures of European colleagues. There was a real sense that power was present.

The ministers assembled had the ability to take decisions for their countries; the time for negotiation had passed. It was a heady, and unusual, feeling. The experienced foreign ministers, led by Douglas Hurd, Leon Brittan and the Americans, drove the process steadily through. It did not end until around 4am, when we repaired to the EU Ambassador's residence for what was rather a late supper. Then I had to give an interview to the *Farming Programme* for the BBC about two hours later, before flying back to the UK. But at least the matter had been concluded, and several years of patient negotiation had come to fruition.

Other meetings were more difficult. In the early 1990s Britain was somewhat isolated in her position on social policies in the EU. I became involved in these matters when, as Secretary of State for Employment, there was negotiation at EU level of a Directive on Working Time. This particular row became known as the forty-eight-hour week, with the tabloids and the CBI taking up strong positions against any change to the operation of the successful and liberal labour market that had developed in Thatcher's Britain. It was clear from the outset that many of the other Member States saw this as a competition issue. They resented the greater freedom of operation for employers and employees in the UK, and the fact that substantial inward investment had resulted. An atmosphere of extreme hostility developed each time the matter appeared on the agenda of the Council of Ministers. I decided that the best way to deal with this was to form alliances where I could. The French employment minister at the time was Martine Aubry, who was clearly destined for great things. She was also the daughter of Jacques Delors, at that time the President of the European Commission and the bogey man of Britain's right-wing press ('Up Yours, Delors', said *The Sun*). We got on well. I had the feeling that she got little fun out of her job, and that she enjoyed exchanging political anecdote and experience with someone who was clearly no threat to her. We swapped stories of the most outrageous chauvinist behaviour we had experienced. She won, easily, with a tale of having had a red bra thrown at her by a male deputy during Questions in the French Assembly. I visited her a number of times in Paris, and spoke at a conference she had arranged on health and safety. While we were politically opposed, she was more than capable of seeing the domestic problems posed for the British by the forty-eight-hour week issue. She agreed tacitly to help delay the whole matter, and to support sensible modifications, and she was as good as her word.

The issue came to one of its conclusions at a Council of Ministers meeting in Luxembourg. This was never my favourite location. Flights there were less frequent than to Brussels. The other ministers had personal jets, courtesy of their governments. We were dependent on scheduled flights, and if meetings overran, confusion followed in Whitehall. This discussion was clearly going to run late. I was not prepared to compromise on an issue we regarded as more appropriately settled between employer and employee, not at national level and certainly not at European level. I also had some kind of respiratory infection, which did not make for sparkling form. To avoid being submerged in racking coughing attacks, I had a large bottle of Actifed cough medicine on the table in front of me.

The meeting dragged on. The room grew cold. At around 6pm we were told that no more food or drinks would be served. I took refuge in the Actifed, which was more nourishment than anyone else had. It was eventually decided that we should go into a session attended only by ministers and their interpreters. Our EU Ambassador, the glitteringly clever Sir John Kerr, attended as my interpreter, bizarrely, and between us, with Martine Aubry, we manufactured a deal that let Britain off the hook for five years. By then it was nearly midnight, no one had eaten or drunk since lunchtime, and wearily we trailed off to a hotel.

The next morning we arrived at Heathrow to find a battery of cameras and microphones. The combination of no sleep, overdosing on Actifed, no food and rage made this set of media appearances less than successful. However, I was much cheered, a few days later, when a huge parcel arrived at the Department. It contained about a stone of Fisherman's Friend lozenges, with a letter to the effect that the company had noticed I had been taking Actifed throughout the European meeting, and in their view their product would have been more effective. They were therefore sending a good supply so that I could judge for myself.

A particularly grim form of time wasting in the European decision making process was the Informal Council. These events were designed to allow ministers (and their spouses) to get to know one another in a more relaxed atmosphere, and to experience something of the daily life of the country being visited. The country holding the presidency of the Council was expected to host the series of Informals. During my time, such occasions became more and more elaborate. Our own Informal, held on the Welsh Borders in the autumn of 1993, unfortunately coincided with Michael Heseltine's announcement on the mines closures, so the press conference to conclude the Informal was derailed in front of the world's press. At least the meeting itself had been conducted on a modest scale.

Quite different was the Informal held by the Irish during their presidency. They staged it at a luxurious hotel in the west of Ireland. The nearest airport was at Knock, where a fleet of black limousines awaited the delegates to convey them to the hotel. We travelled there at speed, attended by teams of outriders, sweeping through a chain of astonished Irish market towns, scattering cattle and hens as we went. The Irish Employment Minister was a man of enormous good humour and shrewdness. He put on the most incredible show of warm hospitality, unspoiled by the equally incredible security measures he had been obliged to adopt: each minister had their own police officer, and police divers emerged from the lake in front of the hotel like so many large seals. Food and drink flowed, the microphones for the interpreters failed, although this seemed to make no difference to such outcomes as there were, and the whole event was crowned by an uproarious evening of music and song. The Irish minister brought tears to every eye with his deeply soulful rendering of *Danny Boy*. The event was only slightly marred for me by a hostile encounter with the Portuguese minister – we had fallen out over the forty-eight-hour week. Overall, I have no doubt that the Irish were well satisfied with their occasion. Indeed, its wholehearted embrace of the concept of an Informal Council was more successful than others, where attempts were made to railroad through decisions while people were over-refreshed.

All of these distractions should not deflect attention from the fact that the European process, with its demands on ministers' time and energy, was an obfuscation of the democratic process as we see it in the UK. Decision-taking in a forum representing fifteen Member States, at the level of detail required in, for example, Agriculture, is impossible, and worse because it renders ministers impotent, and unaccountable domestically. 'We can't do anything about it. It is a matter for Europe,' was too often the cry. Had one struggled to be in a position to take decisions, and the flak for them, only to find that someone else was calling the shots, or worse, that the process itself delivered fudged decisions that pleased no one?

The summits, attended by prime ministers, were perhaps less of a waste of time, although they absorbed a great deal of energy. I remember seeing the hall of Number 10 literally filled with boxes and briefing material, which was on its way to accompany John Major to the Edinburgh Summit. I wondered if he had mastered all the material inside them. Probably. Summits were sometimes used to resolve issues that had proved incapable of resolution at Council of Ministers level. One such issue was the infamous Italian milk quota. The Italians had claimed cash for more milk quota than their dairy industry was capable of producing. It is true that Italy is also the country that unaccountably found its olive trees were peripatetic; other Member States were found to have operated similar scams. But milk quota was a serious matter. Never mind that British dairy farmers had demonstrated against the introduction of the system, locking the poor Agriculture Minister, Michael Jopling, inside a school in Wales and overturning a milk tanker. Times had changed. Milk quota had become a valuable commodity and that the Italians should have cheated on such a scale was not acceptable. By this time, they had a woman Agriculture Minister. Her explanations were operatic in scale and intensity. She explained that if Italy had to repay what it was claimed it owed to the EU for the fraud the state would be bankrupted, taxes would have to be raised and many other disasters would follow. She would explain this with much hair tossing, and eye flashing. She was altogether too much for her colleague agriculture ministers on the Council. Meanwhile, the British tabloids, and the *Daily Telegraph*, were loud in their justified condemnations of Italy's behaviour. At the same time, the EU split on who should replace Jacques Delors as President of the Commission. The decision on this appointment had to be unanimous. John Major refused to back the Belgian De Haene, using the Italian milk quota as his lever. The final compromise included some payments by the Italians of their debts to the EU, and the appointment of Jacques Santer, from Luxembourg, as the Commission President. In order to fight this particular corner, John Major had not only to master the issues of the day for the Summit, but all the twists and turns of the Common Agricultural Policy as well.

On occasion, the Commission itself, and the Council of Ministers, could be used to good effect. In the autumn of 1993, a German health minister, a Herr Seehofer, raised alarms about the safety of British beef. In the first instance he was not supported by the German Agriculture Minister, but he caused a great deal of fuss among German consumers, to the extent that British beef exports to Germany, never very high, fell almost to nil. Despite evidence from all the relevant scientific committees, including the World Health Organisation, Herr Seehofer continued and concerns were raised at EU level. Germany was acting illegally – of that, there was no doubt – but until she formally banned our products, we could take no action. Herr Seehofer was invited to Britain for talks on the issue, his officials came, and left apparently reassured. The German reluctance to use our beef continued. Then came a trade fair in Frankfurt, in the spring of 1994. To our amazement we found that not only was our beef refused, but Scotch whisky and shortbread too. At this stage, I enlisted the support of the Agriculture Commissioner. He saw at once that the German action was illegal, and not *communautaire*, in that it militated against the Single Market. Obviously one Member State could not operate an unjustified unilateral ban on another Member State's products. We had to get the backing of other Member States, to take legal action against the Germans, and I set about it.

Wheeling and dealing became the order of the day. There were different bargaining counters for different Member States. The French, I recall, wanted support for electronic devices to be used to identify pets crossing the Channel. The Irish, as they always did, promised undying support. The Belgians were uncertain, until I pointed out that the same thing could happen to them. It eventually did, of course, over their poultry products.

The Dutch were always good allies, the Danes wanted support on an environmental issue, and so it went on. The day of the Agriculture Council came. On the whole, colleagues reacted as they had promised, apart from the Irish, who seemed inclined to change their minds. I had to threaten them, at the eleventh hour, and we got the vote. The Commission took the Germans to court, and won.

As a Cabinet minister I undertook travel for other reasons, which gave me a quite different view of attitudes to power in other countries. In France, all senior ministers were entitled to bodyguards and outriders. When I visited my opposite number at Agriculture, Monsieur Puech, in his constituency in the Massif Central, we were attended by a huge police presence, on the not unreasonable grounds that farmers' demonstrations encircled Paris at the time. It was also cold and snowy, so in addition to the out-riders and police, we were preceded everywhere by a snow-plough, which made for slow, if majestic progress.

As Agriculture Minister, I visited Paraguay, Uruguay and Argentina. In Paraguay, which had only recently introduced dem-ocratic elections for the President, and opened up its press, the con-trast with what I had left was almost comic. The President was enormously popular, a heady and new experience for me as I swept along in his wake. By extension, anyone who visited him was also very popular, and I was presented with flowers and gifts of all kinds, and treated to amazing hospitality. The press was uncritical, just delighted to be around. The President took us in his own plane to his ranch where he had a million head of Brahman cattle. At least a hundred journalists came too, separately. The President wanted us to see his prize beasts so he piled us into a Land-rover, packed many of the journalists into an open trailer behind, and set off, fast, over bumpy ground. Our journey was attended by shrieks and bumps as the journalists and their cameras fell off the trailer and were left behind in the distant pampas. The whole event, including a huge barbecue on which several whole animals were cooked, was recorded ecstatically in the press the next day. Such was power.

The distinction between official and political activities for min-isters was strictly observed by John Major's government. It has been less strictly observed by the present government, whose Prime Minister was able to say from the dispatch box that the principle objective of his official spokesman, paid for by the taxpayer, was to 'knock hell out of the Tories'.

Of necessity, that distinction becomes more marked as a general election approaches. If one had, mistakenly, developed a close relationship with officials at ones Department, all illusions were dispelled as politics intervened. My own memories of the Department for Education and Employment were a little soured by an absurd incident during the 1997 general election campaign. About two weeks into the campaign I was due to speak, as Secretary of State, to the annual conference of the Secondary Heads Association. It was an official engagement which I felt obliged to honour. In any case, I was still Secretary of State until the day after the general election. The Department refused to provide typing for my speech, maintaining that it was a political engagement. A number of hours were wasted in futile argument, and in the end I had to have recourse to the Cabinet Secretary, Sir Robin Butler. It was a sad and silly end to what had otherwise been a positive relationship.

The imminence of general elections brings other changes for ministers to remind them of their transient status. If a government stays in office for a full term of five years, the Official Opposition is entitled to access to civil servants to prepare it for government, should that be the outcome of the election. This must be a difficult period for civil servants, with loyalty to the present incumbents and excitement about who may be the new ones.

When the election is called, ministers are asked to empty their desks and pack all the paraphernalia from their offices into boxes. This is a curiously chilling moment, but no more chilling than the standard letter received by all Members of Parliament telling them that they have no access to parliamentary premises for the duration of the election period. If one ever had illusions about the provenance of power, these procedures dispel them utterly.

Parliament and Opposition

The duty of an Opposition is to oppose everything and propose nothing.

LORD DERBY

FOR MOST POLITICIANS, the point of politics is the exercise of power, and some politicians see a period in Opposition merely as a period of impotence to be endured until the next election victory.

Despite the importance of the Opposition's role, it is an area 'relatively neglected by scholars', as Peter Hennessy observes in *Whitehall*.[26] The reason for this is not hard to find: politicians want to govern. Few wish to dwell on the mixture of failure, humiliation and disappointment that is electoral defeat. Even fewer would admit to enjoying Opposition. As Margaret Thatcher once put it, 'When you are in Government, five years is a very short time. When you are in Opposition, it is a hell of a long time.'[27]

Yet there is a positive job to be done. Apart from playing its role in the democratic process, a political party can use a period in opposition to refresh its structures and policies, and to get back in tune with the electorate. It can introduce new people and thinking, and form new alliances. It is one of the disadvantages of the macho, confrontational nature of British politics that no one can say so, much less prepare for it while still in power.

Eighteen years is a long time in politics. The general election result in 1992, the problems of the Major Government between 1992 and 1997 and, indeed, the consistent message of the opinion polls during that period, gave force to John Major's comment that to expect a fifth Conservative term in office was to 'stretch the elastic of democracy too far'. In political life, however, it is unthinkable for contingency plans to be made for what everyone strains to avoid, even when they can see that electoral defeat is on the cards. Operating at a high level in politics sometimes unavoidably militates against what would be common sense in any other situation. And the electorate has, on occasion, surprised the political establishment.

Tories Out!

> A Conservative is a man who will not look at the new moon, out of
> respect for that ancient institution, the old one.
>
> DOUGLAS JERROLD

The mood in the country before the 1997 election was to get the
Tories out as a first priority, notwithstanding Party manifestos. The
scale of the defeat in terms of parliamentary seats was enormous; in
terms of actual votes cast, less shattering. Not surprisingly, the
Conservative Party took some time to start functioning again as a
political force.

In the days following the election, the media were triumphant.
Had they not predicted this? Was it not time that the country rid
itself of the wicked Tories? Was it not, yet again, 'the *Sun* wot won
it'? No less triumphalist were the opinion pollsters. Having been
spectacularly wrong over the 1992 Election, it would have been
more than their business was worth to get it wrong again. The sun
shone every day, the new Prime Minister and his untried ministers
smiled untiringly. More than one naïve quality journalist opined
that a new day had dawned for Britain.

Many who had not before been tried in Opposition felt that to
creep under an appropriately sized stone might be the right
response. It took a little time before we realised that losing an election is not only part of political life, it also presents challenges and
even opportunities for renaissance. But in the early days, the overwhelming feeling was of powerlessness.

Adjusting to Opposition

It has been said that England invented the phrase 'Her Majesty's Opposition'.

WALTER BAGEHOT

One of the first lessons we learnt in Opposition was that all the support systems to which we had been accustomed vanished. I mused on this, a few days after the election, as I waited in a queue behind some part-time catering staff for my new parliamentary pass. I had come back to the House of Commons after an audience with the Queen to hand in my seals of office. The Palace, of course, had met this particular situation before. Everything was handled with the perfect light touch. Back at Westminster, however, I had the strong feeling that we were in uncharted waters, which was strengthened by the number of new faces around the House, new Labour faces, mostly, clamped to mobile phones and pagers, and uniformly beaming. And they had reason to do so.

I crawled into the House. Everything looked the same, but somehow strangely unfamiliar. Our Whips' Office was now the Opposition Whips' Office, located on the opposite side of the Members' Lobby. It was almost empty, with a few stray papers drifting about, and an almost palpable sense of Situation Vacant. I asked for a list of Conservative MPs who had been returned at the election, together with their phone numbers. 'Sorry, we don't seem to have one,' I was told.

I rang Central Office, to be told the same thing. 'Who did you say you were?' the voice enquired, not unkindly and rather accurately.

The mood was one of *nostra culpa*. It would have been hard for it to be otherwise, given the mood of the country, which was

173

euphoric that we had gone at last, and the triumphalism of the new government at its victory after so long in the political wilderness. At first it was worse than that. It was as if, at a stroke, the Conservative Party had lost all the skills and experience that, collectively, we possessed, and in addition as if we had suddenly become invisible. Journalists who for years had besieged our offices to talk to us no longer quite recognised us in the street. Our views were not only not valued, they were not sought. For a short time, there was a collective crisis of confidence.

Help and advice were available. Old hands at Opposition, like Michael Heseltine, Norman Fowler and John MacGregor, had been there before. They told us that what we were experiencing was what we could expect. They gave good advice. The wisdom offered by Heseltine was that the only way to get attention in Opposition was to issue a press statement every Saturday morning, and await press reaction on Monday. Fowler warned that we would find it hard work with little public reward. John MacGregor reminded us that the Opposition during the previous Labour administration in the 1970s had kept the Government up for night after night, with vote after vote, and that such persistence had worked in the end. While none of these scenarios was appealing, at least they reminded us that there is life, in government again, after Opposition, and here were the living proofs. At the same time, we were learning at first hand why political parties strain every nerve to avoid losing elections.

A Major Shock

The duty of an Opposition is to oppose.

RANDOLPH CHURCHILL

The mood of Situation Vacant was heightened by the first Shadow Cabinet meeting after the election, presided over by John Major. For many of us, it was the first time we had seen him, or each other, since the defeat. The mood, as can be imagined, was grim. For one thing, our numbers were sadly depleted by the colleagues who had lost their seats – Michael Portillo, Tony Newton, Roger Freeman, William Waldegrave, Malcolm Rifkind, Michael Forsyth, Ian Lang, James Mackay and Paddy Mayhew had all left. So many absences seemed more substantial than our presence.

Our collective mood was not enhanced by what we found on entering the Shadow Cabinet premises. Almost none of us had known where they were or what they comprised. In fact, they occupy what was formerly the residence of the Serjeant at Arms, with an outside entrance into the Speaker's Courtyard. Inside the House, they are reached from the Official Corridor behind the Speaker's Chair, via a long corridor leading past the Table Office and the Foreign Secretary's suite. Upstairs there is a large conference room and a set of smaller ones, which had been used by John Prescott before the election and during the campaign. There were empty pizza boxes, drinks cans, overflowing ashtrays. It looked as if it had just been vacated by an occupying army, which in a way it had. None of us was in a mood to ask the House authorities why, during a six week election campaign, there had not been time at least to clean the rooms but it was a disgrace, nevertheless, and not boosting to our collective self-confidence. The insight it gave us into the eating and recreational habits of our predecessors was also deeply unpleasing.

On the day of the Shadow Cabinet meeting we crammed into the Shadow Cabinet room, with its broken lamps and spaces on the walls where pictures or charts had been hung. John Major was in sombre mood and clearly did not want any kind of post-mortem discussion, although Virginia Bottomley, who had been consistently loyal throughout our period in government, delivered an impromptu lecture on the perils of disloyalty. She was heard out in a resigned silence. Then John Major said, as was evident to us all, that he would be standing down as leader, that he would be prepared to do Questions, and other parliamentary occasions until his successor was appointed, and that for the time being the rest of us should continue to hold our pre-election portfolios. With that he concluded the meeting, and we trailed out.

His reluctance to do anything other than the bare minimum was understandable. He would certainly have wished to avoid rows and accusations which, had he allowed the meeting to run, would undoubtedly have surfaced in the press the next day. He might have been unsure too of whether he could have avoided losing his temper in the presence of some colleagues whom he perhaps thought more responsible than others for our plight. He would have been conscious, as we all were, of the leadership ambitions around the table. Whatever the reason, the meeting was highly unsatisfactory, and gave no leadership for the period to come.

I consulted the Chief Whip, Alastair Goodlad. Always a man of few words, he pointed out that he was having to do double duty as Shadow Leader of the House, and the best thing all of us could do was to shut up, get on and leave him alone.

There were, of course, things to do. The new government, flushed with its triumph, announced even before the House had assembled that henceforth there would be only one Prime Minister's Questions per week, and that the Bank of England would become independent. Furious, we rang our usual journalists to make statements about abuse of Parliament. We could almost hear their *So What* shrugs over the phone. Hey, we were in new territory, man. All that stuff about Parliament had no place in the exciting world of New Labour. There had been a press conference, had there not?

There was a Queen's Speech. No one wanted to hear what we thought about it. John Major did a manful job in his response. We sat behind, the new invisible army as far as the media and public were concerned.

As was their right, the new government was determined to make an impact. They planned to make an announcement a day for months, not often including the House of Commons in their list of announcement venues. There was early Education legislation. I was not helped by the fact that exhaustion and the election campaign had left me with a raging ear infection, which not only made me ill but also picturesquely deaf. Former Education colleagues, notably Cheryl Gillan and James Paice, with our adviser, Elizabeth Cottrell, now unemployed, met in Cheryl's Millbank office to draft amendments and plan tactics for the forthcoming debates on the Bill in the House. It was a revelation of the resilience of these colleagues, and the newly elected Members of Parliament we drew in, to see how they tackled the work with no help, no resources, and no Party back-up. In some ways it was refreshing to work on our own, with no lines to take, no Question and Answer briefing, just our own views and convictions. We spent a little time laughing about how new ministers were currently being overbriefed and overcircumscribed, just as we had been, by the same officials who had worked with us.

Given the small size of the new Parliamentary Party, I felt we must draw in new MPs to help. We needed them, and they needed to get stuck in early. We got them over to Millbank, and trained them in how to intervene, ask questions, and translate such briefing as we had into parliamentary-style speeches. These new Members were wonderful – fresh, inventive and courageous. They were also constructive about the task in hand. After all, Opposition was all they had known. I began to see positive possibilities about our changed role. Among the most outstanding in those early days were Theresa May, MP for Maidenhead, who had come into the House with a strong background as an effective councillor, Nick St Aubyn and Graham Brady. Keith Simpson also made a strong impact. We made sure that they would not be cowed by the inevitably hostile parliamentary atmosphere. They were not, and under Cheryl Gillan's leadership, actually kept the House up until the small hours, with relentless questioning on the Bill. They did rather better than I, as I succumbed to my deafness before the parliamentary process was completed.

There were all the usual irritations to be experienced at the start of a new Parliament. This time, we were not in charge. Thus every change, every development seemed to be one designed to put us in our new-found place, the No Lobby.

One of the sillier nuisances that attends new sessions of Parliament is the battle for the allocation of rooms. It is well known that new MPs have to wait up to a month before they are allocated a room. Until that happy moment, you trail around carrying mountains of mail, leaving it in unsuitable places and grabbing the chance to use a telephone when one becomes free. What is less publicised is the reason for this delay, which is that senior MPs are negotiating with the whips for their own rooms, changing their minds, throwing tantrums, and generally being grand, so that those lower in the pecking order have no choice but to wait their turn.

Each generation of new Members is routinely outraged by this treatment, especially those who have come from exalted positions in the private sector or local government – academics, of course, are used to scrabbling for space. 'Don't you know who I am?' or 'I haven't been treated like this since I was at university,' are the repeated cries one hears at these times. The more people complain, the more grimly determined are the whips to exercise their power as parliamentary disciplinarians – in other words they start as they mean to go on. I remember being ridiculously pleased when I was finally allocated a coat peg in the Members' Cloakroom, and even more delighted when, in advance of actually having a chair and a desk, I was given a locker and key in the Library Corridor. Ken Livingstone, who entered the House in 1987 when I did, famously was not given a room, desk or phone for at least a year after his election. The whips, who decided to treat him in that way no doubt to teach him some humility, as they thought, must since have wondered if their tactics were a success.

The situation, of course, is much worse when a party goes into opposition. In our case, in 1997, the whip who had done our room negotiations before the election, the genial Derek Conway, had lost his seat and with him had gone the folk memory and bargaining positions. I was given a tiny room in which no more than six people could stand at once. I knew better than to complain: instead I fixed a meeting for fifteen people, among them the new (and until then stupidly intransigent) accommodation whip. He and ten or so others had to stand in the corridor, unable to hear what was going on. Curiously, and with no more being said, I was given a larger room. Others had a similar experience. The feeling of rootlessness it engendered permeated the parliamentary party through to secretaries and helpers. While these kinds of matters are trivial, and soon forgotten once a Parliament gets under way, they are undoubtedly worse when a Party is newly in Opposition. Everything seems designed to underline one's powerlessness.

Electing a Leader

Politics is the art of the next best.

OTTO VON BISMARCK

Our spirits were soon lifted, even if in an illusory way, by the exercise of political power at its most raw. We had to engage in the election of a new leader. Whether in government or opposition, Members of Parliament, backbenchers and office-holders, are equal in the power they hold in the election of a leader. Most find it a heady experience. It was particularly so when we were newly in Opposition. Here, at least, was an issue over which we had control.

It brought back memories of the last time we had engaged in a leadership election and inevitably, some thoughts of the 'if-only' variety. I had been an inexperienced Parliamentary Under-Secretary when Margaret Thatcher fell. It was from there that I had engaged in the leadership campaign for John Major.

I had observed then the interesting change that comes over those involved. The candidates themselves are touched with the potential for greatness, and for the duration of the campaign, at least, are courted eagerly, listened to, quoted and supported. That is to be expected. More fascinating is the transformation of back-bench politicians as they realise that for the period when their votes are needed it is they who wield the power. They form camps, swirl into plots, and take on more or less important roles in the campaign teams. Some go off into self-appointed tasks, doing their own vox pop opinion polls in the House of Commons, and revelling in the media attention, speaking to Radio Copenhagen or Cairo, not minding in the least that no one listening will know or care who they are. The important thing is the attention. Overhanging the whole procedure is the whiff of possible preferment – 'If I support him, what will be in it for me?' is clearly the motivation of many. Among their number are those whom preferment has so far eluded. But there is a scent of real power, potential on the part of the contenders, actual on the part of those whose votes are being courted.

Such preoccupations were very much under wraps in the period immediately preceding the fall of Margaret Thatcher. While she had been undeniably a great Prime Minister and world figure during at least the first ten years of her term in office, there were many in the parliamentary party, and among our activists, who felt that she should have stepped down at the height of her popularity. I recall her being interviewed by Sir Robin Day on this point – only he would have had the temerity to ask if she did not agree that it was time she left. She leant forward, fixed him with a piercing gaze, and said sweetly, 'Sir Robin, I see no reason why I should. I enjoy the work.'

Apart from anything else, her answer revealed how differently she saw her role from the way in which many male colleagues would have perceived it. She did indeed enjoy the work, possibly more than she enjoyed the power. But she had become a very controversial figure by this time. She inspired great admiration, and great loathing, even on the part of our own activists. Many felt that she had slain her dragons, and that it would be better to have a less confrontational figure in charge of the party. There was undoubtedly plotting in and outside the Parliamentary Party, although I was too humbly placed to be aware of just how much.

There was much tut-tutting when Sir Anthony Meyer, the gentlemanly but eccentric MP for Clwyd North West, announced in the autumn of 1989 that he would stand against her in the annual leadership election. Most of us felt that this was ridiculous but, of course, he was a stalking-horse, and a forerunner of the challenge to come.

When I arrived in the House in 1987 Michael Heseltine was a backbencher, having resigned eighteen months earlier over the Westland debacle. He made occasional appearances, stalking through the lobbies with his blond mane visible above the general scrum. There were those said to be 'in his camp', like Julian Critchley, Michael Mates and Keith Hampson, but apart from the odd rude reference to the 'Great She Elephant', or 'She Who Must Be Obeyed', from the naughty Critchley, much of what went on was below the surface.

The challenge, when it came in the autumn of 1990, electrified the party and the country. Some colleagues, like Emma Nicholson, immediately declared for Michael Heseltine. Edwina Currie was equivocal. During the period leading up to the first vote, the Conservative women MPs had arranged a dinner to discuss policies and approaches for women. It was cancelled because loyalists like Jill Knight would not sit at the same table as Emma and Edwina. With hindsight, it is clear that the divisions in the party which his supporters hoped John Major would be able to heal were already present, and too deep for easy bridging.

Margaret Thatcher's helpers included Peter Morrison, her PPS, and John Moore, whom she had sacked from her Cabinet only a year earlier. On the night before the first vote, they were in the Tea Room, not their usual habitat. I remember asking them if they needed any help. 'Oh, no thanks,' they chorused in unison. 'We have everything under control.' That's good, then, I thought. Alas, events proved that they had not. Margaret Thatcher was on an official visit to France. When the result came, it had to be broken to her, and she was obliged to carry out an official engagement with the French President at Versailles in the full glare of international media attention. Political life is rough and tough.

The next day, Wednesday, 21 November, we as junior ministers were consulted by our boss, Tony Newton, on whether we thought Margaret Thatcher should stand down, or, as she had put it, fight on. My own view was that she had been irremediably damaged by the whole affair. I was also aware of growing discontent in my own constituency with her style, encapsulated by the handling of the Poll Tax issue. I said, with a heavy heart, that I thought she should stand down. All members of the Government were consulted in this way, and the results fed back to Mrs Thatcher.

On Thursday, 22 November, I was in my office at the Department of Social Security. It was obvious that it was going to be a momentous day. I had rung a close colleague, Andrew Mitchell, to join me so that we could consider what should be done next. He was with me when someone from the Private Office came in to tell us that the Prime Minister had resigned. We were living through an historic shift and we realised that, junior as we were, we had power to use in the next step.

I rang John Major's office, and said that Andrew and I would be over to offer our help. In the event, we did not get to the Treasury until an hour or so later, bearing sandwiches in plastic bags in case Major had not had time to eat. We were immediately subsumed into the fast-moving process of his leadership campaign. There was no time for regrets. Politics came to the fore, and phones rang all over Whitehall for hours. In the House of Commons Press Gallery,

journalists waited in vain for departmental press notices but ministers had reverted to being politicians, and were plunged deep into
the process they loved best, pure politics.

Quickly, John Major's campaign took shape. A house in
Westminster, which belonged to Alan Duncan, who was not then
an MP, was identified as the headquarters, and phone lines were
rushed in. By the hour, it seemed, more helpers poured in, and tasks
were allotted. Norman Lamont, at that time Chief Secretary to the
Treasury, became campaign leader. Richard Ryder, then a junior
Treasury Minister, was also heavily involved. He had been in the
Whips' Office and at MAFF, and was a natural plotter and conspir-
ator who could make an invitation for a drink sound like a request
to take part in the Gunpowder Plot. Volunteers from Central
Office, like Angie Bray, resigned their posts to help. After the first
few days, Gordon Reece, who had been one of Margaret Thatcher's
image-makers, appeared in our midst. Journalists like Bruce
Anderson joined the party.

Although the process took only a few days from start to fin-
ish, it seemed an eternity to those of us involved. Margaret
Thatcher had resigned at a meeting of the Cabinet at 9am on
Thursday, 22 November. By the following Tuesday, John Major
had been elected as her successor. In between lay a lifetime of
political experience for all of us.

My own constituents were strongly behind John Major as the
new leader. Margaret Thatcher had attracted great admiration, and
there was general appreciation of all that she had achieved, but the
Poll Tax had gone down very badly locally. Many people felt it was
unjust. They also felt that the Conservative Government did not
want to hear their views about that or any other issues. What had
been seen as strong leadership by Margaret at the start of her time
in office was now interpreted as uncaring arrogance.

At the start of John Major's campaign, days were organised on tight schedules. There were early planning meetings to decide who should do what in terms of media appearances. My main tasks were at first to persuade people to join the Major campaign, and to collect intelligence as to who was supporting whom. Considerable weight was placed on senior colleagues and their declarations. Cheers went up in the headquarters as names were announced. Gordon Reece decreed that since there were few other female Major supporters, I should be fielded in interviews as often as possible. This led to a number of sexist encounters, during the course of which I was asked why women found John Major attractive, and so on but all of us revelled in the chance to speak to journalists and interviewers, no matter how remotely they were placed, in the belief that everything must help.

It was all breathtakingly exciting, and took over our lives. Fortunately, the main activity took place over a weekend, otherwise little government work would have been done. We found ourselves taking part in numerous interviews on radio and television, sometimes discussing the qualities of the candidates with colleagues from the other camps, sometimes extolling the virtues of our candidate with interviewers from every radio station, it sometimes seemed, in the world. We should have realised, and no doubt many did, that the end of Margaret Thatcher's career as Prime Minister was what was making the news, rather than the election of her successor, at that stage of the process. There were discussions on whether Major should take part in debates with the other candidates, a good deal of jockeying to get good interviews for him in the press, a lot of attention to his photo image. On one occasion, he and I had a televised photo-call walking down Whitehall. The resulting pictures of us bore the legend 'Mr and Mrs Major campaigning.' Such was fame. The real Mrs Major must have been mortified.

When the result was announced I was in a television studio with David Hunt, who was supporting Douglas Hurd. I was a nervous television performer at that stage in my career. I recall wondering what on earth I should say if the result went against Major. In the event, I had the easy script. David's immediate reaction was, 'I will be very happy to support John Major in any way.' I thought this a complete turnaround from what he had been saying, on air and live, one second before. On reflection, I realised that this was the correct response of 'The King is dead, long live the King.' We shot out of the studio, an impromptu building on St Stephen's Green opposite the House of Commons, to where the action was. In the House of Commons there was uproar, people rushing in all directions, shouting the voting numbers and answering media calls.

By word of mouth I discovered that there would be a celebration at Number 11 Downing Street later that evening. Times and arrangements were vague, since we were still, unbelievably, in the pre-mobile, pre-pager era. By the time I turned up, an extremely large party was under way, fuelled by very generous measures of gin, whisky, or whatever was requested. I do not remember any champagne. Given John Major's modesty, and perhaps superstition, he would have been unlikely to order any.

The noise level rose steadily, until eventually someone whose face I recognised, but whose name I did not know, came over and said, 'I think we should go and have something to eat, don't you?' He marched off, collecting James Arbuthnot on the way, and we went downstairs to climb into the most enormous Rolls-Royce. Its owner turned out to be Jeffrey Sterling, who took us to Wilton's, where miraculously, a dinner in the private room had been arranged. Those present included Sir Terence Burns, now Lord Burns, then a senior Treasury mandarin. Others arrived – Andrew Mitchell, Michael Jack, Andrew Tyrie, and finally John Major himself. Now the champagne flowed. Photographs of the occasion reveal that all present looked, at the least, bemused, and at the worst, overrefreshed.

Meanwhile, back at the House of Commons, a debate was under way on the School Teachers Pay and Conditions Bill. Hansard honourably records a normal debate, ending at 10.45pm, with a few Opposition references to the Rt Hon. Member for Huntingdon. Most of us remember flowing back into the lobby with so much noise and uproar, everyone congratulating John Major and each other, that the Speaker called a vote to calm things down. He was right in thinking that there would be no more sense from anyone that night.

After the 1997 election such euphoria was absent. We were in Opposition, and were not choosing a prime minister, but someone who would have an enormously difficult job. Yet the issue of who should succeed John Major was of key importance for the future of the party. Major began by stating firmly that he would play no part in the process, and would support the party's eventual choice.

Contenders for the position then emerged. They had clearly been preparing for this eventuality since the last days of Major's Government because some of them had well organised teams of supporters already in place. William Hague, in particular, had support systems from the earliest days of the new Parliament, somewhat diminished by the electoral loss of leading lieutenants like Andrew Mitchell. John Redwood, of course, had a number of supporters from his leadership bid against John Major in 1995.

Stephen Dorrell, Kenneth Clarke, Michael Howard and Peter Lilley were a little less organised, but quickly got into position.

This was a curiously unreal period. I was in any case unwell, and alternating between periods at home with a raging ear infection and time in London crawling about, trying to function normally while not hearing much of what was going on. But it was unreal because as long as it lasted, we felt that we mattered, almost as if the election had not happened. The media and our constituents wanted to know what was going on. We were in demand again, even if we were looking inward. But it helped our recovery process as we engaged in some real politics, and exercised real power.

The activity was fast and furious. The usual canvassing of colleagues took place. The contenders established headquarters from which to run operations, and appointed chiefs of staff. I joined Peter Lilley's team, despite blandishments from the others. We met in offices on the corner of Tufton Street, with a super-efficient organiser in Christina Dykes, who went on to head the Listening to Britain exercise from Central Office. Constituency chairmen and Area Chairmen were canvassed. We visited Wales and Scotland to talk to Conservatives there, and to elicit their support. The allegiances of the new Members of Parliament were eagerly sought. Some of the wisest, like Theresa May, never said, and have not said since, whom they were supporting. Others, and it always happens, offered their support to more than one candidate, not knowing that this always comes out afterwards and means that you are never trusted again. We found ourselves asked to give opinions to journalists, to take part in photo calls. Perhaps we mattered after all.

What did matter was the eventual outcome. Peter Lilley, Michael Howard and Stephen Dorrell did not do well enough in the first ballot to continue. Michael Howard's campaign had been dealt a mortal blow by a parliamentary attack from Ann Widdecombe, during the course of which she described him as having 'something of the night' about him. They had fallen out at least a year earlier when working together at the Home Office, over the fate of the then Director of the Prison Service, Derek Lewis. If Ann Widdecombe had been seeking revenge, she succeeded.

With three contenders still in the ring, feverish canvassing of colleagues continued. The Conservative peers, the activists and the MEPs, all supported Kenneth Clarke but MPs were doubtful that with his views on Europe, he would be able to unite the Party. Others took the view that it was time to skip a generation, and favoured William Hague. John Redwood attracted solid support from activists. On one interesting occasion all three contenders were put up to speak in front of the 1922 Committee and peers. The meeting was chaired by Robert Cranborne and was an important parliamentary milestone. When the vote came, it was influenced by the fact that Kenneth Clarke and John Redwood had made an extraordinary pact of agreement. This was regarded at best as a lapse of judgement, but at worst as a cynical ploy on the part of two experienced people who should have known better. It certainly harmed the prospects of both. In the end, William Hague won by a comfortable majority.

During the contest there had been a series of bizarre media occasions. Redwood and Clarke had posed together uneasily in celebration of their pact. Peter Lilley and I were photographed on a staircase, framed by greenery, at the back of the St Stephen's Club. William Hague held a press conference the day before the final vote at the Atrium Restaurant at 4 Millbank. Afterwards we streamed back to the St Stephen's entrance of the House of Commons for a photo call. Margaret Thatcher made a staged exit from the House to join us, sweeping down the steps, immaculately dressed and coiffed as usual.

I was asked to persuade her to come to the Commons Tea Room. 'Yes, dear,' she said, 'but I don't have any money with me.' Charging her for a cup of tea was far from our minds. We swept through the House, with her in the vanguard, and entered the Tea Room to the amazement of the new Labour women MPs clustered there. Sir Richard Body was seated behind a newspaper. She went straight up to him, snatched away the newspaper, to his terror, and boomed, 'You do support William, don't you, Richard?' It would have taken a brave man indeed to have entered into discussion on the proposition but fortunately for all, Richard Body did support Hague. It was a splendid episode, and taught some of the new MPs a thing or two about style and verve.

So William Hague became Leader of the Conservative Party. The first building block was in place. Now we needed to persuade colleagues and supporters that a period in opposition, no matter how painful, could also be an opportunity to refresh and renew ourselves and our policies. The difficult thing, after a shattering defeat, is to achieve the necessary positive state of mind to use the time in opposition to good effect. But given that the point of politics is the exercise of power, Opposition is the time to prepare for its return. There is no time to waste.

Renewing the Party

A Conservative is someone who believes in reform. But not now.

MORT SAHL

An analysis of the 1997 defeat indicated that we needed to modernise the Party, to get back in touch with the electorate, and to renew our policy base. We were powerless as politicians for the moment, but we could at least achieve change in those areas we controlled.

After his election as leader, Hague addressed a large meeting of the Conservative Party at Central Office early in July 1997. He said, 'Political parties do not succeed through good organisation alone. But they certainly do not succeed without one.' He went on to describe how the Party had declined throughout his lifetime, and pointed out that the average age of members was sixty-four. He said that the local government base had thinned, and the number of professional party agents who organised the party associations in the constituencies had halved since 1970. In launching a programme for renewal and reform of the Conservative Party, he said, 'Our current organisation is not up to the job. No change is not an option. We need to renew our organisation, rebuild our membership and rejuvenate our Party if we are once again to become the dominant political force in the land.'

For the past eighteen years, we had been busy governing and it would be no exaggeration to say that we had lost touch with many of the changes affecting the lives of the electorate, some of which were the result of our own policy successes. The country was in a sound economic condition. The power of the unions had been curbed, although it was arguable that other elements in society, the media, for example, and pressure groups, were in danger of becoming over-mighty. By and large the population was enjoying the fruits of our work: there were more home owners, more car owners, more holiday makers, more people aware of their rights. The public services had become more customer orientated but also more stretched. And significantly, compared with 1979, the importance of the political process and of politicians, relative to the other activities and personalities in people's lives, had waned markedly. Compared with the celebrities whose every exploit was shouted from the tabloids and *Hello!* magazine, politicians were tame indeed. Communications were immeasurably more rapid. Globalisation was upon us, as was the technology revolution. People were more informed and less impressed. The Labour Party in Opposition had had the time to take account of these changes, and used them to their advantage. Their vocabulary, of 'new' and 'modern', chimed with the voters of 1997.

Within the party, as Hague pointed out, membership had declined. We were not unique in this: all political parties were finding that their membership was dropping. People no longer had sufficient free time to give to organising the kind of money-raising efforts popular in the 1950s. They did not necessarily want to discuss and take part in politics as a leisure activity. With the majority of women under pension age working, they were no longer available to support party activities as they had in the past. People were very busy with work and family. Older people were often involved in caring for grandchildren. Politics was being squeezed out of people's lives.

And there were other problems. The Party had a big overdraft, partly the result of spending £28 million on the general election, compared with the £6.7 million spent on the 1983 general election.

Our activists, though still loyal and supportive, were demoralised and inclined to blame the parliamentary party for sleaze, disloyalty and the 'brown envelopes' affair, which they believed had played a large part in our defeat. Our professionals – agents, Central Office workers and regional staff – were similarly demoralised, although certainly not terminally so.

It was clear that the whole party structure would have to be recast, taking the activists, professionals and politicians with us. William Hague brought clear-sighted energy to plan the strategy and follow it through.

One of the quainter characteristics of the earlier arrangements had been that there was no legal entity entitled the Conservative Party. The party machine was composed of the National Union – the activists – with its own structure of constituency associations and its own career ladder, and the professional side, Central Office, and the Party Chairman heading paid officials throughout the country.

Then there was the parliamentary party – which included MPs, Peers and MEPs – Conservative councillors and the Young Conservatives, who, although declining and with a shifting nomenclature, were also part of the equation. This management nightmare had worked in more leisurely days, when, as someone put it, we all knew each other, but became severely strained during the sleaze and brown envelope period when everyone, not least Prime Minister and Cabinet, was demanding that something be done. The brutal truth was that the structure provided no mechanism to do it.

If an individual MP was found wanting, the only means of getting rid of him lay with his constituency association, and MPs had become very good at creating constituency associations in their own image: the most Eurosceptic would surround themselves with like-minded activists; the most Europhile would do likewise. So they were perfectly justified in saying, as many did, that their associations would not countenance them supporting this or that point of view. They forbore to add that, in a way, they had created their associations' opinions. No one – not the Prime Minister, the Party Chairman, the chairman of the National Union, the Chairman of the 1922 Committee or the Chief Whip – could oblige the constituency association to act if it was disinclined to do so. The independence of individual local associations, in some ways such a strength of the Conservative Party, had been a factor in damaging the prospects of the whole organisation. The Party paid lip service to the concept of unity, but its sense of unity had been severely strained during the troubled 1992–7 Parliament. Many activists were incredulous when told that the Prime Minister could do nothing to call rebellious MPs to account, and that apart from a good telling off from the whips, the only people who could hire and fire were themselves. Something had to be done to introduce power and accountability into the structure of the party.

William Hague set about bringing the three parts of the party together, under the title of the Conservative Party. This was easier said than done. There was some resentment between the three elements. MPs felt that they had soldiered through the 1992 Parliament working to the best of their ability, with a diminishing majority, an increasingly hostile press and with a far from certain future in their own careers in prospect. They could not see why individual associations could not take their misbehaving MPs in hand, thus removing the common problem. The National Union could not understand why there was such difficulty on policy issues like Europe within the parliamentary party, and why MPs could not just shut up and conform in the interests of the party. The professionals, naturally sore at the reduction in their numbers, wanted the politicians to read the runes provided by every local government election and every by-election.

All of this added up to more than the blame apportioning that might be expected after an election defeat. It was the result of eighteen years of electoral success and government, during which there had been neither motivation nor time to look at a party machine that appeared to be delivering the goods. It was also the result of a truly British dislike of institutional reform.

But it would not do, and Hague set out six principles by which reform would be achieved: Firstly, unity of the three component parts of the party. Secondly, decentralisation, whereby constituency associations would henceforth be regarded as essential building blocks of the Party, with a much more direct contact between them and the Party leadership. Thirdly, democracy, through which the membership would be consulted on the manifesto and policy change. Members would also be more directly involved in the election of the Leader. Fourthly, involvement, and thus a move to national membership. Fifthly, integrity, giving, through a disciplinary committee, the party itself the power to suspend or expel. As Hague put it, the party would not again find itself in a position 'where sustained controversy in a single constituency blackens the name of the whole Conservative Party.' And finally, openness, on party funding.

Hague set out these proposals in July 1997, and laid out a rapid timetable for consultation on their adoption. He asked that by the end of September 1997 members should endorse his leadership and the principles of reform, and that the results of the exercise should be announced at the Party Conference that year. A Green Paper on the principles would be published before the Conference, it would be debated there and, if adopted by the Party, it would become the new constitution, to be launched at a special conference the following spring

This exercise could only be undertaken by a Party in Opposition, and the amount of energy that went into it was impressive: 22,000 copies of *Blueprint for Change* were circulated; 150,000 executive summaries were sent to party members; each constituency association was asked to complete a detailed questionnaire; twenty-six roadshows were held around the country, attended in all by 3,000 Party members; 1,200 feedback forms and letters were received from individuals, officers of associations and various Party organisations.

MPs and others rightly perceived this as a shift in power towards the activists. Many MPs had misgivings, not least because they felt that they might have to face reselection in their constituency associations. They had observed, with some anguish, the gyrations of the Labour Party when reselection was introduced. Many were the tales from Labour colleagues of the meetings and grillings they had had to endure on the road to reselection. Now Conservatives were worried that they were to face the same examination by their activists. Fears were expressed, not without foundation, that some associations would use the opportunity to force their views on to the local MP as a price for his or her reselection, with Europe, for or against, in the forefront. In the event, there were no deselections of sitting MPs. Some vengeance, however, was wreaked on those who sought to be chosen again after they had lost their seats. Many experienced great difficulty.

The most effective change, because it empowered the party, was the introduction of the new constitution, which would, for the first time, establish a single Conservative Party. To oversee the constitution, which, it was recognised, would need revision from time to time, there would be a Constitutional College. This would be composed of the National Conservative Convention, Conservative Members of Parliament, Conservative Members of the European Parliament, House of Lords front bench spokesmen and the Executive of the Association of Conservative Peers. The aim was to ensure that different interests within the party be kept in balance. In the same connection, special safeguards were introduced for the arrangements for election of the Leader, the make-up of the single ruling board, and of the Ethics and Integrity Committee.

The new board's members were the Party Chairman, appointed by the Leader as his representative, two deputy chairmen, one elected by the National Conservative Convention, and the other appointed by the leader. In addition were, four further members elected by the Convention, the Conservative leader in the House of Lords, the elected representative of the Scottish Conservative and Unionist Party, the elected co-ordinating chairman for Wales, the elected chairman of the Conservative Councillors Association, the Party Treasurer (appointed by the Leader), a senior member of the professional staff of the Party (nominated by the Party Chairman), and a further member nominated by the Leader, subject to the endorsement of the board. The board can add one further place.

The board's responsibilities are wide-ranging, but it has the power to 'refuse membership of the Party, replace or remove any officer of a Constituency Association or Recognised Organisation and establish or replace Constituency Associations'. Its power to oversee all aspects of party management and administration is made clear, including 'the resolution of any disputes within the Party' and 'implementation of the decisions of the Ethics and Integrity Committee'.

The principles underlying all the party's reforms are under-pinned by the determination to have decisions made by one member, one vote, wherever possible.

The election of the Party Leader is a case in point. While, in the first stage of the process, Conservative MPs will present a choice of candidates to the whole Party, the second stage of the election will involve every member of the party voting for his or her choice. There had been much criticism that in the leadership contest which resulted in William Hague's election as Party Leader, Kenneth Clarke had emerged as the clear winner in the polls of activists, MEPs and the House of Lords. Some activists were left with a sense of injustice, although many others felt that a fresh start had been called for and were happy with the final choice.

The endorsement of William Hague as Leader and of his policies also included endorsement of his stance on Europe. He was conscious that divisions on European policy had cost the Conservative Party dear in votes and public esteem under John Major, and subsequently at the 1997 election. Meetings were held up and down the land to present the policies to members in September 1997. Returns were sent in to Central Office. These resulted in an overwhelming expression of support for William Hague as leader, and also for the policy of 'In Europe but not ruled by Europe', which he had coined. Thus, as a result of the reforms which he had introduced, and had ensured were fast-tracked, he became the first Conservative Leader to have received a one member one vote endorsement from his Party membership. While this did not remove altogether a variety of opinions within the party on the European question, it did enable the leadership to pray in aid the support they enjoyed.

There was opposition to the reforms from what some might have thought an unexpected quarter. When the plans for the new organisation of the party were published, and sent out for consultation, it was clear that one whole branch of the party had apparently gone out of existence: the Conservative Women's National Committee. Tory women, of course, have their own mythology and bibliography and their power and influence is legendary. Although caricatures paint them as blue-rinsed and out of touch, they have played an impressive part in the party's history for many decades. The CWNC had its own organisation, with separate arrangements for Scotland. There was a National Committee, which has provided many a formidable member of the House of Lords and Chairman of the Party Conference. There was a network of regional and constituency committees, all of which raised money, ran functions, and contributed to political debate. When I entered the Commons in 1987, I was quickly absorbed into the speaking round demanded by the many women's functions, as were all women MPs. We were all grateful for this, as it gave us valuable experience, knowledge of the way the Party worked and thought, and got us known among the activists. The Women's Conference was an important date in the Party's calendar. The Party Leader, and Cabinet ministers always spoke at it, and it was chosen as the occasion on which important announcements of policy were made. It is impossible to overstate how impressive were the achievements of the CWNC at the height of its powers. Its influence – for example against any kind of change in child benefit – was very strong. How then, could the Party have got things so terribly wrong as to imply the abolition of this body?

Some in the party believed that women-only organisations had had their day. If the party was to modernise, it must be wholehearted about it, and sweep away this vestige of the past. Also women had done well on the voluntary side of the Party, and did not seem to need the CWNC to advance. None of this thinking actually grasped the point, which was that the CWNC did not exist in order to provide a career structure for women in the party. It existed because women valued it, regarded it as their way of contributing to the Party, and because it did a good job.

William Hague appointed a Tory activist, Peta Buscombe, as Party Vice-Chairman with responsibility for women, and put her in the House of Lords. This, too, caused real resentment, not because people disliked her but because she had not come up through the CWNC, and therefore, it was thought, did not understand the importance of what she had been put in place to change.

There was a row. The Conservative Party is not normally discreet about its rows, more is the pity, but the women were made of loyal stuff. Above all, they did not want this row to surface unpleasantly in the media, believing correctly that William Hague had plenty of other things to worry about. But the discussion was vigorous. The then chairman of the CWNC, Caroline Abel-Smith, stood firm, and with the support of the women, continued as before, with a Women's Conference and regional and constituency functions. The CWNC is still in place. Baroness Buscombe has become a respected opposition spokesman in the Lords.

This is an interesting example of how a reforming tendency can get carried away with itself. In this case, everyone saw sense in time, and a potential waste of goodwill, expertise, and enthusiasm was averted. But it is also an example of how real power, born of experience and self-respect, can prevail.

The time and energy spent on modernising the Conservative Party, although of only internal importance, was an important first step in recovering from electoral defeat. It will be a lasting monument to William Hague's ability to set a course and see it through.

Hague's New Team

No government can be long secure without a formidable Opposition.

BENJAMIN DISRAELI

Hague appointed his first Shadow Cabinet on 20 June 1997. It combined familiar faces with new ones. Thirteen of its members had held Cabinet posts, although not all under the last Government. John Redwood was brought back as Shadow Trade Secretary. Norman Fowler, revived for the umpteenth time, as he himself said, became Shadow Environment Secretary. Hague rang me from Yorkshire to ask if I would become Shadow Leader of the House. Initially I was not keen, feeling that I could do more for the party by being out and about and not tied up in the House of Commons. However, he prevailed, and I found not only that I enjoyed the job, but also that it used some of the skills I felt I had in helping to weld together the Parliamentary Party at a potentially difficult and vulnerable time.

Newer faces included John Maples, who had been a Treasury minister before losing his seat in the 1992 election, and who became Shadow Health Secretary, Francis Maude, who had also had a period out of the House, as Shadow Culture Secretary, and Andrew Mackay, a former Deputy Chief Whip, as Shadow Northern Ireland Secretary. It was a master stroke to make Cecil Parkinson Party Chairman. I had never worked with him but, like everyone else, soon saw that he was invaluable. Not only was he charming and self-deprecating, but he knew everyone and had seen everything before. This made his presence peculiarly comforting, and his contributions weighty. He saw the funny side of his resurrection, saying, at the Conference, that cabbage always tastes better boiled twice. Another great source of strength was Norman Fowler. He had been in opposition before, during the Labour Government from 1974 to 1979, when he had had to shadow Barbara Castle among others. He told us that no one would be interested in anything we had to say for a very long time, that we should prepare ourselves for a long haul, a year or more, before we would feel we were making headway. He also observed that in the end the shine came off all governments. How right he proved to be! Michael Heseltine, although not a member of the Shadow Cabinet, and not often seen in the House, gave experienced advice when he was there. His own standing also ensured that when he chose to make a speech on any issue, it was given maximum coverage – which was not always helpful to Hague, especially with his stance on the Millennium Dome.

All the old hands understood from the start that Hague would wish eventually to have his own team, which might not include colleagues who had served in the Major Cabinets. Any new leader has the right, and indeed duty, to stamp his own authority on his inheritance. It is also self-evidently the case that, in our new situation, new people should take the party forward, and should have their chance, as we had had. Nevertheless we were a little startled by the briefing against 'the old faces identified with the failures of the past' that appeared in the press. Several of us were picked out for special treatment – Michael Howard, Norman Fowler, John Redwood, and me. This seemed a little unjust, given that when asked to serve any of us might well have said, 'I've done my bit. Good luck, you get on with it,' as many did. It was not as if it was a special pleasure to slog away in Opposition after doing the job 'for real', as one colleague put it. But my own view was that having had the privilege of office, I ought to repay my debt to the Party and to the system by serving on the front bench at least for a period in Opposition. That was why I accepted a Shadow Cabinet post. I also believed that a few old hands might be useful to support William Hague in his early days as Leader. It was clear that it would be an interesting challenge, but I did not feel it was my future life's work. It was irritating, therefore, to be depicted by those briefing the press as clinging to office for dear life, out of one's own grandiosity. It was even more irritating that such briefing could be taken at face value by prominent journalists, who should have known better. But the briefing had a more damaging effect than mere irritation on the part of its targets. It also allowed William Hague to be portrayed, inaccurately, as ungracious towards the colleagues with whom he had, after all, also served in the Major Cabinets and as rejecting a past of which he had been part. It was not worthy of his courage and big-heartedness. He was clearly not the source, but on one occasion, the briefing was so blatant that I had it out with William, and insisted that it stop. It did, and after a month or so, I announced that I would stand down.

He handled Shadow Cabinet meetings briskly and skilfully. He introduced Shadow Cabinet 'Away Days' so that we could take a longer look at strategic issues, examine opinion polls and present, in a more leisurely way, policy options. A series of Shadow Cabinet sub-committees was established, to look across a range of policy areas where co-ordinated approaches were required.

Renewing and modernising the Party organisation had to be achieved. William Hague, to his great credit, saw the need to do that, threw his weight and organisational capacity behind it, and achieved it in double quick time, with the support of all the disparate elements that made up the Conservative Party. He pursued this objective, the media found too dull to report, because he believed passionately that the Party should be run on democratic lines, and that it could not survive as it was. Many other Leaders might have had more glamorous-seeming initial aims but Hague doggedly pushed on with reform of the Party.

Listening to Britain

If they want to survive, they've got to start listening.

MICHAEL SANGER

In the same way, he perceived that the party had to rid itself of the uncaring, non-listening image attached to it after eighteen years in power, so he launched *Listening to Britain*. In the introductory document he said,

> When I became Leader of the Conservative Party, I promised a fresh approach to politics. I said that Conservatives would no longer be afraid to acknowledge where we had made mistakes in the past. I recognised that, proud as we are of the achievements of the last Conservative Government, the world has moved on. New problems demand fresh thinking, and new solutions. Above all, I promised that never again would we let ourselves get out of touch with the British people.

The idea was a simple one. A small unit was set up in Central Office to co-ordinate what eventually became a huge exercise. Non-Party meetings were to be set up across the country, with an independent chairman, well known locally, on specific issues, such as planning, taxation, education, transport and so on. Questionnaires would be sent out to local opinion formers before the meetings, which would be open to press and public, and views would be aired in the presence of local Conservative MPs and, if possible, a

Shadow spokesman. Hague took part in the first one, held in Shrewsbury, and the rest of us followed suit. I attended meetings all over the country in connection with my shadow brief, by then Environment, Transport and the Regions. I truly believed that I was not out of touch with people's preoccupations and concerns, but experience of the meetings proved me wrong. People were furious about what they perceived as the failures of the planning system, the opacity of the local government system, inaction on transport problems and, generally, about their own impotence in achieving change.

With the help of other local MPs I organised a *Listening to Norfolk* meeting, the first, and one of only two, county-wide *Listening to Britain* exercises. More than three hundred people attended, at the local agriculture college, on a freezing February morning. The meeting was admirably chaired by a well known local journalist, with help from the Dean of Norwich and the Director of the Rural Community Council. Despite all our efforts to make sure that the meeting was run without political bias, the local Labour Party thought otherwise, and, on the day, cobbled together a gathering for a few Labour activists, at which a hapless minister was obliged to appear, just to spoil the story, as they saw it. We saw it, and their reaction, as a success for us.

Listening to Britain was an overall success for the Party. 40,000 people attended over 1,400 meetings; 250,000 responses were received to the questionnaires, consultations and other requests for information. The national media was bored by the whole exercise, but local newspapers and media gave good coverage. We all learnt a great deal. Under the same 'Listening' banner, we organised specialist meetings with health and education professionals, parents, people working in all parts of the legal system, business people, those engaged in religious activities and all faiths. The Conservative Christian Fellowship alone conducted 200 *Listening to Britain*'s Churches meetings.

The final document summarising the exercise and its findings covered fifteen different policy areas. There were some hard truths about politicians and the political process. Government was seen as 'wholly irrelevant to people's needs'. 'There are too many politicians, too much government, too much red tape', we were told, and 'Why don't politicians see problems coming rather than just deal with the things that go wrong?'

The subject areas explored were People First, Education, Safer Communities, Earning and Spending, the Countryside and the Environment, Business and Industry, Travel and Transport, Security in Retirement, Work and Welfare, the Family, Health, How Britain is Governed, Britain and Europe, Defending the Nation, and Britain in the World. Given the huge number of responses, and the general enthusiasm at local level engendered by this work, the party leadership had cause to be pleased with a useful job well done.

It was conducted alongside a programme of other policy-making activities. These included discussions conducted by front bench teams and Shadow Cabinet members. There were also high-level commissions, which so far have worked on House of Lords reform, monetary policy, the benefits of keeping the pound, and strengthening Parliament.

Those who mock such an exercise are mistaken. The scale of the work undertaken, and the mere fact that Conservative politicians and activists sat down to listen to and discuss people's preoccupations would have been positive enough achievements. Would that we had had the time and inclination to do more of it when we were in government, and in a position to do something about what we had learnt. But it has also meant that the policy changes we bring forward are now based on what people think needs to be done, rather than what the narrow circle of metropolitan-based opinion formers tell us should be done. It has been interesting to see the present government increasingly enmeshed with the views of the latter. When we return to government, we must ensure that we escape this form of institutionalisation.

Getting Used to Opposition

If you take yourself seriously in politics, you've had it.

LORD CARRINGTON

Being in opposition at this time has meant dealing with the special problems of our age. The accelerating pace of media communications has meant that even if policies have not been thought out, there are constant demands for an instant policy response to all government initiatives, policy changes and, of course, events. After the Conservative defeat in 1945, Winston Churchill was able to tell his colleagues that the electorate would not wish to hear from them for four years. In 1997, although we knew that that might well have been the electorate's preference, we had not the luxury of silence that our predecessors had. Nor is this a British phenomenon. My former colleague Jacques Barrot, Employment Minister in France until the election of the present Socialist Government of Lionel Jospin, had found the same problem in France. And no one could accuse the French Right of inexperience in opposition.

The new Labour Government plunged into frenzied activity. Every day brought fresh announcements, statements, initiatives, consultation exercises and the publication of Bills. While none of

207

these brought great surprises, in our depleted state it was sometimes hard to keep up, and I began to understand what David Blunkett had meant as Opposition Education spokesman when he told me I was running him ragged with the many education initiatives I launched as Education Secretary.

Predictably the media were dazzled by all the new faces, and by the fact that the Government, quite simply, were not us. They consistently ignored almost all of what we had to say on any issue, as the old hands had warned us they would. They also published tables showing how infrequently we were quoted in the press, forgetting that such mentions were in their power, not ours. Michael Fallon, one of our Treasury spokesmen, was asked to go to the Millbank Studios to do an interview on why the Opposition was failing to get its message across. When he arrived, he was told the interview had been cancelled. There were many new tricks to learn. One was to keep trying.

On the policy front, we had begun by thinking that we would have time to prepare policy papers, to consult widely, to take our time. We soon realised we had been wrong. While we could look forward to the duration of the Parliament before we had to prepare a manifesto, many areas required our attention immediately.

We tackled this in a number of ways. Clearly, Government legislation, policy announcements, Green and White Papers could be responded to on an *ad hoc* basis, after Shadow Cabinet discussion and agreement. Other areas, where new thinking was required, would need a different and more thorough approach.

In the past, our predecessors had used Party Backbench Committees as vehicles of policy formation when in Opposition. These Committees, not to be confused with Select or All Party Committees, shadow each department of state, have officers, and a weekly programme of meetings, visits or discussions. When I entered the Commons, election to office in the Committees was hotly contested, with different wings of the party putting up slates. Some exercised real power and influence. An example was the Backbench Finance Committee, which was always addressed by the Chancellor of the Exchequer immediately after his Budget speech. Another was the Foreign Affairs Committee, which played a key role in the debate on Europe. In government I attached so much importance to the influence of the Committees that the Chairman of the Backbench Education Committee, James Pawsey, was an *ex-officio* member at my weekly 'prayer' meetings in the Department for Education and Employment. At MAFF, I met the Backbench officers each week.

To our mild surprise – because we had thought that Backbench Committees would assume even greater importance in Opposition than they had in the past – we found that attendance at and interest in the work of the Committees, with some exceptions, greatly diminished after the election. The reason for this is not hard to find, and it is a practical one: the parliamentary Party is small, 169 MPs in all. It is quite stretching for such a relatively small number of colleagues to do all that has to be done in Opposition. Attendance at Standing Committees, membership of Select Committees, work in the Chamber to keep the Government on its toes, representing the Party outside the House, speaking engagements, all these normal activities for MPs take precedence over Backbench Committee work.

Scoring Points

Politics is a blood sport.

ANEURIN BEVAN

Shadow Cabinet members therefore used other means of taking forward policy development. As Shadow Leader of the House, a post I held for just under a year, I worked closely with constitutional experts, involving those colleagues with a natural interest, to prepare our views on strengthening Parliament, and on the constitution generally. As Shadow Environment Secretary, the task was awesome. During the year I was in the post I had contact with more than 200 organisations, all with direct connections to the brief. It was important to be in touch with people who were expert in their fields and keen to talk about new policies.

The organisations ranged from the Royal Society for the Protection of Birds, and Shelter, through every kind of transport lobby, to the Country Landowners' Association, and all aspects of local government. I organised meetings through the Backbench Committee system every week with the aim of educating myself and my shadow team, more than from any hope that colleagues would have time to come. While all this was a strain on our administrative resources, which consisted of myself and a less than full time secretary, we worked well together, and the shadow colleagues worked with a will to form their own connections.

It became obvious that the Government would be making a policy announcement on the Right to Roam, in accordance with their manifesto commitment. We were often asked how we had found out what was going on, given that in government whole departments are devoted to setting the agenda and intelligence gathering. It was easy: some colleagues had retained contacts with the Civil Service, others were so involved with lobby groups that they were fully informed, while journalists, in seeking a reaction from us, naturally had to give information. We really were able to get information about anything we needed to know and, to that extent, were a little less impotent than we had expected to be.

From contacts with the National Farmers Union and the CLA, I began to piece together what the Government was likely to say on the Right to Roam. At the same time, I mounted a full consultation exercise, with a questionnaire to all the relevant organisations and to colleagues in both Houses of Parliament. This culminated in a conference in Central Office, with an independent chairman, involving the Ramblers Association, the CLA, the NFU, conservation bodies, local government interests and so on. We then produced a dossier to back up our own approach, in good time for the Government's announcement.

Unusually and fortuitously, we had had adequate time for preparation in this instance: we needed a sound party position in an area important to Conservatives. Less easy, because of the timescale, were responses to Government announcements and statements in the House. The convention on these occasions is that the minister making the statement faxes through a copy about half an hour before it is due to be given in the House. When the statement is likely to be complex, much preparatory work has already gone into second-guessing its content.

This was the situation when on 20 July 1998 the Government published its White Paper on Integrated Transport after many leaks and somewhat misleading press briefings. We knew from all our contacts that the White Paper had been endlessly delayed, that there had been internal disagreements about the funding and the

211

general thrust. But we also knew, from our own experience of government, that the Treasury would be bound to hold out until the last minute, as they had done with us, and that the conservation versus motorist debate would have to have final Number 10 approval. This was the last day of the parliamentary session before the House went into its summer recess, and was chosen, no doubt, to stifle the wails from Labour backbenchers, who had been hoping to return in triumph to their constituencies, claiming their success in obtaining a new bypass or road improvement scheme. We were familiar with this kind of ploy, too, having been in that position more than once ourselves. The key point was that we were prepared, not only from the contacts we had built up with the various lobbies but from the work we had done to get our own party stance right. On the day, I was armed with all the correct questions, and all I had to do was check them with the content of the statement.

Rather different is the annual statement on the Revenue Support Grant for local government. Local government finance is, of course, complex, and few ministers have the time while in post to grasp every last nook and cranny of it, although some, like David Curry, get close. The advantage for an Opposition in preparing for this occasion is that one normally knows when it is likely to take place, around the end of November. Our own contacts in local government in turn have their own links into the department, so that by the time the statement comes the bones of it are fairly clear. Nevertheless, we put a lot of effort into getting our response right. I held a number of meetings with experts, and our own local government leaders, preparing a series of 'what if' style questions.

The day dawned. It was 2 December 1998. I had a raging cold. I had to deliver a memorial service oration at noon for the much loved president of my constituency association, who had died the previous August. I returned to the Shadow Cabinet room, where we had assembled our own Central Office number crunchers, young men of awesome application, members of our Shadow team and colleagues from local government. The statement started to come through on the fax at the start of Prime Minister's Questions, which, of course, I had to miss.

I also received on my pager a message from Robert Cranborne, whom I had been going to see that night. The message said, 'Lord Cranborne regrets he is unable to dine tonight.' Shades of Miss Otis, I thought, and got on with the briefing. I had been so occupied throughout the day that I had totally missed reports of the immense row between William Hague and Lord Cranborne over the future of the House of Lords, which had come to a climax on that day.

I went up into the Chamber, clutching my questions. I also had points to make, which I was confident were relevant, and awkward for the Government. They were, but the Revenue Support Grant was not what was preoccupying colleagues. The Prime Minister and William Hague had just had a shouting match about the House of Lords, its future, and Cranborne's part in it, all of which I had missed and of which I knew nothing. Our own side was agog. There was just time for someone to whisper that Blair had been having a go at William over Cranborne's behaviour, and I was on.

Hansard records that the Opposition acquitted itself honourably on that occasion. I have to say that my own memory of it is hazy and of the autopilot variety. I was intensely curious to know what had happened. Whatever it was, given the whispering on our side and the stifled giggles on the other, it was serious.

Cranborne Sacked

> Nothing is so admirable in politics as a short memory.
>
> J. K. Galbraith

After the statement, I rushed into the Tea Room for a few moments before Shadow Cabinet started at 5pm. On the way I bumped into Liam Fox, and asked him what had been going on. 'Cranborne has been negotiating direct with Blair about the future of the House of Lords, and it all came out in Prime Minister's Questions. William is furious about it. He knew nothing of it. He's in the House of Lords now,' explained Liam.

Shadow Cabinet started without William. We were told that he and the Chief Whip were in the House of Lords, meeting the Association of Conservative Peers. There had been an immense, if courteously conducted, row between him and Cranborne, before the interested gaze of the Conservative Peers. After about fifty minutes William arrived. He was clearly in a rage, bright pink, eyes shining with anger. 'I've just sacked Robert Cranborne,' he announced without ceremony. 'He has behaved duplicitously and without my knowledge or the agreement of the Shadow Cabinet. So I've sacked him.' Silence followed. He then set out the sequence of events, explaining that Cranborne had put forward a plan to retain a number of hereditary peers, elected by themselves, as part of a reformed House of Lords, and until the second phase of reform was in place. This idea had been rejected by a Shadow Cabinet sub-committee, but apparently Robert Cranborne had gone ahead and negotiated it direct with the Government. He had had at least one meeting with the Prime Minister and with his Press Secretary. There were sharp intakes of breath around the table. No one spoke.

I decided to break the silence. I said that Robert would certainly know that he had behaved unacceptably. On the other hand, he strongly believed that his plan was supported by his colleagues, and that, in the absence of any sort of thinking from the Government on the future of the House of Lords, it was the best, indeed the only way forward. I added that Cranborne had given outstanding service to the Party and to the country over many years, and we could ill afford to do without someone of his ability.

At that stage my views received little support. And none of us knew then that some months later we would be told to support the deal, or something like it, when the legislation finally came before the House of Commons. Cranborne's four hundred years of experience of power would finally bear fruit.

We left the Shadow Cabinet room. I need hardly have bothered with my careful preparation on the Revenue Support Grant. Never a glamorous political issue, it had dropped completely out of sight because of another great Tory row.

Robert Cranborne is an outstanding man, by any standards. Born to great wealth and a prominent position, which might have seen him comfortably through life, he chose to become a Member of Parliament in 1979, resigned from his position as PPS over the Anglo-Irish Agreement, and left the House of Commons in 1987. He was a junior Minister of Defence from 1992 to 1994, and came into the Cabinet as Lord Privy Seal, or Leader of the House of Lords, in July 1994. He brought with him the accumulated experience of his family, operating at the highest level of the state for the past four hundred years. He played the central role in John Major's leadership election in 1995 – an episode he consistently referred to as 'the unpleasantness' – and again at the 1997 election, when the final sad pictures of the retreat into Conservative Central

215

Office show his arm round John Major's shoulders. Capable of operating on a number of levels at once, he was a brilliant strategic thinker, and brought an important constituency to the Tory leadership.

Nevertheless, on this issue he accepted that he had behaved, as he put it, like 'an untrained spaniel that keeps running in', a remark that had to be translated for the benefit of some of the more callow members of the Party and all of the London-based media. He maintained, and still does, that the deal he negotiated, first with his opposite numbers in the House of Lords and then, it emerged, with the Prime Minister and Alastair Campbell, was the right deal for the moment.

Was William Hague right to sack him? Could things have been arranged another way? Perhaps not, given the character of both men. But the Conservative Party cannot do without the experience, wisdom and sheer style of people like Robert Cranborne and, for the moment, we are the poorer for his loss.

On the other hand William Hague surprised some by the forceful and decisive exercise of one of his few powers as Leader of the Opposition, and his standing in the Parliamentary Party went up as a result.

Parliamentary Opposition parties have power and can wield it, which is always more apparent to governments than to oppositions, especially to a party newly in opposition, but it is, nevertheless, a fact. Moreover, an effective Official Opposition is as integral a part of a parliamentary democracy as Parliament itself.

The Neill Committee, examining party political funding in October 1998, pointed out in its report that 'in a parliamentary democracy, the party in Government should be held to account and kept in check by a vigorous and well-prepared Opposition.'

Jennings, in *Cabinet Government*, went further, asserting that, 'if there be no Opposition, there is no democracy. Her Majesty's Opposition is no idle phrase. Her Majesty needs an Opposition as well as a Government.'

It is obvious that there is a real job for the Opposition to do. By its vigour, it can focus the public's mind on important issues, can oblige the Government to explain and justify itself, and can act as a conduit for public opinion on legislation. Through Parliament itself, it reminds the Government of its democratic obligations. Between elections Parliament provides the vital link between the electorate and the government. The Hansard Society, in a document prepared for its own Commission on the Scrutiny Role of Parliament, points out that 'Parliament is the principal means by which the government can be held to account for its activities.' This important and constitutional task is one of the most vital an Opposition can perform.

Parliament provides the most obvious arena for the Opposition. The Conservative Party had had its own parliamentary difficulties during the dying days of John Major's government. Now we had to learn new skills, against a majority of 179. Wits pointed out that quite a lot of our own MPs had had plenty of practice in opposition against their own side. Some of the best advice came from the experienced old hands, procedure men like Sir Patrick Cormack, who became the successful Deputy Shadow Leader of the House, first to me and then to Sir George Young. Another expert was Sir Peter Emery, and yet another the formidable Nicholas Winterton, whose frequent expressions of outrage were now turned, to excellent effect, against the new government.

It was obvious to me that we needed to use all the skills available in the Parliamentary Party and to involve as many as possible

217

in everything that was going on. We therefore established a weekly planning meeting to discuss the week's parliamentary tactics. The 1922 Committee meeting, so often either a mere formality or, when we were in government and a row was brewing, menacingly long and heavily attended, was used to present policy options or examine other longer term issues. Progress was slow, but gradually we began to learn how to oppose.

There is no shortage of procedural opportunities for a party in opposition. One useful source is to be found in *Parliament: Functions, Practice and Procedures*, by Griffiths and Ryle, with Michael Wheeler-Booth, Clerk Assistant to the House of Lords. They produce their own version of the duties of an Opposition.

> The Opposition . . . must look critically at all policies and proposals brought before the House by the Government and then oppose, and, if possible, delay or even prevent the implementation of those proposals it considers desirable. It will also take the initiative in seeking to bring to the public's attention aspects of the Government's policies and administration which would not otherwise be brought before Parliament. And it will present its own alternative policies and proposals in the most favourable light. It will either make promises about what it would do if it came to power, or will seek to avoid making such promises in areas where it feels less secure or where its popularity might suffer.[28]

They might have added, 'or where it thinks the Government might steal them'. They go on to list the opportunities available for the Opposition to question with greatest effect the policies of the Government. They include the debate on the Queen's Speech, which affords the Opposition Leader the chance to criticise the forthcoming legislative programme in front of a full House. The same shop window is provided by the Opposition Leader's response to the Chancellor's Budget Statement, curiously deleted by BBC television coverage in the Budget of 2000. Some, even now, recall Margaret Thatcher's brilliance when she was replying for the Opposition to the Budget in 1979. Her response was so well informed and fluent that someone called out, 'This is meant to be off the cuff,' to which she answered, 'It is a very good cuff.'

The most obvious opportunity for the Opposition leader to make his or her mark is provided by Prime Minister's Questions. That is why the present government's slick and cynical replacement of the twice-weekly slot by an over-choreographed and sycophantic photo opportunity for fawning Labour backbenchers to earn a few approval points once a week was a real blow for democratic accountability. What is immediately clear from all this is that an Opposition Leader ideally should be able to score in the Chamber. While it takes time for his or her superiority to be noted in the country, it rattles the government of the day, and depresses its supporters.

It is an area in which William Hague has acquitted himself consistently well. His critics say it does not matter to the country at large, since people take little interest these days in the Chamber of the House of Commons. However, with the cynicism of experience, I feel that if he was not good at it, commentators would find that it did indeed matter a great deal.

Parliamentary Ambushes

> When political ammunition runs low, inevitably the rusty artillery of abuse is always wheeled into action.
>
> ADLAI STEVENSON

Other opportunities abound. They range from set piece debates, where a well-drilled Opposition can tease out the flaws in the

Government's arguments, to the more opportunistic Private Notice Question, where a minister is called to the Chamber to answer a particular point of concern on a current issue, and to explain why he was apparently unwilling to offer a statement on it. The great advantage of successfully tabling a Private Notice Question is the chaos it induces in the minister's office. Almost by definition, the issue raised is one they will have been hoping to conceal. The Speaker is not obliged to give her approval or otherwise to the Question until at least midday, so all morning, the Private Office of the minister's department will have been in a ferment of indecision, wondering whether to cancel the day's engagements on the off-chance that the Question will have to be answered. The media, of course, know that a Question has been put down, and the hapless minister will have to decide whether or not to accept radio and television bids. Whatever else, the issue is brought thoroughly into the open. For an Opposition, it is a first-class weapon. The process in the House lasts only thirty minutes from 3.30pm. While the Opposition will hope to shred the minister in the Chamber, the damage will already have been done. The issue has been aired, the minister's reputation for openness, and the Government's, will have been questioned, the minister's day will have been ruined, and there should be positive press coverage for his tormentors.

Opposition Day debates are another useful tool to harry the Government. Opposition parties are entitled to a set number of days in the parliamentary year on which they can propose the business. These are slotted into the programme, and the subjects chosen for debate are those most likely to embarrass the Government, like hospital waiting lists, or police numbers, where broken promises can be shown up and lavishly illustrated. Opposition Day debates afford time for preparation with the appropriate lobbies, colleagues and the press. They are most effective if they also coincide with lobbying activity on the part of the affected group, such as rural postmasters and postmistresses. A lot of effort is put in, and although the results are not always commensurate, such debates can trap ministers into making unwise promises, or unsympathetic statements, which are then usefully recorded in Hansard.

Planned and concerted attacks, against, for example, a minister under threat from his own side, or a policy where Government MPs are likely to rebel, are also useful weapons for the Opposition. Scalps are claimed gleefully if a minister is forced to resign after a series of unanswerable onslaughts in Parliament, backed up by unrelenting work with the press. This is an area in which John Redwood excelled, but he did not succeed by magic, rather by vigorous conviction and constant alertness.

An Opposition would be unwise to measure its successes in terms of government defeats, particularly when it is pitched against one with a vast majority of 179. Some of the most effective tactics are those which cause Government backbenchers to complain bitterly to their Whips. Especially successful in this area has been Eric Forth, the flamboyant former Education Minister, with a dandyish taste in clothes and a passion for Elvis Presley. Like Dennis Skinner and Bob Cryer before him under a Conservative Government, Forth has made himself an expert in procedure, and a formidable advocate for full debate of certain issues. In this he is well supported by David MacLean, an extremely able Minister of State in a number of departments before the election. They have frequently kept the House up until the small hours debating this or that point, with a clever use of procedure to ensure that they are not reprimanded by the Speaker for wasting parliamentary time.

On 25 January 2000, they executed a brilliant coup on the Disqualifications Bill by keeping the debate going throughout the night, and until 2.30pm the following day. The result was that the day's business was lost, and with it, the Prime Minister's planned celebration, at Question Time, of his first thousand days in power. Nor was this merely a procedural matter. There were strong feelings on the Opposition side about the principles at stake in the Bill, which was one of the reasons why Forth was able to summon enough speakers to keep the whole thing going. The tactic and the principles were largely ignored by the press, who did, however, manage to mention that during the night a mouse had joined the proceedings.

This kind of tactic, usually ignored as too difficult to write about by journalists, is down to internal House of Commons politics. There is a variety of opinions about the value of keeping the House up all night. Few outside know about it, and if they do, are unlikely to be impressed. But as a weapon it has the effect of raising the profile of an issue within the House, and better, of irritating the Government as they trail wearily through the lobbies, not knowing when they will be allowed to go home. Nothing has got further under the skin of new Labour backbenchers than this sort of Opposition activity. We wait, mischievously, for the first plaintive comments from – usually women – Labour MPs, as they wail about uncivilised hours, and family-unfriendly procedures. As these surface in the press, we know we have succeeded. Members of Parliament are regarded by the public as having a cushy life, with long holidays and no perceptible product. For them to complain about the few hours they are perceived to work does not add to their lustre, or to that of the Party they represent. And the complaints inevitably give rise to suspicions that those making them do not understand the purpose of Parliament, which is not the same as that of a District Council. The attitude 'We won the election, what more do you want?' betrays a contempt for the democratic process surprising in those who never stop talking about it.

Delaying tactics are one of the Opposition's few weapons. They are also important because legislative proposals may have been hastily drafted and therefore be flawed, or causing outrage in the nation. Parliament must have the time and flexibility to scrutinise what is passing before it. This was why there was some concern, and not only in the Conservative Party, when the Modernisation Committee seemed close to recommending the timetabling of all Bills. The Committee backed away from this proposal, not least because even a recently elected government with a huge majority has clear memories of its own time in opposition and the certain knowledge that it will return to it sooner or later. It would in any case be a constitutional outrage to suggest that the passage of a Bill through the parliamentary process was merely a matter of time, and rubber-stamping by a compliant House.

The House of Lords has shown the way to scrutinise legislation. It defeated the Government no fewer than seventy times, between the general election and the time of its reform. Since then, it has so thoroughly scrutinised legislation passing before it that the Government has been obliged to cut short various recesses and has had to timetable a large number of Bills when they have returned to the Commons. One of the results has been that the Parliamentary Labour Party, and in particular, a large number of new women MPs, are loud in their condemnation of broken promises from their own side that the conduct of House of Commons business would be made more family-friendly.

In opposition, a political party is torn between two approaches. It must undertake careful planning of policy initiatives, organisational change and thoughtful presentation of political philosophy.

But it must also take opportunistic advantage of the moment, in Parliament and through the press and media. It is no good saying you have no comment on some issue or another because you have not had time to think out your position, even if that happens to be so. The two approaches are obviously not mutually exclusive, although they sometimes come close, given the lack of manpower available. The problem diminishes as time and experience in opposition increase. At first, we discussed the need to be perceived as presenting serious alternative policies, and planning our activities, while quite frequently missing tricks. That did not last long. Apart from criticism from other quarters, our own activists were the first to point out that we should be raising the profile of this or that unpopular government policy, and we became more flexible in our responses. In the end, as systems were put into place and there was more research support, we found we could have a go at both.

Organising the Opposition

> Every government is run by liars and nothing they say should be believed.
>
> I. F. Stone

Like our predecessors, we quickly ran into the problem of the resources with which to do the job. Shadow Cabinet members, in particular, found that they were required to attend conferences, make visits, keep a high profile and, of course, oppose. Many entered the Shadow Cabinet with a part-time House of Commons secretary and a gap year researcher. This, of course, was just not adequate to shadow, for example, a department like Environment,

Transport and the Regions, where there are ten ministers, each with a Private Office and press officers.

Since 1975, 'Short' money has been available for the parliamentary work of Opposition parties, named after the then Leader of the House, Edward Short. The Leader of the Opposition and the Opposition Chief Whip receive a salary. Front bench spokesmen are entitled to some support for their work. In the past, the amount of cash each Opposition party received was calculated on a formula worked out from the number of seats and votes each got in the previous general election. In 1997–8 a total of £1.5 million was made available, of which the Conservative Party received £987,000. This sum, given the important role played by Opposition in our Parliamentary democracy, makes an interesting contrast with the total spent by all political parties on their general election campaigns in 1997, which amounted to £56.4 million.

The whole position was investigated by the Neill Committee, and its report on the Funding of Political Parties in the United Kingdom recommended a substantial, perhaps threefold, increase in Short money; a fixed amount for the Official Opposition; extra funds for the Leader of the Opposition; an increase in 'Cranborne' money for the work of the Official Opposition in the House of Lords.

The Government agreed the main proposals of the Neill Report, with the result that the total amount in 1999/2000 for Opposition activities is £4.8 million, of which the Conservatives receive £3.3 million.

I appeared before the Neill Committee when it was deliberating and pointed out that the political process had changed out of all recognition since 1975. The Committee accepted that the raised expectations of the media, special interest groups, and the inexorable rise in the amount of legislation all placed on Opposition spokesmen burdens they could not carry with the current levels of finance. It would be interesting to know if they were also influenced by the amount the Labour Government was spending on political advisers, in addition to the megalithic Civil Service. Despite the welcome Neill increases, that development has further shifted the balance in favour of the Government in defiance of the constitutional principle that both sides' activities are equally legitimate.

The Role of Her Majesty's Opposition

> Politicians are the same all over. They promise to build a bridge even when there's no river.
>
> NIKITA KHRUSHCHEV

The Hansard Society Commission on the Scrutiny Role of Parliament has as its objective to examine how effectively Parliament scrutinises and holds government to account. In the document published by the Society to seek views on this matter, the following statement is made about Parliament:

> Parliament performs a number of roles in British democracy. Parliament makes the law and decides on how much the government can raise through taxation. Crucially, it also creates and sustains the government. Parliament provides the vital link between the electorate and government. Governments are accountable to the people through general elections. Between general elections, Parliament is the principal means by which the government can be held to account for its activities. This form of accountability is generally termed Parliament's scrutiny role. Parliament performs this role by obtaining and publicising information

about the government's performance and future plans. On the basis of the information, Parliament and others form a judgement as to whether the government is discharging its mandate effectively, economically, and in the best interests of the electorate.

It is clearly the task of the opposition to lead this important scrutiny role. The Houghton Report on Financial Aid to Political Parties puts it thus:

> The parties in opposition have the responsibility of scrutinising and checking all the actions of the executive.

British Government and the Constitution points out that

> The legitimacy of opposition parties is confirmed by law, convention and the political culture of the United Kingdom. Opposition is recognised as having rights and is part of the constitutional system – as much part of it as is the government.[29]

Ivor Jennings expands on the principle:

> Democratic government demands not only a parliamentary majority but also a parliamentary minority. The minority attacks the Government because it denies the principles of its policy. The Opposition will, almost certainly, be defeated in the House of Commons because it is a minority. Its appeals are to the electorate. It will, at the next election, ask the people to condemn the government, and as a consequence, to give a majority to the Opposition. Because the Government is criticised it has to meet criticism. Because it must in course of time defend itself in the constituencies, it must persuade public opinion to move with it. The Opposition is at once the alternative to the government and a focus for the discontent of the people. Its function is almost as important as that of the Government. If there be no Opposition there is no democracy. Her Majesty's Opposition is no idle phrase. Her Majesty needs an

Opposition as well as a Government.[30]

This important statement, however, presupposes a view of the importance of Parliament, which may be becoming outdated. By how much is the power of an opposition reduced by a government that has scant regard for the parliamentary process, and by compliant media that seem to share that view?

Abusing Parliament

> Government is only as good as the men in it.
>
> DREW PEARSON

Madam Speaker's view is clear. On 5 April 2000 she reprimanded the Government for yet again announcing a policy change on the *Today* programme, followed by a press conference, without informing Parliament. She said,

> It seems to me that there is a situation developing in some departments in which the interest of Parliament is regarded as secondary to media presentation, or is overlooked altogether. I hope that Ministers will set in hand a review of procedures right across Whitehall to ensure that the events that took place this morning are never allowed to happen again.

The newly elected Labour Government, even before the new Parliament had met, began as it meant to go on, in announcing by press conference its intention to make the Bank of England independent. The widely reported remark of Peter Mandelson in a speech in Germany in March 1998 that 'the era of pure representative democracy is coming slowly to an end'[31] gave substance to the obvious truth that this Government regarded Parliament as an outdated, slow moving means of getting its way, and not much more. Peter Riddell commented, 'Government is becoming divorced from Parliament. For Blairites, Parliament is no longer central, it is merely one means of communication. Once in office, many ministers treat Parliament as secondary.'[32]

The Prime Minister gives the lead in his own attitude towards Parliament. Peter Riddell revealed that Tony Blair had voted in just five per cent of divisions. This is in striking contrast with Margaret Thatcher's record. Even when her majority was great, in the mid 1980s, she voted in about a third of divisions. Blair lost no time after his election in announcing that he would answer Questions only once a week. For John Major and Margaret Thatcher, Questions were an important twice-weekly occasion. It is true that preparation for them took a great deal of time, but for serious parliamentarians, the constitutional necessity of answering to Parliament justified it.

Riddell explained Labour's position as a new constitutional practice, 'if not yet a doctrine'. He continued:

> Parliament exists to translate an election result into a Commons majority, to supply ministers and to implement its programme. But the executive then governs largely independently, consulting interest groups and the public directly through focus groups and citizens' juries. On big issues, the Government seeks public approval through referendums, whose results have, in practice, to be accepted by Parliament.

New constitutional practice it may be, but it is not one endorsed by the electorate.

He concluded that increased use of the referendum and direct consultation is inevitable and desirable. As he put it, 'Parliament cannot any longer claim to be the sole repository of political wisdom, particularly in an age of constitutional change.' This conclusion is questionable: Parliament may indeed not be the sole repository of political wisdom – it may never have been – but it is accountable to the electorate, which cannot be said of focus groups and the like. Its place within the democratic framework of Britain goes beyond being a repository of wisdom. For those who believe in parliamentary democracy, the Government's treatment of Parliament is at the least worrying, at the paranoid worst, sinister.

Madam Speaker's rebuke of the Government on 5 April 2000 was not her first. On 3 December 1997, in reply to a complaint from Liam Fox, MP for Woodspring, she said,

> What is happening is that the status of this House is being devalued, which I deprecate most strongly. I hope that senior Ministers present will note my remarks and ensure that there is no recurrence of such events. It seems that I have to make statements such as this every two weeks.[33]

This kind of sentiment is echoed by Tony Benn:

> I do think we are now in a political society where we're managed, when democracy really is about being represented. There's all the difference in the world between being a representative of your constituency and your convictions and being a sub-agent of the Millbank Tower Corporation, whose job it is to pass the message on to the faithful and tell people what to do. As I've got older the thing that has really come home to me is the democratic question. Are people spectators of their fate or participants in their future?[34]

Such sentiments sit ill with Peter Mandelson's views that 'plebiscites, focus groups, lobbies, citizens' movements and the Internet' are alternative means of representation to Parliament.[35] It is likely that if a minister as influential as Mandelson makes such a remark it is the view of the Government itself.

The cost of government has increased from £13.3 billion in 1997–8, to an estimated £14.4 billion in 1999–2000. But much of the increase seems to have been incurred on non-accountable Government machinery. Since the last election the cost of quangos, by definition not accountable, has risen from £22 billion to £24 billion. The Sixth Report of the Committee on Standards in Public Life, quoting Cabinet Office figures, noted that,

> The number of special advisers did not vary much for about 20 years. At the beginning of 1997, there were 38 in Government. However, the number in December 1999 stood at 74. Taking the position at Number 10 alone, the respective increase has been from eight special advisers to 25 (including one unpaid special adviser). The paybill for special advisers has accordingly risen in the last four years, from £1.8 million in 1996–97, to £3.9 million in 1999-2000.[36]

Their role is at least questionable. Tam Dalyell MP, writing in the *Scotsman*, said,

> Special Advisers have become an abomination. They cause little but sickness in the body politic. They intrigue and chatter, causing misunderstandings about policy. Many special advisers have now become little more than media operators. Their business is about leaking for the alleged advantage of their Minister. I just do not think that those who engage in this kind of activity should be paid for by the taxpayer.[37]

According to a study called *Ruling by Task Force*, around 320 task forces have been appointed, which are by definition not accountable to the electorate.[38]

But it is the assumption that Parliament is just another means of communication, and not a very effective one at that, rather than the centre of democratic accountability, that is the most breathtaking.

Modernising Parliament

> The Commons, faithful to their system, remained a wise and masterly inactivity.
>
> SIR JAMES MACINTOSH

This attitude underlay many of the comments made in the early sittings of the Select Committee on the Modernisation of the House of Commons, by newly elected MPs, freshly made-over and full of zeal to transform the old-fashioned place to which they had fought to be elected into some kind of People's Palace. On one occasion, a particularly caring member of the Committee delivered herself of a diatribe on the demeaning fact that House Messengers are obliged to wear a uniform. On cue, a messenger entered the room, and we were able to ask his opinion. While this was courteously delivered, it was clear to the more experienced of us that storms would follow. They did. The Serjeant at Arms and Madam Speaker were invoked. The messengers like their uniforms and wear them with pride. And some of us, including large numbers of the public, like some of the quainter aspects of the workings of the House of Commons.

While sensible changes should be made to ensure that its procedures are transparent, it should not be equated with some newly established Unitary Council. It is not Parliament's traditions and history that are an affront to the democratic process, but the present Government's abuse of it. With such attitudes permeating the whole of the Government, it is not surprising that the Opposition have found it difficult to use the arena of Parliament to full effect. If the Government itself finds Parliament an irrelevance in the era of mass communication, then what goes on there is likely to lose some of its importance in the eyes of the public.

In this respect, the media have been the Government's willing partners. Sadly, and in the case of the BBC, shamefully, they have been less than interested in the erosion of the accountability of Parliament. The BBC abolished *Yesterday in Parliament* on Radio 4 FM, consigning it to long wave, although after protests from many, including Madam Speaker, there is now a chatty item included in the *Today* programme. The broadsheets have all but dropped serious coverage of Parliament, which was still a regular feature when I came into the House in 1987, in favour of sketches and diary pieces. *The Times* and the *Daily Telegraph* have now reinstated coverage of Parliament, in such a self-congratulatory way that one would have thought they had not abolished it in the first place. Television continues to cover rows in the Chamber, or, in the spring of 2000, the appearance of a mouse in the House, but little else of substance. It has proved ominously difficult for Opposition politicians to get coverage. While the media are loud in their praise of themselves as champions and saviours of free speech, it is the more ironic that the heart of our democratic process, Parliament, is increasingly regarded by them as too dull to cover.

233

The Power of Spin

Truth is the most valuable thing we have. Let us economize it.

MARK TWAIN

But the compliant attitude of the press towards the present Government is regarded in some quarters as more sinister still. Peter Oborne, the political columnist on the *Sunday Express,* gives a devastating analysis of the reasons for what he calls 'the unique tractability of today's Fleet Street.' He explains this tractability as the result of more than a decade of conscious effort by two new Labour media chiefs, Peter Mandelson and Alastair Campbell, the Prime Minister's press secretary: 'Between them they have worked ceaselessly to place friends in powerful and senior positions in the political teams of each Fleet Street paper.' He points out, somewhat chillingly, that *The Times'* political team has been 'ethnically cleansed of Tories', and adds that the unprecedented readiness of the parliamentary lobby to give the Government the benefit of the doubt is a matter of the highest political importance. He quotes Mandelson as having said when he took the job of Labour Party Director of Communications in the 1980s, 'Of course we want to use the media, but the media will be our tools, our servants; we are no longer content to let them be our persecutors.'[39] That such a statement could pass almost without comment demonstrates why the Opposition sometimes finds it hard to get their scrutiny of the Government reported. It is also a sad reflection on the current state of our parliamentary democracy, not to mention the press, the self-appointed watch-dogs of our freedoms.

Perhaps linked to this is the fact that since the general election in 1997, sixteen of the eighteen most senior press officers in

Government departments have either been removed, moved side-ways or pensioned off. The *Daily Telegraph* remarked,

> Many press officers privately complain that they have come under pressure to take an increasingly 'political' role and that the boundaries between promoting Labour and Government policies have become blurred at times. The changes coincide with the creation by Tony Blair of a slick PR machine and information and rebuttal system designed to promote his core messages. Many civil servants have privately complained that they have come under pressure to stretch the boundaries between Government information work and political 'spin'. This may or may not be so. Whatever the truth of the allegation, however, there is no doubt that before the last election, most of the public were not familiar with the term spin-doctor. Now they are.[40]

Their Lordships' House

> The cure for admiring the House of Lords is to go and look at it.
>
> WALTER BAGEHOT

One part of the parliamentary process has proved resistant to this onslaught: the House of Lords. It has been difficult for the Government to grasp that the important contribution of the House of Lords is its independence – not to mention its expertise and wisdom on many issues. Equally if the House of Lords were to be replaced, it would be important to put in place an institution as capable as their lordships have been of real legislative scrutiny. The Government should have noticed that during the last three months of John Major's administration, the House of Lords defeated the Government six times. So much for a compliant Upper House. Their fate has been similar.

235

Before the reformed House of Lords came into existence through the House of Lords Act 1999, the Government had already felt the force of the Lords' disapproval, frequently expressed from an all-party front. During the passage of the Teaching and Higher Education Bill in July 1998, Conservative peers persuaded the Government to set up an independent inquiry into the tuition fees anomaly it had created between treatment of student fees in Scotland and the rest of the UK. A cross-party alliance of peers won an amendment in the Welfare Reform and Pensions Bill in October 1999 obliging the Government to make later concessions before the Bill became law. Their opposition to the Sexual Offences (Amendment) Bill forced the Government to invoke the Parliament Act to get their legislation through.

If the Government had thought that its reformed House of Lords would be more compliant, they have been disappointed. Since the reformed House came into being, the Conservative leader in the Lords, Lord Strathclyde, has pointed out that the Government had 'declared that the interim House is more legitimate, and its decisions have more authority.' He remarked,

> We have a duty now to put those words to the test. For, after all, in the old House, when the Government was defeated by a range of political and independent opinions, it simply ignored it. If it would have been defeated without a single Tory vote, as on Lord Ashley's Welfare Bill amendment, it simply ignored it. If it was defeated on the votes of life peers alone, as it has been several times this Parliament, it simply ignored it.[41]

And the reformed House has been as good as its word, frequently and massively defeating the Government on a range of issues, most dramatically perhaps on trial by jury, in the Criminal Justice (Mode of Trial) Bill with a cross-party alliance of peers, including the Labour Baroness Kennedy of the Shaws. Threatened with rebellion in the Commons, the Government made amendments to the Bill and was obliged to reintroduce it in the Commons as a No. 2 Bill.

Opposition is an important part of our parliamentary democratic process. It may be distasteful for those whose principal interest in politics is to exercise power. But for those who believe that Parliament, and its role of holding to account the government of the day on behalf of the electorate, is central to our democracy, any diminution in the power of Parliament is a threat to democracy. In the Lords debate on the report of the Royal Commission on Reform of the House of Lords Lord Strathclyde put it this way:

> We on this side of the House do not fear a stronger Parliament. If a government carries confidence in a free, independent and respected Parliament – one not cowed by patronage or by party whips – then that government is more authoritative and respected. What destroys respect for any government is backstairs arm twisting, trading of favours, a culture of cronyism, the bypassing of Parliament and the handing of power to unelected and unaccountable advisers.[42]

Every opposition has its own problems, born of the age in which it operates. It can and must use its time to make necessary reforms in the areas over which it has control. Its leader must unify and motivate its parliamentarians, activists, and professional staff. A new opposition must have patience, be content at first with small victories, and combine careful planning with clever opportunism. Above all, through Parliament, and the media, it must restore the confidence of the public in its ability to represent their views, and hold the Government to account.

It is, of course, more difficult to achieve these objectives in a situation where there is a diminishing interest in the political process, and where a government itself prefers focus groups and people's panels to the constitutional instrument from which it take its power, namely Parliament. It is even more difficult to operate if the press and media are compliant to the government of the day. But oppositions have to work within the conditions they inherit. If the present Opposition has to work within a climate where Government attitudes demean and devalue the parliamentary process, then the Opposition's task may be more difficult, but ultimately it is also that much more important for the future of the democratic process.

Constitutional Battles

A constitution should be short and obscure.

NAPOLEON BONAPARTE

THE UNDERLYING THEME of this book is that power is conferred through the ballot box on governments, and bestowed by Parliament. There may be constraints on the exercise of power by government, because of the personality and attitudes of those in charge, of circumstances and chronology, events, policy inheritance, and party baggage.

Essentially, however, while a government retains control of Parliament, it can continue to exercise power, and can be held democratically accountable for what it does. For decades the power of the executive has outstripped parliamentary control, but until now we have not experienced a situation in which the executive has made a virtue, a policy, of reducing the power of Parliament. It is important to explore what happens when the authority of Parliament itself is challenged, by constitutional change and the modernisation of its procedures, the implications of which for democratic accountability have not been sufficiently thought through.

Discussion of the constitution does not make for a lively evening at the Dog & Bottle. Considerations about its future may not be at the forefront of everyone's minds. However, everyone is an expert on law and order, health and education and the effect of constitutional change on the means by which policies on these issues are delivered is far reaching and ultimately affects us all. If the democratic process of Parliament is weakened by blurred account-ability, then we may one day wake up to find the constitutional landscape irreversibly changed, and our part in it reduced. That will be the day when the Dog & Bottle finds, too late, that the demo-cratic process as we know it cannot be saved.

The Role of Parliament

> In questions of power, let no more be heard of confidence in man, but
> bind him down from mischief by the chains of the constitution.
>
> THOMAS JEFFERSON

The Hansard Society Commission on the Scrutiny Role of
Parliament, working under the chairmanship of Lord Newton of
Braintree, describes the role of Parliament as follows:

> Parliament performs a number of roles in British democracy. Parliament
> makes the law and decides on how much the government can raise
> through taxation. Crucially, it also creates and sustains the government.
> Parliament provides the vital link between the electorate and govern-
> ment. Governments are accountable to the people through general elec-
> tions. Between general elections, Parliament is the principal means by
> which the government can be held to account for its activities. This
> form of accountability is generally termed Parliament's scrutiny role.
> Parliament performs this role by obtaining and publicising information
> about the government's performance and future plans. On the basis of
> the information Parliament, and others, form a judgement as to whether
> the government is discharging its mandate effectively, economically and
> in the best interests of the electorate.

Bagehot, on whose views the Hansard definition is based, identifies
six roles for the House of Commons in his seminal work *The
English Constitution*. First, it is an electoral chamber, in that it is the
assembly which chooses, as Bagehot puts it, 'our President'. He
adds, 'Because the House of Commons has the power of dismissal
in addition to the power of election, its relations to the premier are
incessant. They guide him, and he leads them.'

Second, Parliament has what Bagehot calls an 'expressive

function. It is its office to express the mind of the English people on all matters which come before it.'

Third is what Bagehot calls 'the teaching function'. 'A great and open council of considerable men cannot be placed in the middle of a society without altering that society. It ought to teach the nation what it does not know.'

Fourth, it has an informing function: 'In old times, one office of the House of Commons was to inform the Sovereign what was wrong. Since the publication of Parliamentary debates a corresponding office of Parliament is to lay these same grievances, these same complaints, before the nation which is the present sovereign.'

Fifth, the function of legislation: 'of which it would be preposterous to deny the great importance and which I only deny to be as important as the executive management of the whole state or the political education given by Parliament to the whole nation'.

Sixth, a financial function, although Bagehot considers that financial legislation is, in effect, no different from any other. He concludes that 'Parliament conforms itself, accurately enough, both as a chooser of executives and as a legislature, to the formed opinion of the country.'

The Hansard Commission document defines the role of government in relation to Parliament:

> Effective scrutiny relies not only on the role of Parliament and MPs, but also on the role of government. The Government has a duty to account for its policies, decisions and actions. The structure of Government and the context within which it operates, has changed enormously in recent years. The increased use of executive agencies by central government, devolution to Scotland and Wales, the growing influence of the courts, the extension of EU involvement across wider areas of policy-making and the burgeoning power of the media have all had an impact on the influence of Westminster.

It might have added, although that would be to pre-empt the outcome of the inquiry, that the wholesale adoption of constitutional
change with no apparent thought for the consequences to the
power of Parliament and the accountability of government has
been a remarkable feature of Government policy since the 1997
general election. This wholesale change has been described by ministers in various ways: modernising Government, making it more
accessible, bringing it closer to the people. What has not been taken
into account, as yet anyway, is the overall effect on the democratic
process in Britain. As David Marquand points out,

> The process of constitutional change will almost certainly generate a
> dynamic of its own, carrying the transformation further than its authors
> intended or expected. [43]

This is undoubtedly so, but if it is combined with Peter
Mandelson's view, that 'the era of pure representative democracy is
coming to an end' it has worrying implications for parliamentary
democracy as we know it.

Certainly the scale of constitutional change is wholesale. Nor
should the electorate be surprised. After all, it was presented in the
1997 Labour manifesto. The country is facing the consequences of
the establishment of a Scottish Parliament and a Welsh Assembly
and new devolved arrangements for Northern Ireland. The
Freedom of Information Act will have implications for central and
local government and all public bodies. A strategic Assembly for
London and an Executive Mayor are in place. Regional
Development Agencies have been introduced, perhaps as the precursors of elected Regional Assemblies. The House of Lords has
undergone the first stage of its reform, with the expulsion of hereditary peers, save for the hundred or so who remain as part of the

interim arrangements. Modernisation of the procedures of the House of Commons is under way. A commission on electoral reform for the Westminster Parliament has reported. Elections with proportional representation to the European Parliament have taken place. The Neill Committee is considering the funding of political parties. The European Charter of Human Rights has been incorporated into UK law. Preparations are being made for the electorate to consider Britain's entry into the single currency. We are assailed by change on all fronts.

The most surprising element in all of this is that change on such a monumental scale is being introduced piecemeal by the Government, with apparently no thought of its impact on the overall democratic process, on the constitution, or on its own accountability and powers. As the Select Committee said, of Scottish and Welsh devolution, 'We hope that the Government will not be overtaken by events, and that when the pace of reform slackens, it will be found that all the separately constructed pieces of the jigsaw will fit together.'

Some explanation for the Government's seeming insouciance on the whole matter has been provided by Peter Riddell. He believes that the Prime Minister is not interested in constitutional matters, thinking that they barely register in opinion polls compared with education, health, and law and order. He has therefore left his Home Secretary and Lord Chancellor to deal with them, and concentrates himself on issues he thinks have more voter appeal.[44]

If this is so, it is deeply irresponsible. Apart from other considerations, one might have hoped that a political leader would have been conscious of the provenance of his power and the effect of his own policies upon it, and his own accountability. As Riddell points out,

245

> There are big questions about where constitutional reform is going. Are
> we creating a written constitution which will be interpreted by the
> judges? Is the unitary, or rather union, state being replaced by a quasi-
> federal structure? The Government often acts as if changes such as devo-
> lution or the Human Rights Act need not disturb the inward-looking
> world of Westminster. [45]

In fact, the inward-looking world of Westminster, in the shape of
the Opposition at least, is the only place that is disturbed by these
changes, if press coverage is anything to go by, with the honourable,
but spasmodic, exception of Riddell, of course. He continues,

> What ministers really fail to address is the dynamic nature of their pro-
> gramme. They treat each individual Bill like an item to be ticked off on
> a check list. But there are loose ends: not just issues which have yet to
> be resolved like electoral reform, but also the consequences of measures
> already enacted.

Quite so.

The Spectre of Separatism

> The beauty of Scotland is that it is big enough to be important in the
> UK and small enough to know everyone else.
>
> GEORGE YOUNGER

It is no secret that the present government introduced the idea of
devolved government in both Scotland and Wales to secure for
itself electoral advantage in those countries in the light of growing
electoral success for the nationalist parties. The appeal of a devolu-
tionary message was not confined to the Labour Party. Before the

last election, the Conservatives and the Liberal Democrats introduced measures or proposals to underline their respect for the separate identity of Scotland. Michael Forsyth, the last Conservative Secretary of State for Scotland, brought in a number of measures designed to demonstrate Conservative commitment to Scottish separateness. Among other measures, he introduced the Scottish Grand Committee, and returned the Stone of Scone to Edinburgh, in an important symbolic gesture. He argued powerfully for Scotland in and out of Cabinet. It is at least arguable that had he been promoted earlier to Scottish Secretary the Conservatives would have fared better in Scotland at the election. In the event, they were devastated, and lost every Scottish seat.

As a minister in a number of posts whose responsibilities extended to Scotland, I spent a lot of time north of the border during my time in government. There was no doubt about the separateness of Scotland. Scottish Tories felt isolated from London, and the peculiarly southern brand of Conservatism that was represented by Margaret Thatcher. John Major was popular with them, and was assiduous in his visits to all parts of Scotland, and to the Scottish Conservative Conferences. By then, though, it was too late.

I recall an extensive tour I made as Minister for Agriculture in support of our candidates for the European elections in 1994. It included visits to the west coast, meeting fishermen and crofters and potato growers on the east coast, and a huge meeting of farmers, about 400 of them, at a motel near Stonehaven.

I watched the four-wheel-drive vehicles come into the car park, and the rather serious looking men pour out, and into the hotel. Apart from the female chairman of the meeting there was barely a woman to be seen. I had got used to chauvinistic and difficult meetings in the Agriculture portfolio, but I thought this one would be something else, watching the demeanour of those arriving. It was. In the event, I was able to say some genuinely complimentary things about the quality of agriculture I had seen on my journey, adding a few jokes about the number of Scottish farmers who had come to East Anglia in the 1930s to help us farm. This got us off to a reasonable start, and by the end of the meeting, they seemed almost reluctant to leave. The experience taught me a lot about respect for the separateness of Scotland, as did my frequent encounters with Scottish fishermen.

Contact with Welsh farmers was easier. This was not because Wales has a less distinct character than Scotland, but because the volume of agricultural trade between England and Wales, especially in livestock, means that there is common cause between English and Welsh farmers. Again, during the European election campaign, I spent a long wet day travelling the length of Wales, holding meetings with farmers, either in the open air or standing on a bale of straw in a windy cowshed getting wetter by the second.

In the event, the message of devolution was popular in Scotland. It was very much less so in Wales, where the vote for an Assembly was won by a whisker or, in some parts of the country, not won at all. I was struck when campaigning in north Wales before the Assembly elections not only by the apathy towards the whole proposal but also, in some areas, by the downright hostility. Very different attitudes prevail between the south and north of Wales, as well as in the rural western areas, and it seemed to me that people preferred to feel hostile towards the common enemy, London, rather than to award power to Cardiff.

This is a more important point than it seems. All MPs, particularly those who represent far-flung rural constituencies, are expert on the territorial disputes and wars that exist within different parts of their areas. Towns and villages have different allegiances – they relate to different larger centres of population – but most are united in their dislike and resentment of the county town and, in particular, London. It is not hard to whip up separatism. Any of us could do it, in our own village, town or county. In my own area, in 1996, the County Council consulted the population of Norfolk on whether it wished to have unitary councils. In the west of the county, this would have meant rule from Kings Lynn. When this concept was put to the people of Downham Market in a public meeting there was a unanimous vote against. People preferred to unite against the common enemy, Norwich. Norwich and the west of Norfolk were, after all, on opposite sides in the Civil War.

When such strong feelings of territorialism are exploited for political, rather than real reasons, it is not hard to understand that separatist movements may result but other more menacing feelings may also emerge. There has been much anecdotal evidence from Scotland of racist activity against English people living there. My own cousin, who is married to a Scot, and has lived in Scotland for the last fifteen years, describes having had to adopt a Scottish accent in order not be sneered at in shops. A young Scottish Labour back-bencher with an English wife told me that his wife dare not attend Scottish-English football matches, in case people find out that she is not a Scot. A traditional old Labour Welsh MP told me that there was racism in the Welsh valleys, following the establishment of the Welsh Assembly, which he found immeasurably distressing. It is ironic that a first fruit of 'bringing the Government closer to the people' should have had the effect of engendering a particularly unpleasant and intolerant form of political correctness.

All of this was far from the Government's mind as it plunged into its ill-thought-out programme of constitutional reform shortly after the 1997 election.

Early on, it introduced skeletal legislation to hold referenda in Scotland and Wales, skeletal in the sense that ministers were unable to explain during the passage of these Bills how devolution would affect the constitution and the powers of Parliament.

We were not sure, at first, how best to arrange our Opposition resources to respond to Scottish and Welsh issues. We were keenly conscious that we had no Conservative Scottish or Welsh MPs. On the other hand, we felt that these issues were not merely the business of the Scots and the Welsh, but of the whole country. That very point was, indeed, the basis of our argument. In the end, Michael Ancram was made spokesman for Constitutional Affairs, and led for the Opposition in the constitutional legislation that followed. We decided, given the emphatic 'yes' given by the Scottish electorate to a Scottish Parliament, that we must accept the will of the electorate. We were determined, however, to expose the effects of this piecemeal breaking up of Britain on the rest of the constitution, the English and, most importantly of all, on the power of Parliament. We were supported in our misgivings about a Welsh Assembly by a strong lobby of traditional Welsh MPs, who opposed the whole idea, and whose courage in the face of Government briefing against them was magnificent. As the legislation went through our task was to tease out how the new structures would work, and their effect on the accountability and transparency of the democratic process in Westminster. The fact that the referenda were held before the legislation to set up devolution arrangements had even been drafted did not bode well for the democratic process, or for the Government's regard of it.

The broad questions of principle remain unclear, even now that the Scottish Parliament and the Welsh Assembly are in place.

As far as Scotland is concerned, the so-called West Lothian Question is unanswered and unanswerable. It is this: why may

Scottish Members of Parliament vote on matters affecting only English constituencies, such as the Revenue Support Grant for local government, or the roads programme for England, when English MPs may not vote on similar matters affecting Scottish constituencies because they are devolved to the Scottish Parliament? There is not only no answer to the West Lothian Question: as a result of its headlong rush to devolution, the government has created for London the West Hampstead Question.

All Members of Parliament are responsible for raising taxation – it is one of Parliament's principal tasks – but they have no right to scrutinise how that money is spent in Scotland or Wales, as that scrutiny is devolved to the Scottish Parliament and the Welsh Assembly. The Scottish Secretary, Dr John Reid, said,

> There is genuinely a partnership of Parliaments. It is the most radical constitutional settlement for 300 years. There is no route map for it and no textbook that we can consult. The First Minister and I are already involved in discussions to see that there is a symmetry of conventions . . . it means that both sides have equal rights and responsibilities.[46]

These are weasel words. Translated into normal language, they mean, 'I haven't a clue how things will work out, but I suppose we will muddle through.' It is not good enough, and such an imprecise, not to say sloppy attitude has already landed the Government in a number of ludicrous situations. During the passage of devolution legislation through Parliament, it was unwilling to spell out what would happen if on devolved matters, Scotland and Wales took a different view from the UK Government. They have now experienced this in the issues of beef on the bone and student grants. The Agriculture Minister, Nick Brown, received advice from government scientists late in 1999 that the beef-on-the-bone ban

251

should be lifted. He was unable to do so, because neither the Scottish nor the Welsh Governments would follow suit, on the grounds that their scientific experts took a different view. That another of the first fruits of devolution should be to render the UK Government impotent was an irony indeed. Government ministers were unable to justify the ridiculous position in which they found themselves, apart from saying lamely, 'That's devolution'. Naturally.

More serious has been the debate on student finances, which has resulted in Scottish (and EU students) attending Scottish universities being treated differently from English students at the same universities. Another first fruit of bringing government closer to the people was surely not intended to be a glaring injustice to the English – or was it? As the minister said, there is no route map.

New arrangements have had to be made to deal with the conventions of Scottish and Welsh matters in Parliament, not least to give some form of occupation to their unfortunate Secretaries of State, who languish palely in the House with no visible means of employment, and to give some reason for MPs with a dual mandate to visit London, to justify taking their Westminster salaries and travelling expenses. In the *Daily Telegraph* on 24 May 2000 Benedict Brogan gave colour to the sad charade that is now Scottish Questions in the House of Commons:

> Dr John Reid is a man of action now reduced to observer status by Tony Blair's decision to hand nearly all of the Scottish Secretary's traditional responsibilities to the new talking shop up north. The 25 minutes devoted to Scottish Questions were probably the longest engagement in his diary this week. Scottish Questions are fast becoming one of the non-events on the Commons Order Paper. With no powers worth mentioning to shape the lives of the people of Scotland, Dr Reid is left to answer general questions about Government policy.

His Welsh counterpart, the excellent and talented Paul Murphy, has fared no better. He took the liberty, in April 2000, of announcing a set of agriculture statistics to the Welsh Grand Committee sitting in Westminster. The view from Wales was that he had had no right to do so. The figures should have been announced in Wales, to the Welsh Assembly, by the Welsh Agriculture Minister. Much time was spent that day in justifying or attacking what he had done. The debate advanced not a jot the fortunes of agriculture in Wales, which at the time were low.

So one result of devolution has been a reduction in the sum of the whole, which is the government of Britain. Concentration on issues affecting the parts has inevitably reduced the importance of issues affecting the whole. This is a sorry state of affairs. Did the Government really mean to reduce a discussion of Scottish matters to a 'non-event' in the national Parliament? Was one of the purposes of establishing a Welsh Assembly to render the Welsh Secretary powerless to speak even on Welsh issues? If so, that is a curious way of recognising their importance. These questions have been examined by the House of Commons Procedure Committee. In their 1999 report 'The Procedural Consequences of Devolution', while making clear that their position is an interim one, they made an innovatory recommendation. Bills relating exclusively to Scotland, England, Wales or Northern Ireland should have their Second Readings and Committee Stages taken by a Committee of MPs representing seats in that part of the UK. This recommendation was rejected by the Government, at least partly because

> at a practical level, there is no room in the precincts large enough to accommodate all 582 members sitting for English seats. If all such Members were to be able to take part, the Second Reading Committee

would have to sit in the House itself. From such a sitting it would be difficult to exclude any other Members of the House – though if they wished to be called in a debate, they would presumably be less likely to catch the Speaker's eye than Members with a constituency interest.[47]

So there is no room large enough in Westminster to accommodate the results of the Government's constitutional changes! As Richard Littlejohn might say, you couldn't make it up. This is the kind of ludicrous muddle visited upon constitutional conventions and democratic rights by a government determined to push through reform with no interest in its consequences for the democratic process. The Government continued, in its response,

> None of the devolution legislation affects the House's ability to pass legislation on any matter. For all public Bills, the government would expect that a convention would be adopted that Westminster would not normally legislate with regard to devolved matters without the consent of the devolved body.[48]

There are more weasel words that fail to deal with eventualities that, over time, are bound to emerge. Translated, they mean, 'We're in rather a mess with all of this, but let's hope we can cobble something together without too many people noticing.' Sadly, such is the almost universal boredom induced in the population by constitutional matters that not many have – yet.

They surely will, however, when the UK government and the devolved parliaments are under different political control. There are no mechanisms, beyond certain constitutional deadlock and paralysis, proposed in the Lord Chancellor's Department Memorandum of Understanding and Supplementary Agreements between the UK Government, Scottish Ministers and the Cabinet of the National Assembly for Wales. This memorandum established concordats which are written on the premise, a false one if there ever was, that each of the devolved administrations will wish to work with one another.

Does all of this matter? It does to those who are concerned to preserve the principle that power should reside in the ballot box, and be bestowed on politicians by Parliament. If that process is obscured by the imposition of additional layers of government with imprecise power, then the vital element of transparent accountability is lost and, with it, much of the democratic strength of the structure.

What of the effects of all this change on the eighty-three per cent of the UK's population so far left out? While it would not be true to say that there has yet been an English backlash, there is certainly resentment at grass roots level, particularly towards Scotland. What is more serious is the democratic deficit that the Government has created for England, and the damage it has done to the standing of the Westminster Parliament, apparently by inadvertence.

The position of London illustrates the point. Londoners voted narrowly in favour of an executive mayor and a London Assembly. The Act to enable elections to take place and other changes to be made gave no fewer than 277 additional powers to the Secretary of State for the Environment. So much for decentralisation of power. Worse, as a result, Londoners will be asked to vote for Borough councillors, Assembly Members, the Mayor of London, Westminster MPs and Members of the European Parliament. They will also need to understand the functions and responsibilities of the Government Office for London, the London Regional Development Agency, the London Police Authority, the Fire and Emergency Planning Commission and so on. Will all these individuals, bodies and structures help them when they want to know where to turn to report a hole in the road? They will not, and that is the true test of accountability.

Undeniably there was an appetite in Scotland for devolution. The response of the Welsh and of Londoners was so equivocal that the Government has no justification for further weakening electoral accountability and the power of Parliament by foisting elected regional assemblies on England, reportedly their 'solution' for the English democratic deficit they have so thoughtlessly created. There seems little enthusiasm for this kind of change, even in the South West and North East of England, areas normally quoted as those most likely to want their own assemblies. Rather there is deep division in those places and elsewhere in England, on where the regional centre would be, what would happen to the rest of local government, and even, in the case of the South West, the South East, and East Anglia, what would constitute the region.

It is conceivable, however, that the Government is less enthusiastic about devolution after practical experience of what it actually means. They have been made to look ridiculous by the pantomime of candidacies for the post of Welsh First Secretary and for the London Mayor. In the end, Number 10's control-freak approach was defeated in Wales, by the forced departure of the centrally imposed First Secretary, Alun Michael, and his replacement by Rhodri Morgan. In London, the Government's humiliation was complete when its candidate for mayor, Frank Dobson, came a bad third to the Independent, Ken Livingstone, and the Conservative, Steven Norris. It could also be that the ruling coalition between Labour and the Liberal Democrats in Scotland was not what ministers had in mind to run the country, especially when illness forced the replacement of the Labour First Minister by his deputy, a Liberal

Democrat. Even the most determined moderniser might pause before taking on eleven regions in England, in the light of devolution experience so far. No wonder John Prescott sounded hesitant about the Government's plans for regional assemblies when answering a question from Jim Cousins, MP for Newcastle upon Tyne Central. He said,

> Let us be clear: I will argue for regional government. That is how parties make their decisions. There are different views, there are democratic debates, and we come to decisions. [49]

A less than ringing endorsement. In practice devolved democracy has been bruising for a government that has made such a virtue of it. Even so, the promise in the 1997 Labour manifesto remains. It says:

> In time we will introduce legislation to allow the people, region by region, to decide in a referendum whether they want directly elected regional government. Our plans will not mean adding a new tier of government to the existing English system.

Their plans do, however, mean the abolition of county government – in other words, more constitutional change. They are also remarkably meagre in their examination of the implications for the democratic process at Westminster.

Reforming the Lords

> When I'm sitting on the Woolsack I amuse myself by saying 'Bollocks' *sotto voce* to the bishops.
>
> LORD HAILSHAM

The reform of the House of Lords was described thus in the Labour manifesto:

> The House of Lords must be reformed. As an initial self-contained reform, not dependent on further reform in the future, the right of hereditary peers to sit and vote in the House of Lords will be ended by statute. This will be the first stage in a process of reform to make the House of Lords more democratic and representative. The legislative powers of the House of Lords will remain unaltered.

This statement perfectly encapsulates what has been this Government's problem with the constitution. Finding reform of it imperative for political reasons, in the case of Scotland, Wales and London, or in the case of the House of Lords, to throw ideological red meat to the Left, it has focused on reform and not on function. Thus even in its manifesto the Government gave no hint that it had thought about the function of a second chamber. Clearly it should have done so, if only because there would be a need to ensure its independence, that having been a principal characteristic of the House of Lords under all previous governments.

What is a second chamber for? Is it principally a revising and scrutinising chamber? Is it to be a further check on the executive? Should it concentrate mainly on debate? All of these questions should have been considered, because the answers would influence the composition of a reformed House of Lords. Sadly, the Government has given the impression in this matter that it is concerned only with the composition of the House of Lords, and not with the contribution that a second chamber makes to the democratic process.

While it would be hard to justify an unelected and hereditary House of Lords as part of a modern constitution, there can be little doubt that it has been precisely the unelected and hereditary element of the House of Lords that has given it its formidable independence. Equally, the qualities of many life peers, appointed for their intellect, expertise and achievements, have made the House of Lords a scrutineer *par excellence*, exposing anomalies and forcing government rethinks before flawed legislation reaches the statute book.

Select Committees in the Lords, composed as they are of some of the country's greatest living authorities on the subject in question, are a powerful means of holding governments to account. The Wakeham Commission report, in bringing forward, as widely predicted, merely a series of options, has been the disappointing result of many months of work and consultation. The Government's announcement that they intend no further reform for three years has led many to conclude that, after all, it was only about class envy, and not about serious attention to the effective and democratic scrutiny of government.

Lord Cranborne, in his essay 'The End of the Era of Representative Democracy?' sums up the arguments as follows:

> There are arguments for a directly or indirectly elected House, there are arguments for at least a partly nominated House, there are arguments for a House which represents the nations of the United Kingdom and local government. There are arguments for a House made up of a combination of all of these. What there is no argument for is a House which cannot act as a check on an already over-mighty Prime Minister, a Prime Minister whose piecemeal and headlong dismantling of the present constitution looks increasingly like an attempt to rig the new system to his own advantage.[50]

Unless the reform of the House of Lords eventually improves opportunities to hold to account the government of the day – unless, in other words, it strengthens the power of the democratic parliamentary process – then the public will be forced to conclude that this government is not interested in that process, but only in being able to say that it had got rid of hereditary peers.

Lord Cranborne also writes of the need to strengthen Parliament, which he describes as 'the response of the British people to over-mighty governments for 700 years.' As he points out, any examination of Parliament should start with the House of Commons.

The Government came to power promising the public that it would make the proceedings of the House of Commons more open and comprehensible for them. It also promised its own new MPs that it would make the workings of the House more women- and family-friendly.

It set up a Select Committee on the Modernisation of the House of Commons under the chairmanship of the Leader of the House. Not unreasonably, a number of newly elected MPs were placed on the Committee, so that it could have the benefit of see-ingthe House as others see it. These were counter-balanced by other Members who were experts in procedure and some of the more arcane ways of the Commons. It has proved difficult to strike a balance between making the procedures of Parliament easy to understand while preserving the traditions and courtesies that have served democracy well in the past.

Some of the changes made by the Modernisation Committee have been sensible, and in line with its objective of making the procedures of the House easier to understand. They have built on the solid work done by Tony Newton as Leader of the House in the last Conservative Government. The Modernisation Committee has introduced a revised, more comprehensible Order Paper, clearer explanatory notes to accompany Bills, and the carry-over (from one parliamentary session to the next) of certain Bills where they are subject to consultation or where they deal with particularly complex matters. This last proposal was regarded with some suspicion by Opposition MPs, naturally aware that delaying tactics are one of their principal weapons: the prospect of the House being made to sit into August because of Opposition dissatisfaction with a Bill is always a powerful incentive for a government to offer amendments. However, the Committee wisely concluded that all-party agreement would be required if a Bill were to be carried over, and agreement ensued.

Another proposal formalised the practice often adopted in the past by the Treasury with complex legislation: pre-legislative scrutiny. The Modernisation Committee went a step further, by establishing *ad hoc* Select Committees to do this work. It was also agreed that, provided there was agreement 'through the usual channels', that is between Government and Opposition business managers, there should be more timetabling of Bills, so that their passage through the House could be conducted in an orderly fashion. Again, the Opposition had misgivings about this, believing that its power to scrutinise and delay Bills might be curtailed. In the event those misgivings have been justified: in just three years, the Labour Government has used the guillotine sixty times. Margaret Thatcher's governments, in eleven years, used it forty times – each time in the face of outraged opposition from the Labour benches.

Other reforms introduced by the Modernisation Committee were perhaps less controversial. One did away with the practice of members being required to put on a top hat, or cover their heads in some other way, if they wished to raise a point of order during a division. This device had caused those watching proceedings in the House to wonder if they were instead at a Whitehall farce. In the past, Dame Irene Ward, a formidable Member who always wore a hat, was occasionally asked by a colleague if they could borrow it to raise a point of order. Since she usually wore a serviceable beret, the result, atop a male face, must have been singular, to say the least. The top hat in use when I first came into the House was battered and squashy and gave a rakish air to those who donned it.

Other reforms gave the Speaker more flexibility. There had been growing resentment that the Speaker, by custom, had been required to call Privy Councillors to speak first in debates. The Committee agreed that the Speaker should have more room to manoeuvre, in this matter, and on the length of speeches. It was also agreed that Members' constituencies should be shown on monitors when they were speaking in debates.

There was some debate about the establishment of a chamber parallel to the main Chamber, in the Westminster Hall. However, a number of colleagues felt that for some debates to take place out of the main Chamber would mean that they were regarded as unimportant, would not be covered by the media, and, perhaps, would detract from the dignity of Parliament. Others were unhappy that Westminster Hall would be set out, not confrontationally, but in a semicircle. They felt that such an arrangement was foreign to the nature of traditional parliamentary debate. In fact, Westminster Hall debates have taken on their own character. They are indeed less confrontational than those conducted in the main Chamber but they enable issues to be aired, constituency matters to be explored, and a thorough debate of Select Committee reports, all of which had had to be previously squeezed in round official government business. There is also the advantage that Adjournment Debates, which were formerly confined to the half hour after the conclusion of the rest of the daily business, at whatever time that might be, can now take place in Westminster Hall during the day on Tuesdays and Wednesdays, at a time when they can be covered by the press and supported by colleagues.

One proposal, strongly supported by some of the newer MPs on the Committee, was that the House should consider voting by electronic means: it was thought that it would be more accurate and efficient. Indeed, if electronic devices could be installed in MPs' offices, or even on their pagers, they would not need to come into the House at all. Apparently in the early days of the new Parliament, the sheer numbers in the Government lobby made voting a crowded experience, and, for more sensitive souls, an unpleasant one: the new women Labour MPs complained that their colleagues smelt and pushed unacceptably close to them – they had evidently led very sheltered lives. The other side Opposition MPs were vehement in their rejection of the idea. For a start, voting in the lobby is not inaccurate. The number of mistakes resulting from the present combination of clerks recording names and Whips counting heads has been minuscule over the years. For another thing, contact between MPs, back and front benchers, during votes, is a positive advantage of the current system, indeed one that would be the envy of business and other organisations trying to find systems to help them build a corporate identity. The unmentionable possibility of MPs cheating an electronic system loomed. Finally, it was pointed out that large electronic machines would have to be installed in the lobbies, through which MPs would pass with their swipe cards. The clerks explained that from their experience of MPs' expertise with electronic matters, they would have to be on hand to help, even if they were not required to record names. The words 'Planning Permission', and 'Listed Building' were voiced. The idea was dropped. However, a much less radical and extremely sensible measure was adopted, namely, the installation of a third clerk's desk in the lobbies so that MPs passed through three instead of two exits.

Other useful reforms have been approved in the area of European legislation. The Committee felt that scrutiny of such legislation was adversely affected by the mismatch between the Westminster and Brussels timetables, that there was insufficient notice of what could be expected from Brussels in terms of changes in the law, and that such changes were often paid scant attention with the existing arrangements. A designated official is now in place in each department to ensure the smooth running of scrutiny business. A national Parliament office has been opened in Brussels, so that liaison can be improved. The Chairman of the Scrutiny Committee tables a Written Question to the relevant minister, so that earlier information of the outcome of European Council meetings can be made available. The number of European Standing Committees has been increased, so that business can be adequately dealt with. None of these arrangements can stem the flow of sovereignty from Westminster to Brussels, but they mean that at least Parliament knows more about it. All in all, this has been successful work, accepted on all sides of the House.

Some changes suggested themselves and one affected the device known as a Ten Minute Rule Bill. This enables backbenchers to introduce, in the space of ten minutes at 3.30pm on Tuesdays and Wednesdays, a proposal to change the law, addressing an abuse or problem he or she has identified. A Ten Minute Rule Bill is useful in that it is short and sharp, and takes place in prime time when the House is normally full. When I first entered the House in 1987, Members had to apply and queue for such Bills. Amazing as it now seems, the queuing had to be done overnight: you were obliged to spend the night in the House of Commons, in a dusty stationery room somewhere above the Chamber. You arrived, armed with duvet and pillow, and spent an unusual night, in proximity to Big Ben, regularly inspected by security patrols.

Ambushes were common. If you left the room during your waiting time, to vote or whatever, your place might be taken by someone else. The whole thing became a cult, each political party vying through the insomnia of its backbenchers to have more Ten Minute Rule Bills than the rest. On one occasion, I ambushed Frank Cook, the fiery Labour Member for Stockton North. He went off to vote, and I shot into the room and took his place. When he returned he was displeased to put it mildly, and for a time, the air was indigo with parade ground language – not all of it from him – which could be heard several floors down. I would not give way. In the end, the Whips were summoned to separate us. They decided that I had been unfair, and awarded the honours to Frank. We have remained firm friends ever since. Ten Minute Rule Bill behaviour rose to even greater heights of absurdity when MPs began to queue all weekend to secure a prime spot just before a big parliamentary occasion, like the Budget. In the end, under the last government, it was decided, rightly, that there should be a ballot for the privilege.

The Modernisation Committee, which set out with high hopes at the start of the Government's period in office, has now attracted criticism on a number of fronts, despite the valuable work it has done, not least in improving the scrutiny of European legislation. The reason is that while it has dealt, for the most part, sensibly with a number of important but peripheral matters, it has fiddled while accountability burned. The thirty-three strong Liaison Committee, composed of the chairmen of the Select Committees of the House of Commons, and therefore a House of Commons heavyweight, examined the question of accountability in a report published in March 2000. The Report begins:

> Select Committees have been used by the House of Commons for centuries to investigate, judge, assess and advise. As governments have

become more powerful, the work of select committees has increasingly focused upon the Executive: the quality of its policies; the effectiveness of its administration; and its expenditure of the taxpayer's money. But in practice governmental power has always outstripped parliamentary control.

The Liaison Committee points out that the 1979 Select Committee system has been a success. They say,

> At a bargain price, it has provided independent scrutiny of government. It has enabled the questioning of Ministers and civil servants, and has forced them to explain policies. On occasion it has exposed mistaken and short-sighted policies and, from time to time, wrong-doing both in high places and low . . . it has also shown the House of Commons working at its best: working on the basis of fact, not supposition or prejudice; and with constructive co-operation rather than routine disagreement. . . . As a committee consisting of all Chairmen of Select Committees our concern is the effectiveness of the system. After two decades – and especially in the present climate of constitutional change – we think it is time for some further reform and modernisation.

The proposals of the Liaison Committee are moderate. This is an all-party group, representing vast collective experience, whose members are realistic. They accept that in the British system executive and legislature are linked, and that strong party discipline is an influential factor in MPs' attitudes and work. But it is clear that these experienced and wise people are concerned that a combination of constitutional change and centralisation of power, and the implications of devolution, are weakening Parliament's ability to hold the Government to account.

They suggest that Select Committees should be independent of party whips, and have a strengthened scrutiny role. This is not revolutionary: it is a sensible way in which to strengthen the House's power to hold a government to account, by using a system set up for that purpose, which has proved its worth over the past twenty years. The Government's response to the Liaison Committee's proposals has been illuminating. Never mind that it is the self-proclaimed guardian of the people's rights, it rejected all the Committee's main recommendations, in a manner described by Peter Riddell as 'evasive and mendacious'.[51] The Government turned down the notion of Select Committees holding confirmation hearings, in public, of major public appointments. It even rejected the idea of half-hour spots after Questions for debates on issues raised by Select Committees. How times change. What happened to the Labour Party which proclaimed in its 1997 manifesto, 'Unnecessary secrecy in government leads to arrogance in government and defective policy decisions'? As Riddell points out,

> In a perverse way, the Government has done the reformers a favour. By adopting such a contemptuous attitude, ministers have made it easier for MPs to respond forcefully and publicly, to show that the Government cannot always ignore the Commons.[52]

Blair's Babes: Poor Dears

> The *weak* are the second sex.
>
> ELIZABETH JANEWAY

The Government has been criticised for its indolence in modernising House of Commons procedures by another source, and a rather unexpected one. Who would have thought that the new army of women Labour MPs, just three years into the life of the

Parliament, would be castigating ministers for 'selling them a pup', as one woman backbencher described it?

One of the most memorable features of the 1997 general election was that it resulted in the election of 121 women MPs, 101 of them Labour. For the first time in history, one in five Members of Parliament was a woman. Linda McDougall, the TV producer wife of Labour MP Austin Mitchell, describes the mood:

> And so they arrived at Westminster, in the first week of May 1997. 120 bright-eyed British daughters. Smart, well-educated, experienced in the ways of the world. Many of them came from political families, so they had been dealing with politics and politicians all their lives. Many had been councillors, council leaders, teachers, heads, senior doctors, lawyers, barristers, journalists, consultants, carers and mothers.[53]

The appearance of so many women at once in the House of Commons led to a media-fest. Some of the early victory pictures of the Prime Minister show him surrounded by the 101 women Labour MPs, who were clearly thrilled and excited by their new roles. I had a lot of fellow feeling for them: it is an achievement to become an MP, and given, still, that only one in five is a woman, it is a particular achievement for a woman. Some were surprised by their victory, but their hopes were high.

The press went into overdrive. A *Daily Mail* editorial said, 'Never before have women been so well represented in a parliament, and even though some of them are there thanks to a quota system, that must be a cause for celebration.'[54] Pages were written about them: they appeared, made-over, in countless women's magazines. They transformed the look of the green benches in the Chamber, with their bright hair and clothes. Linda McDougall summed it up:

> 1997 will be remembered for ever as the election which produced a critical mass of women at Westminster. For the first time, women MPs are a group too big to be counted quickly. Too big for everyone to know everyone else.[55]

Some of the press coverage was less positive. The most critical comments came from female journalists, among them Jane Shilling of *The Times*. Shortly after the new Parliament had assembled, she wrote a trivialising article about the cheap shoes and synthetic fabrics worn by the new women MPs, their vivid, vulgar colours, their awful hair and make-up.

I was enraged. Political opponents they might be, but they did not deserve such treatment. I faxed a reply to *The Times* on the lines that since the women had spent the previous six weeks on the stump, they might not have had time to get their minds around this season's necessity – according to Shilling – of dressing in natural cottons and linens, and handmade shoes. It was conceivable that some of them might not have had the money either. Curiously, although my fax was headed 'From the Rt Hon. Gillian Shephard MP', *The Times* afterwards said that they did not know it was from me. They did not print it.

Sadly, that first early promise of a transformed House and a transformed legislative programme did not last the summer of 1997. Like their predecessors, the new women were whipped into line and became, mostly, compliant and hopeful of preferment. Few rebelled, even when the issues were of obvious relevance to women and families. The press, bored with those who had been their creatures, began to turn against them, which was sadly predictable. When Virginia Bottomley and I were Health and Education Secretaries respectively, the press criticised us and the Conservative Government, because we had been put in charge, as they put it, of soft issue departments. There are now five women in Tony Blair's Cabinet, but men are in charge of the soft issue departments, Health and Education. Blair and, by extension, the women were criticised because women were not in charge of big spending departments, like – wait for it – Health and Education! Sometimes in politics you just can't win.

But there were other problems with the new intake of women. I had become aware of them during the deliberations of the Modernisation Committee, in 1997–8. It was clear that some of the new MPs had been promised more reform of the proceedings of the House than the Government could deliver. And they appeared amazed by what they discovered about the demands of their new calling. Some of their comments were to be expected from people getting to grips with unfamiliar surroundings and curious work conditions, but strikingly absent was any realisation that the House of Commons is not like other workplaces, nor is it meant to be. While there should be reasonable comfort and courteous treatment of its Members, that is not the purpose of the House. Its purpose is to scrutinise the government of the day, and hold it to account, in the name of the democratic exercise of power. This cannot always be achieved between the hours of nine and five. Its demands are unpredictable. How could they be otherwise? Did those who fought hard to be elected as Members of Parliament not know what to expect? Or in their attitude towards Parliament and its function, are they taking their lead from the top of their party?

The work of the Modernisation Committee has gone some way to improving working hours. It has introduced a new timetable for Thursday sittings, with the House starting at 11.30am and finishing at 7pm. In the view of the Opposition, it has over-enthusiastically embraced the timetabling of Bills. But this is not enough, apparently, for some new MPs. Some seem to see the House principally as a vehicle for getting the Government's legislation through, and have missed the fact that scrutiny of legislation is not a time-wasting exercise designed to irritate backbenchers, but Parliament's principal purpose in the name of democracy. Thus the MP for Gloucester, Tess Kingham, elected in 1997, said,

> Many of us feel that it is difficult to do a good job for our constituents when we have to sit up all night or are called in at the whim of a few others to take part in such silly activities. That does our constituents no credit and involves putting off appointments to the next day or rejigging them completely, which causes unpredictability – we never know where we are.[56]

Ms Kingham announced shortly before this speech that she would not be standing at the next election, blaming the conditions of work at the House of Commons.

Her colleague, Julia Drown, elected as MP for Swindon South in 1997, complained in May 2000 about the lack of facilities for mothers and babies at the House. She reportedly requested of the House authorities that mothers should be able to breastfeed their babies anywhere in the House, and was turned down by the Speaker. It was alleged in one newspaper diary that Madam Speaker had said she would have more sympathy when she saw check-out girls at Tesco breastfeeding their babies while doing their jobs.

Criticism can certainly be levelled at some of the sillier aspects of the working conditions at the House of Commons. All-night sittings as a regular feature of our lives, time-wasting points of order and other procedures, the rough and tumble of the place are among its less attractive characteristics. But this has been no secret. There can hardly be a workplace in Britain whose conditions are better known in advance of new entrants arriving. If such conditions are unacceptable, and they may be to parents of young children, then it is better to wait to get elected until it is an easier proposition. Other professional women, lawyers, accountants, teachers, do not demand the right to breastfeed while in court, with clients, or in front of a class. I imagine there would be uproar if they did. Why, then, do women MPs choose to give their own profession a bad name by demanding privileges not available to other women? They should remember that all politicians, and especially MPs, do not have the kind of public image that makes others indulgent towards them. They do not enhance the reputation of MPs and by extension, that of the democratic process, by giving the impression that they expect special arrangements simply because they are MPs. Worse, they have in some ways let down the expectations of women across the country, many of whom must have believed that new common-sense polices of particular interest to them would result from such a large influx of women into Parliament. Instead, press interest has focused understandably on the complaints of those who, women might have hoped, existed not to express their own discontents but to do something about the discontents of others. What would Mrs Pankhurst have thought?

The Democratic Deficit

> Democracy means choosing your dictators, after they've told you what it is you want to hear.
>
> ALAN COREN

The question of what Lord Cranborne elegantly calls the 'dispersal of authority' is a difficult one. Notwithstanding the arrangements put in place by the Government to scrutinise European legislation there is a growing democratic deficit between the institutions of Europe and the people whose lives they affect. And the central question remains: what happens if a Directive from Brussels is unacceptable in the UK? The answer, under the present Government as under the last, is usually, 'This was implicit in the European Act', but in the absence of democratic accountability, in the sense that we know it, doubts and fears will remain and be exploited by the likes of the Referendum Party and the United Kingdom Independence Party. The best and most realistic hope seems to be that Europe should proceed through inter-governmental co-operation, given the unlikelihood of the Commission becoming accountable to some kind of supra-national institution. Thus, the strength and accountability of our own parliamentary and democratic process assumes even greater importance. This is a point overlooked by some commentators. The greater the threat to British sovereignty posed by EU membership, the more important it is to have a powerful and effective parliamentary process to support a government fighting its corner in the European Council of Ministers. That Britain's entry into a Single Currency, even if it were economically essential, would further weaken democratic accountability is almost too obvious to state.

We have not yet seen the effects of the incorporation of the European Convention of Human Rights into our law. The best Armageddon-like description of the possible national reaction, when the implications become known, is expressed by Peter Hennessy. He says:

> Just wait until the Human Rights Bill is law and a judge issues a 'declaration of incompatibility' in relation to an old or a new statute which he or she deems out of kilter with the European Convention as incorporated by the Human Rights Act. If the relevant minister pleaded lack

of parliamentary time even for the fast-track remedial procedure envisaged, or takes refuge in the 'almost certain' to act, but not quite let-out
provision, a most marvellous and hugely public tussle could ensue
between the executive and the judiciary. This is where the problem of a
disinterested minister could really bite. Other people's rights can be irri-
tatingly inconvenient to busy and executive minded ministers.[57]

And the electorate will become crashingly aware that there is an
authority, for which they have not voted, that is higher than parliament. As John Griffith has said of judges and incorporation,
'Whereas previously they have been acting quasi-politically in an
indirect way, now they are going to be required to make political
decisions. This is what it's about.' Hence the Government, again for
political reasons, has introduced a constitutional change with no
consideration for the effect it will have on democratic accountability, indeed on the power of Parliament and thus on Government.

I have attempted here to lay out the range of constitutional
change introduced over the past three years, and some of its effects
on the democratic process. Other effects will take time to emerge,
but it is unlikely that they will be benign. They are accompanied
by further changes in government practice, which are not benign
in their effect on the democratic process.

The Erosion of Accountability

Power corrupts. You use it, abuse it, then lose it.

HENRY KAISER

Since the Labour Government was elected in May 1997, the number of special advisers has doubled, as has their total salary bill. They
are specifically appointed for a political purpose. The taxpayer,

therefore, is paying for political propaganda in a way that has never been demanded before. This is why the Neill Committee has demanded a Code of Practice for such people. It will not make them accountable but their paymasters, the ministers, will have to answer for their exploits. Neill has also proposed, reasonably, that there should be a limit on their numbers.

In the first three years of its life, the Government has set up more than 300 task forces filled with Government appointees. The worst aspect of their existence is that despite the considerable powers some of them are able to exert, they are not accountable to anyone.

In a report of a study undertaken by Democratic Audit, an independent research group at the University of Essex, the *Sunday Times* said,

> In less than three years, the government has set up at least 318 task forces in the form of policy reviews, action teams, forums and working parties, involving about 2,500 appointees who for the most part are unelected outsiders. They are the favoured ones who have been, as senior civil servants put it, 'invited to the party' at a total cost to the taxpayer of at least £20m a year. Their arrival at new Labour's power-fest has been, if not by the back door, at least untrumpeted. Few know of the task forces, let alone of the people who sit on them or what their personal or business interests may be. . . . Even the Cabinet Office admitted it did not know their extent and refused to give details of their members. Whether it is secrecy or incompetence, it raises concerns about cronyism, vested interests, consumer rights, bureaucracy, and effectiveness. Who are these people? Why are they chosen? What are their agendas?[58]

It is, of course, unacceptable that the membership of publicly-funded bodies should be a secret from those funding them. Worse, perhaps, is the fact that their decisions cannot be questioned.

The new Regional Development Agencies – thought by some to be precursors of Regional assemblies, but as yet appointed, not elected – administer sizeable budgets, making decisions about how regional funds should be spent. If they make an unpopular or even a wrong decision, there is no means of complaint. They are not even representative. When the East Midlands RDA was established, Lincolnshire, the largest and most rural county in the region, had no representative on it. Some even wondered if it was because the majority of Lincolnshire MPs and councillors were Conservative. Whatever the reason, it is clearly an outrage that no place could be found for a rural point of view to be expressed. It is even more of an outrage that the Cabinet Office was unclear about the number of such bodies. Neill has requested that the Cabinet Office conduct a review to establish the number of task forces in existence, and their current status and longevity. That such a request is necessary hardly requires further comment.

There are other concerns about appointments. Early in 2000, the Commissioner for Public Appointments, Dame Rennie Fritchie, produced a report on Political Bias in Public Appointments to NHS Trusts and Health Authorities. Its objective was to establish if non-executive appointments to NHS bodies had been politicised since the 1997 general election. Her conclusions were that while the issue of the politicisation of appointments was not new, it had gained a fresh momentum since the 1997 general election. She added that there were examples where a candidate's political affiliation had been a decisive factor in their early selection and appointment, and that decisions had not always been based on merit. Her conclusions included the proposal that 'In the interests of increasing public confidence in the appointments process, the practice of inviting MPs to comment on shortlisted candidates should stop, and the practice of directly seeking nominations from local authorities should cease.'

The increasing 'control freakery' exhibited by the Government has given rise to fears that even the Civil Service might be becoming politicised. Andy Wood, who was replaced as Director of Information at the Northern Ireland Office after the 1997 general election, commented, 'I think there's the making of a nucleus of an alternative civil service. I'm talking about the trashing of reputations of certain members of the then Government Information Service by special advisers. I have no doubt at all that it happened – quite improper for a temporary civil servant to be passing value judgements on the ability of a full-time established civil servant.'[59] He also wrote in the *Daily Telegraph*, 'At principal and senior information officer level, discontent with the increasingly politicised atmosphere in which they have to work is running at a high rate.'[60]

So since its election in 1997 the Labour Government, much hailed by political commentators as a new dawn for Britain, has, by its unthought-out rush for constitutional change, its desire to control from the centre, its apparent inability to understand the vital importance of the democratic process, brought the democratic process to perhaps its most vulnerable point for centuries. It has done this, ironically, in the name of the people. It has been immeasurably helped in its endeavours by a compliant press, which, in equal parts, shouts its support for openness and rights and ignores their erosion by the Government.

Governments are meant to govern by reason of the power bestowed on them by the electorate, through Parliament. The Blair Government has a majority of 179. It has no need to play fast and loose with the democratic process. Why does it do so? And why does it do so in the name of the people, and of modernity? Only it can provide the answers to those questions.

In the meantime, the power of Parliament, and therefore of the people is daily being eroded, almost inadvertently. After all, the Government could not be doing it on purpose . . . could it?

Power Thoughts

The one and only lesson that our parliamentary party could usefully learn from Labour is the discipline of hunger for power.

MICHAEL HIRST

THIS BOOK HAS sought to examine the nature of power in politics. Power in politics is the power to achieve change. There are many influences on the exercise of power. They include constraints, such as personality, chronology, circumstance, and events. There are other sources of power, such as strong interest groups, the press and media and economic and external circumstances. But the only legitimate source of political power is the ballot box, and the most effective constraint on its use is a parliamentary majority, or the lack of it. That must be the case in a country governed by a system of parliamentary democracy.

But was Aneurin Bevan right? Where is power? Do you arrive at what you thought was its source, only to find, as he did, that 'power had been there, but it had just gone?'

The power of the executive has increased inexorably over the years. Parliament's scrutiny role has been reduced, by a combination of party influence and administrative necessity. But no member of John Major's Government between 1992 and 1997 could deny that Parliament mattered. Some would even say, despite the problems of that Government, that the Parliament it had to deal with was a true reflection of the state of mind of the electorate that put it in place in 1992. A majority of 21 is not a ringing endorsement, nor an expression of overwhelming enthusiasm. It is a recognition that given the deficiencies of the alternative, you should be given a chance. As John Major said in his autobiography, the victory would have been good for the Conservative Party 'had it chosen to behave like a party of government'.

The Labour Government was elected with a majority of 179 in the 1997 general election. This was clearly a ringing endorsement. It was happy to accept the gift of power from the ballot box. But it was not long before Peter Mandelson was musing in public about whether the 'era of pure representative democracy was coming to an end.' Senior and influential figures in the BBC have echoed, in private conversation with me, the view that there are other more participative ways of involving the electorate in the democratic process. Like Peter Mandelson, they seem to feel that local groups, focus groups, plebiscites and neighbourhood forums are somehow preferable to the verdict of the ballot box on the grounds that they are somehow more modern. That none of these arrangements is universal or legitimate does not seem to enter the argument.

Mandelson's analysis was as follows:

> We entered the twentieth century with a very different class structure. In those days, it seemed natural to delegate important decisions to members of the landowning elite, or the industrial elite. When in Britain, Labour emerged as the party that represented the industrial working class, it quickly developed its own elite of trades union bureaucrats, city bosses, and socialist intellectuals. But that age has passed away. Today people want to be more involved.[61]

But which people, and involved in which ways? And how can they be involved in a way which does not also involve the ballot box? What would Bevan have said? At least, in his search for power, from council, to county council, and, one presumes, to Parliament, he assumed that that power was elected. Would he have been shocked by the assertion that the 'era of pure representative democracy is coming to an end'? What would he have thought of the 'big tent' approach?

All political parties in government have friends and supporters. In the past, it has been traditional for business people and landowners to support Conservative governments, and for trade unionists and public sector workers to support Labour governments. While such stereotyping has long ago vanished, not least because of Margaret Thatcher's onslaught on such preconceptions, the purpose of such support groups has been just that: to support the government in question. No government, so far, has attempted to use them to stifle political debate, in effect, to prevent it from taking place, by binding to the cause of the Government all those who might criticise it, or put an alternative view.

With the Blair Government there is emerging a new political grouping, a new class, almost, that seems to have that purpose, of demonstrating that the Government is so unassailably right on everything that we must all agree with it. For the first eighteen months or so of the Government's life, the attitude of ministers, when criticised in Parliament or in media interviews, was one of hurt surprise. 'Hey', they seemed to be saying, 'you can't be criticising us, we're new Labour, remember, not the Tories. We're nice, well-intentioned, and above all, we won the election. What more do you want?' One of their commonplaces was that political debate was confrontational and therefore to be deplored.

While some of these attitudes may be a matter of style, they also undoubtedly stem from the fact that focus groups reveal that the public dislikes political argument, preferring to see those in power getting on with the job. But unless alternative views can be put, the public has no choice – a sinister development.

One of the techniques employed by the Government in stifling debate has been described as the 'big tent' approach. Constitutional reform, devolution, the use of public appointments, including peerages, and aggressive manipulation of the press and media are collectively threatening to the democratic process. This is not only because they reduce the power of Parliament to scrutinise the executive. It is also because they are creating a new elite who in turn influence public opinion and the political process. Deviation from the Government line is not tolerated. Polly Toynbee put it thus, 'Once inside the tent, the law of new Labour omertá is absolute. Criticism is not permitted.'[62] The comprehensive rubbishing of Lord Winston, a new Labour peer, for expressing critical views of the NHS early in 2000 is a menacing case in point.

How is the Government creating its big tent? First, by increasing the number of politicians through the establishment of the Scottish Parliament, the Welsh Assembly, the Greater London Assembly and the promise of elected regional Assemblies; second, by the creation of more than 300 task forces, unaccountable, unelected, and dependent on the Government; third, by the proliferation of quangos – 500 new ones have been created by this government; fourth, by the unprecedented number of party political appointments to public bodies; fifth, in the creation by Tony Blair of more life peers than any other Prime Minister in history.

Thus potential critics of Government policy are co-opted into its pay and patronage. A huge and increasing number of people are subjected to received, politically correct ideas and New Labour-speak, so uniform that the language used to discuss any issue is literally interchangeable, peppered as it is with synergy, partnership, inclusiveness and the like.

One of the most fascinating features of this 'big tent' is how frequently one bumps into the same people inside it. For example, David Puttnam, a Labour supporter and donor, has been made a Life Peer, a member of the Education Standards Task Force, and chairman of the General Teaching Council. Chris Haskins, a long-time supporter of the Labour Party from the business world, has been made a Life Peer, a member of the New Deal Task Force, and chairman of the Better Regulation Task Force. Baroness Young

284

became a Life Peer in 1997, is Chairman of English Nature, member of the Commission on the Future of the Voluntary Sector, and Vice Chairman of the Board of Governors of the BBC. There are countless other examples of the new great and the good within the 'big tent'.

No one would advance the argument that other governments have not promoted their friends and supporters. The difference between this government and its predecessors is a quantitative one: it has created more life peers, more quangos, more task forces, and promoted more of its friends, than has hitherto been known. It is also a qualitative one, in that it appears determined to use the big-tent dwellers to act as its propagandists. Martin McElwee describes the phenomenon:

> A real danger presented by the New Class is its erosion of the foundations of parliamentary democracy. The Government's fondness for side-stepping Parliament and going directly to the television studios, its aggressive news management, its undermining of the independence and integrity of the Civil Service, its reliance on special advisers, and its suborning of experts are all weakening Westminster from within. Those institutions which we once relied upon as bastions of trustworthy independence – the civil service, the House of Lords, the BBC – have all been thoroughly and deliberately compromised by New Labour apparatchiks.[63]

This is perhaps stating the problem too strongly. But the Labour Government's treatment of the press and its use of spin-doctors have been well documented and, in their way, are at least as significant as their use of the 'big tent'. Before the last election, the terms spin-doctor and focus group were, of course, in circulation in Westminster and Whitehall. They were not commonly to be heard on the Terry Wogan and Jimmy Young shows, or seen in *The Sun* newspaper. Now they are. The Government may be less than happy that one of their lasting achievements will be these additions to the language.

The role of the press in this suppression of criticism so far has been less than happy. Of course, there have been honourable exceptions. Moreover, some signs of independent thought are beginning to emerge. In an article in *The Times* pollster Robert Worcester asks how it is that the media can have been manipulated in this way when they were aware that it was happening. He quotes George Jones, political editor of the *Daily Telegraph*, to reply to this question.

> The ultimate function of print journalists is to help their newspaper to compete in the news markets. They cannot afford to reject news, and the same pressures make it more difficult to check stories or consider subtleties of interpretation. The same is true for the commercial broadcasters.[64]

George Jones's brother, Nicholas Jones, of the BBC, comments:

> The multiplication of news outlets is forcing journalists towards becoming processors of stories, rather than investigators of them.[65]

This is undoubtedly the reality for many journalists, even distinguished ones like the Jones brothers. How curious that such a reality should have coincided so exactly with the most manipulative government this country has ever known and what bad luck for the democratic process.

Peter Oborne, in the *Spectator,* comments:

> Mandelson and Campbell know that political reporting in Britain is not about impartial presentation of the facts; it is about the naked exercise of political power. Good luck to them. It is the editors and the political reporters who should question their integrity and allegiance.[66]

The activities of spin-doctors have had one clear effect, which has been to downgrade the role of MPs and ministers. The public have developed a sad scepticism about all they hear from the mouths of politicians. Anyone who doubts this assertion should study the reception of Tony Blair at the Annual General Meeting of the Women's Institute at Wembley on 7 May 2000. The Prime Minister was effectively given the bird by 10,000 country women. The explanation for this behaviour from their chairman was that they had been 'bored' by him.

Even in my own time as an MP, since 1987, there has been a perceptible reduction in public respect for the calling. Journalists hardly need to attend the House of Commons: all they need to know is encapsulated in government press releases and government briefings. If they step out of line, they are bawled out by government press secretaries. They tend not to do so.

The public have become used to the manipulation of statistics, and as a result are cynical about their significance. The Conservative government was frequently accused of changing the way unemployment figures were calculated to give the best interpretation when the news was bad. In fact, to present the numbers of people claiming unemployment benefit, month by month, was surely one way of illustrating what was going on. The Labour Force Survey lagged these figures, thus presenting a seeming contradiction in the two sets. But the present Government have debased the use of statistics altogether. They have made a mockery of their own announcements, for example, by announcing the same spending plans three, maybe four times, each time as if they concerned new money. Parliament is the forum for the exposure of such spin, and has been an effective interrogator of ministers as they struggle to define what is and is not new money, and whether, in the case of

Jack Straw, plans to recruit more police means the same as having more police on the beat. But Parliament is not always fully reported by the media.

Politicians of all generations have to work with the electoral attitudes of their age. At present, those politicians who believe that their work is a matter of overwhelming interest and constant discussion on the part of the electorate are mistaken. People are not interested in politics, they lead busy lives with many demands on their time and energy. They put a government in place and expect it to get on with the job. They do notice, however, if the government in question breaks its clear promises, or if it turns out to be working in a way not foreseen. Thus the centralising presidential style of the Blair Government is starting to be seen for what it is. The term 'control-freakery' has also entered the language. 'It's not democratic, is it?' say taxi drivers. 'They're not royalty, are they?' says the milkman. 'Who do they think they are?' says the man in the Dog & Bottle. Undoubtedly the Prime Minister set out to give the smack of firm government, and to portray himself as all-powerful, making announcements on every conceivable topic, of the 'Blair takes charge' variety. This has two effects, neither welcome perhaps in the longer term. One is that, eventually, the Prime Minister will have to take the blame for everything that goes wrong and however unlikely that may seem in the first three years of his government, it will happen in the end, as it always does. The second is that such an approach renders his ministers mere cyphers – which he may want, but it is not the way to encourage good team-working, the evidence of which is already starting to emerge, with the outspoken departure of Peter Kilfoyle and the briefing from others.

But there is another result of this approach, which is more fundamental, and more damaging in the longer term. It is the case that people have less and less time to take an interest in politics. But this does not mean that people are not interested in the democratic process.

Consider the contact that people have with such a process in their daily lives, quite apart from national or even local politics. One of the many characteristics of British life that differentiates it from, say, French life, is the thread of voluntary democratic involvement that runs right through it. Of course, not every citizen belongs to a group or organisation but many do, ranging from football and bowls clubs, parent-teacher associations, tenants' or residents' associations, allotment groups, Rotary, Inner Wheel, darts teams, pensioner groups, Leagues of Friends of hospitals and other institutions and playgroups. Association with such groups is not only of mutual interest, it also provides first-hand experience of the democratic process, or the lack of it, at local level. Accountability may not be a concept much discussed at the Dog & Bottle. The lack of it, when a club secretary will not reveal club funds, is. In British society there is a concept of what is fair, what is open and what is correct. Parliamentary democracy is all of those things. In the end, those who diminish its effectiveness will pay the price.

Surely, after centuries of struggle to establish elected parliamentary democracy, we shall not see it slip from the ballot box to the focus group and plebiscite. As Bevan found when he was elected to a Council, 'power had been there, but it had just gone.' He did not foresee it escaping the democratic process altogether.

The power to govern is a precious gift bestowed on political parties by the electorate, through Parliament. Each Parliament, because it is human and organic, deals differently with the challenges posed to its authority by the executive. The balance between the two shifts and changes in every age. In the end, Parliament is

289

the only legitimate source of power. It is the only body able to choose and use the weapons appropriate for it to do battle with the government of the day, in the name of the people. In order to do so, it must recognise the importance of its role, and be prepared to fulfil it.

Notes

1. Michael Foot, *Aneurin Bevan*, quoted in Peter Hennessy *Whitehall*, Secker & Warburg, 1989, pp. 326–7

2. Walter Bagehot, *The English Constitution*, Vol. IV: The House of Commons

3. John Major, *The Autobiography*, HarperCollins, 1999, p. 210

4. Anthony Seldon, *Major: A Political Life,* Weidenfeld & Nicolson, 1998, p. 258

5. Ibid., p.257

6. *The English Constitution*, Vol. IV: The House of Commons

7. John Major, op. cit, p. 210

8. Anthony Seldon, op. cit.,

9. Ibid., p. 209

10. John Major, op. cit., p. 212

11. After a formal Cabinet meeting it is common for civil servants to withdraw from the meeting while the Cabinet discusses party political matters. As an election approaches more of these sessions occur.

12. *The Guardian*, 28 November 1990

13. John Major, op. cit., p. 219

14. Anthony Seldon, op. cit., p. 205

15. Ibid., p. 202

16. John Major, op. cit., p. 212

17. Ibid. p. 265

18. Ibid. p. 214

19. Ibid.

20. Anthony Seldon, op. cit., p. 287

21. John Major, op. cit., p. 219

22. Anthony Seldon, op. cit., p. 575

23. Ibid., p. 586

24. John Major, op. cit., p. 311

25. Peter Hennessy, op. cit., pp. 328–9

26. Ibid., p. 280

27. *The Independent*, 14 September 1987

28. Griffiths & Ryle, *Parliament: Functions, Practice and Procedures*, Sweet and Maxwell, 1989, p. 338

29.   Colin Turpin, *British Government and the Constitution,* Butterworths, 1995

30.   Ivor Jennings, *Cabinet Government,* 3rd edn.,1959, pp. 15–16

31.   *The Guardian,* 18 March 1998

32.   *The Times,* 23 March 1998

33.   Hansard, 3 December 1997, cols 390–1

34.   *House Magazine,* 3 April 2000

35.   *The Guardian,* 18 March 1998

36.   Sixth Report of the Committee on Standards in Public Life, Stationery Office, 1999, paras 6.7–6.8,

37.   *The Scotsman,* 14 January 2000

38.   Anthony Barker et al., *Ruling by Task Force,* Politico's Publishing, November, 1999

39.   Article by Peter Oborne in *The Spectator,* 15 January 2000

40.   *Daily Telegraph,* 8 January 2000

41.   Lecture to Politeia, 30 November 1999

42.   Hansard, 7 March 2000

43.   'The Blair Paradox', Prospect, May 1998

44.   *The Times,* 3 March 2000

45.   Ibid.

46.   Hansard, col. 103, 27 July 1999

47.   Government Response to the Fourth Report from the Procedure Committee, 19 October 1999.

48.   Ibid.

49.   Hansard, col. 996, 24 May 2000

50.   Robert Cranborne, *The End of the Era of Representative Democracy,* Politeia, 1998

51.   *The Times,* 22 May 2000

52.   Ibid.

53.   Linda McDougall, *Westminster Women,* Vintage, 1998, p. 24

54.   Ibid. p. 136

55.   Ibid.

56.   Hansard, 22 May 2000, col. 700

57.   Peter Henessy, *Re-engineering the State in Flight: A year in the life of the British Constitution April 1997 to 1998*

58.   *Sunday Times,* 21 November 1999, reporting on *Ruling by Task Force,* op. cit.

59.   BBC Online, 10 January 2000

60.   *Daily Telegraph,* 8 January 2000

61.   *The Guardian,* 18 March 1998

62.   *The Guardian,* 11 February 2000

63.   Martin McElwee, *The Great and the Good?,* Centre for Policy Studies, 2000

64.   *The Times,* 26 May 2000

65.   Ibid.

66.   *The Spectator,* 15 January 2000

Index